FAMILY THERAPY
AN OVERVIEW

FAMILY THERAPY
AN OVERVIEW

Irene Goldenberg
U.C.L.A. Neuropsychiatric Institute

Herbert Goldenberg
California State University, Los Angeles

Brooks/Cole Publishing Company
Monterey, California
A Division of Wadsworth, Inc.

Printed in the United States of America

10 9 8 7 6 5 4 3

Library of Congress Cataloging in Publication Data

Goldenberg, Irene.
    Family therapy.

        Bibliography: p. 258.
        Includes indexes.
            1. Family psychotherapy.   I. Goldenberg, Herbert, joint author.   II. Title.
RC488.5.G64   616.8'915   79-9403
ISBN 0-8185-0361-0

Acquisition Editor: *Claire Verduin*
Production Editor: *Marilu Uland*
Manuscript Editor: *Derek Gallagher*
Cover Design: *Elizabeth Anne Rotchford*
Interior Design: *Katherine Minerva*
Illustrations: *Etc. Graphics*
Typesetting: *TriStar Graphics, Minneapolis, Minnesota*

For our families of origin
       . . . who stimulated our drive and
              sensitivity,

And for the family we created
       . . . who enriched our understanding
              and, above all, taught us
              humility,

And for our children's families
       . . . whose contributions we look
              forward to discovering.

PREFACE

This book is for the increasing number of students and professionals who want to learn more about the theory and process of family
therapy. We have provided a broad introduction to the field, offering
what we believe is a balanced presentation of the major theoretical underpinnings and clinical practices in the field today. Rather than detail a how-to-do-it set of technical procedures, we've given an overview of the evolving viewpoints, perspectives, values, intervention
techniques, and goals of family therapy.

The field of family therapy can claim ancestry in a number of related disciplines. Historically, social workers and various marriage and
family counselors, including religious counselors, have concerned
themselves with understanding and improving interactions between
people. Psychologists and psychiatrists have sought ways of improving individual and group functioning by therapeutic intervention.
Family therapy addresses itself to similar problems, offering a fresh
perspective on human behavior and on ways of helping to achieve
constructive personality and behavioral changes in individual clients
and in the family as a whole. Rather than representing one discipline
or one theoretical viewpoint, family therapy offers a broadly based approach, having emerged from a number of theoretical roots and established clinical techniques that crystallized over the last 25 years into a
unique interdisciplinary therapeutic approach.

To be effective in helping families to change, we believe therapists must first have some grounding in the general principles of fam-

ily living. They need to be familiar with how families operate as a social system, how they develop "rules" for living together, and how they deal with the ever-changing tasks that must be met by a family going through its life cycle. Therapists need some basic theoretical understanding of what causes dysfunction within families and of how to distinguish those families who are undergoing a time-limited crisis from which they will reorganize and recover independently from those families who are severely dysfunctional and who will not recover without therapeutic intervention. Learning about these fundamental theoretical issues should precede the learning of specific family-therapy techniques, and we have organized this book around such issues. However, we recognize that some instructors believe that students or trainees learn best when theoretical conceptualizations are introduced only after the student has had first-hand experience conducting family-therapy sessions. Such instructors may prefer to change the order in which chapters in this book are assigned. We have organized the text in such a way that they may do so easily, without detracting from our pedagogical purposes. We are concerned, however, that the students learn the principles along with the techniques, lest they learn merely to emulate the therapeutic "magic" of a gifted, charismatic family therapist.

We have written this book as a survey of the field of family therapy, covering its historical roots as well as its current major theories and techniques. The book is directed toward readers in the fields of psychology, education, counseling, social work, psychiatry, nursing, and theology. We recognize that, in each of these groups, learning to become a practitioner comes at different points in the educational training. Therefore, this book can serve as a base of information in an introductory or advanced undergraduate course, but it will also be useful in a graduate course and for the practicing professional.

A number of colleagues in various related fields who have an interest in teaching family therapy have been most generous in reviewing earlier drafts of this text in an effort to improve the final product. We wish particularly to thank Richard Bocchini of the Hall-Mercer Community Mental Health Center at Pennsylvania Hospital, Craig C. Gilbert of the University of Nevada, Sandra Guest of the University of Central Florida, Clinton Phillips of the California Family Study Center, and Lawrence Siegel of the University of Missouri at Columbia.

We wish also to thank our personal-support system of secretary (Adeline Butkus), research assistant (Ann Snowhook), and teaching assistant (Cynthia Pearson), without whom we could not have put this book into its present form so swiftly and expertly. Our friends at Brooks/Cole first suggested that a book of this kind was needed in the field of family therapy and that we try writing it together. Our initial misgivings to the contrary, working as a writing team proved to be an-other area for an exciting and stimulating experience together, and we look forward to future collaborations with eager anticipation. Terry Hendrix and Claire Verduin at Brooks/Cole deserve our special thanks.

It is our hope that the reader, having examined the variety of theories and techniques of family therapy presented here, will be in a better position in finding one that fits his or her needs, both theoreti-cally and stylistically. The field of family therapy is still so new and there is still so much innovation and experimentation going on that we can expect many more changes in the years ahead. Having estab-lished a foundation, we expect the reader will continue to grow as the field develops. We would be most happy to have participated in some way in the student's continuing education.

Irene Goldenberg
Herbert Goldenberg

CONTENTS

Part One

FAMILY RELATIONSHIPS   1

1 PATTERNS OF FAMILY INTERACTION   3

Adopting a Family Perspective   4
Changing American Families   9
The Developmental Approach to Family Life   13
    Family Life Cycle   13
    Family Developmental Tasks   16
    Changing Family Roles   20
    The Socialization Process   22
Summary   27

2 FUNCTIONAL AND DYSFUNCTIONAL FAMILY SYSTEMS   28

Some Characteristics of a Family System   29
    Family Rules   29
    Family Homeostasis   32
    Feedback and Information Processing   34
    Subsystems and Boundaries   37
Optimal Family Functioning   38
Moderately and Severely Dysfunctional Families   42
Summary   46

3 EXPRESSIONS OF
FAMILY DYSFUNCTION   48

Developmental Sequences and Family Crises   48
Pathological Communication   50
   The Double-Bind and Mystification   52
   Symmetrical and Complementary Relationships   54
Enmeshment and Disengagement   59
   Delinquent-Producing Families   60
   Psychosomatic Families   62
Scapegoating   63
Persistent Family Myths   65
   Pseudomutuality   69
Summary   71

Part Two
HISTORICAL AND
THEORETICAL FOUNDATIONS   73

4 THE EVOLUTION OF THE
FAMILY THERAPY MOVEMENT   75

Historical Roots of the Family Therapy Movement   75
   Psychoanalysis   76
   General Systems Theory   82
   Schizophrenia and the Family   85
   Marital Counseling and Child Guidance   90
   Group Therapy   94
Developments in Family Therapy   96
   The 1950s: Schizophrenia in the Family   96
   The 1960s: Widening the Focus—New Families,
      New Settings, New Techniques   101
   The 1970s: Consolidation and Innovation   102
Summary   106

5 THEORETICAL MODELS
OF FAMILY INTERACTION   107

Four Paradigms of Family Interaction   107
   Family Psychodynamic Theory   107
   Family Communications Theory   113
   Structural Family Theory   119
   Family Behavior Theory   123
Summary   129

Part Three
TECHNIQUES OF
FAMILY THERAPY   131

6   THE PROCESS OF
    FAMILY THERAPY   133

Basic Characteristics of Family Therapy   133
    Family Therapy versus Individual Therapy   133
    *Indications and Contraindications for
        Family Therapy   135*
Family Diagnosis   139
    Is Diagnosis Necessary?   139
    Evaluating a Family's Functioning   143
    Dimensions for Family Assessment   147
Values and Goals in Family Therapy   150
Stages of Family Therapy   152
    The Initial Interview   152
    The Middle Phase   158
    Termination   162
Summary   163

7   MODELS OF
    CLINICAL PRACTICE   165

Therapies Influenced by Psychodynamic Theories   166
    Nathan Ackerman's Biopsychosocial Therapy   166
    Murray Bowen's Family Systems Therapy   170
Therapies Influenced by Communications Theories   172
    Virginia Satir's Conjoint Family Therapy   172
    Jay Haley's Problem-Solving Therapy   175
Therapies Influenced by Structural Theories   179
    Salvador Minuchin's Structural Therapy   179
Therapies Influenced by Behavior Theories   183
    Richard Stuart's Operant-Interpersonal Therapy   183
    Robert Liberman's Contingency Contracting   187
Two Independent Therapies   190
    Gerald Zuk's Triadic-Based Family Therapy   190
    John Bell's Family Group Therapy   194
Summary   198

8   INNOVATIVE TECHNIQUES
    IN FAMILY THERAPY   201

Multiple Family Therapy   201
Multiple Impact Therapy   204
Family Crisis Therapy   206
Social Network Intervention   209
Videoplayback   212
Family Sculpture and Choreography   214
Conjoint Sex Therapy   216
Summary   218

Part Four
TRAINING AND EVALUATION   221

9   LEARNING, TEACHING, AND
    EVALUATING FAMILY THERAPY   223

Becoming a Family Therapist   224
Training Aids   228
    Didactic Course Work   228
    Videotapes   229
    Marathons   230
    Live Supervision   231
    Films   233
    Looking at Your Own Family   234
Cotherapy: The Use of Therapeutic Teamwork   235
The Effectiveness of Family Therapy   239
    The Question of Psychotherapy Research   239
    Family Therapy Outcome Studies   240
The Future of Family Therapy   243
Summary   247

Glossary   249
References   258
Name Index   268
Subject Index   271

Part One
FAMILY RELATIONSHIPS

1
PATTERNS OF
FAMILY INTERACTION

A family is far more than a collection of individuals occupying a specific physical and psychological space together. Rather, it is a natural social **system**,[1] with properties all its own, one that has evolved a set of rules, **roles**, a power structure, forms of communication, and ways of negotiation and problem solving that allow various tasks to be performed effectively.

By the same token, to understand an individual, we must look beyond his or her internal processes. We need to examine that person's various relationships with other people, especially as they occur within a family context. Despite the persistence of the myth that each person is an autonomous individual who controls his or her own destiny, there is increasing evidence that "man is not as separate from his family, from those about him, and from his multigenerational past as he has fancied himself to be" (Bowen, 1975, p. 369). We believe, along with Minuchin (Minuchin, Rosman, & Baker, 1978), that every human being's sense of identity is largely dependent on the validation of self by a reference group, particularly the family or family substitute. That validation from the family, vital to all family members, is especially important for children, who are in the process of forming identities, self-images they will carry forward into adult lives as they form other families. The way a family functions, then, has tremendous implica-

[1] Terms printed in **boldface** are defined in the Glossary at the back of the book.

tions for how individuals develop and function. Family transactional patterns form the matrix within which the psychological growth of members takes place.

ADOPTING A FAMILY PERSPECTIVE

Psychotherapists have always been interested in their patients' or clients' early family relationships. Ever since Freud's early psychoanalytic formulations, attention has been drawn to family conflicts and alliances (for example, the **Oedipus complex** in boys) as contributing factors in an individual's personality development. However, Freud did not utilize his awareness of the interactional nature of behavior in his psychoanalytic treatment. That is, he acknowledged the influence (and sometimes, the powerful impact) of family relationships, but he chose to help individuals resolve their personal, **intrapsychic** (within the mind) conflicts; he did not deal with changing the properties of the family system. By producing changes in the patient's psychic organization, Freud hoped to change that person's behavior, including changes in response to others, leading others ultimately to change their response patterns to the patient. Thus, most psychotherapists, influenced by Freud, would see a marital partner but refuse to see the spouse, hoping that as the patient changed, a corresponding change in the spouse would occur. Unfortunately, this was not always the case.

Over the past 25 years, an alternative view of human problems and their alleviation has slowly emerged—namely, that an individual who exhibits dysfunctional behavior (for example, excessive anxieties, depression, alcoholism, sexual disturbances, **schizophrenia**) may simply be a representative of a system that is faulty. Moreover, while the causes and nature of an individual's problem may not be clear from a study of that person alone, they often can be better understood when viewed in the context of a family social system that is in disequilibrium.

Understanding what a person does, what his or her motives are for doing it, and how that behavior can be changed, therapeutically, become quite different as we shift from the individual to the broader context in which that person functions. From this new vantage point, **psychopathology** or **dysfunctional** behavior is more the product of a struggle between persons rather than between internal forces within a single person (Haley, 1963). Perhaps the following two examples can illustrate the point. In the first case we are dealing with an adolescent who develops severe, incapacitating schizophrenic **symptoms**, leading the therapist to request that the entire family come as a group for family therapy. In the second case, a more common situation, a young child's difficulties at home and at school reflect some underlying parental tensions.

Jerry M., a 17-year-old high school senior, living at home, suddenly began to show a dramatic change in his behavior. Formerly a friendly person, he now became withdrawn and sometimes stayed in his room, behind a locked door, for several days at a time. He stopped attending school, refused to answer telephone calls from his friends, and demanded that his parents communicate with him only by passing notes under the door. When he did emerge from his room, he acted as though he were being plotted against by his family. He seemed to be hearing voices that were chastising him for his "evil" thoughts. When he finally spoke, he was incoherent and produced a jumble of words that made absolutely no sense to his dumbfounded parents.

Jerry was the only child of a traditional working-class family. The father, 54, worked on an automobile assembly line, a job he had held for over 25 years. He had a tenth-grade education, having dropped out of high school to help support his mother and younger sister when his father died. Jerry's mother, 44, had graduated from high school and attended a junior college at night for one semester before she left her clerical job and schooling to get married. Although the couple was childless for the first eight years of their marriage, Jerry's mother stayed at home as homemaker. There were times when she brought up the subject of returning to work, part time, but her husband was adamant on the subject that his wife would not work.

Roles within the M. family were established early in the marriage and remained more or less fixed thereafter. Mr. M. earned the money, Mrs. M. took care of the house and her husband. He demanded that she keep a clean house, have meals ready on time, and be available for sexual relations whenever he approached her. She expected him to work at a steady job, not gamble, drink, or chase other women. He controlled the money, giving her a weekly allowance for purchasing food. Mr. and Mrs. M. rarely if ever socialized as a couple with other people. Generally on Sunday, Mr. M. would go with his friends to the soccer matches, which his wife found boring and refused to attend. At home, he was likely to watch television nightly, especially sporting events. Mrs. M. preferred reading in another room to watching TV.

When Jerry was born, he became Mrs. M.'s responsibility. Tired at night, lonely, bored, she became increasingly resentful of being neglected by her husband. In turn, her refusal of his sexual advances infuriated him, leading him to withdraw further from her. A stalemate resulted, with Mr. M. beginning to stay away from home more and more and Mrs. M. developing a closer and closer relationship with Jerry, whom she began to use as a substitute for her husband. As he grew up, Jerry had few friends and was considered a "mama's boy." Ashamed of the nonexistent relationship between his parents, he never invited a friend to his home. Increasingly, his schoolmates began to think of Jerry as odd, a loner.

The psychotherapist whom Jerry's parents contacted insisted that the entire family come to his office together for weekly sessions. On first impression, Mr. and Mrs. M. appeared solicitous toward Jerry—if he had a problem they would certainly try to help. However, it was clear from the first session that the parents communicated little with each other. Further sessions revealed that they had little in common with each other, except for their concern over their "sick" child.

Slowly, the therapist began to help them see that "Jerry's problem" was a family problem. It was the system that had broken down; Jerry was merely expressing that fact through his symptoms. As Mr. and Mrs. M., along with Jerry, continued seeing the therapist together, all were encouraged to express their feelings, especially their frustrations and dissatisfactions with one another. As Jerry's schizophrenic behavior was reduced and his symptoms disappeared, Mr. and Mrs. M. were in open conflict with each other. The therapist decided to see the parents together without Jerry, who now was planning to attend college away from home after graduation.

Jerry's "symptoms" represented a desperate effort to hold his family together. Family therapy was able to help his parents to eventually work out a mutually satisfying relationship. Once that was accomplished, his "symptoms," no longer necessary, disappeared.

In the second case, Eric, age 9, is brought to a psychotherapist by his parents because he is causing problems at home and at school. The parents, Laura and Mark T., are a young, upper middle-class, well-educated couple, with two other children: Lynne, age 7, and Patty, age 4.

Eric had been a difficult child as far back as his parents could remember. Bright, oversensitive, socially immature for his age, he frequently would fight with the other children in the neighborhood. At home, he was apt to cling to his parents, sometimes insisting they stay close to him before he would fall asleep at night. As he grew older, Eric began to have trouble at school; he did not like to leave his mother's side and, once in school, he refused to study or do what the teacher requested. By way of contrast, his two younger sisters, both beautiful, were considered by relatives, friends, and teachers alike as "good little girls" and always held up to Eric as models he would do well to emulate. One additional source of family conflict arose from the fact that Eric was extremely unathletic, a fact his sports-minded father found difficult to accept. Eric had previously been in play therapy on a weekly basis when he was six, although the parents terminated his sessions after two months because they believed he was making little progress for the expense involved.

When Eric came for psychotherapy this time, he was given a battery of psychological tests by the psychologist. Test results indicated he was an intelligent child, not seriously emotionally disturbed, but undergoing some current stress, probably of an **interpersonal** nature. When his parents were brought in to hear the results of the testing, they were extremely agitated, indicating they were at a loss to know how to handle Eric. They both agreed that, despite the favorable test results, he was an irritant, and the family would be a happy family if only he were not there.

During this discussion, with Eric not present, Mr. and Mrs. T. admitted they were having marital problems and needed counseling. The therapist suggested family therapy for the parents, Eric, and his sisters together. After two sessions, it became clear that the core problem in the family was the underlying conflict between the parents, which now was surfacing. The children were asked to stop attending, and the parents continued for twenty sessions. As the therapist had predicted to them when the children terminated, Eric's problems began to clear up at home and at school as they worked on their differences in therapy. In addition, the girls, Lynne and Patty, began to act like more normal children, no longer needing to show how "good" they were in contrast to their "bad" brother.

The problems Mr. and Mrs. T. were having were a lot more difficult to resolve. Married right out of high school, they now found themselves ten years later at a quite different place in their lives. The mutual dependence of their early years together was gone, and they had developed very different attitudes and values. Their sexual relations, never entirely satisfactory, had deteriorated further in recent years, so that now they were almost nonexistent. Despite their efforts to make the marriage work, they drifted even further apart and finally decided to separate. After several months, they divorced. The children remained with Mrs. T.

Within two years both Mr. and Mrs. T. had remarried, each to spouses who themselves had children from previous marriages. Some time after his mother's remarriage, Eric's school difficulties flared up once again. When Eric, along with his natural mother and stepfather, came to see the family therapist together, all three were upset and quarreling. The therapist recognized that the old fight between his natural parents had resumed, with their new spouses presumably adding fuel to the fire. True to form, Eric once again offered himself as the family scapegoat by reviving his behavior problems.

The therapist requested that all four adults, Eric's parents and stepparents, join Eric for several joint sessions. While a great deal of quarreling went on, particularly between the two women, each assisted by her husband, some resolution of the conflict occurred and, once again, Eric's symptomatic behavior waned. Later, the therapist was able to help Mr. T. and his new wife to work out some difficulties they were having concerning their differential dealings with their children and stepchildren.

Several points need to be specially noted in this case. Family therapy can occur with subsections of a family and need not involve the entire group. Not all couples live happily ever after; in reality, divorce is a common consequence and often is for the better of all concerned. The family therapist tries to remain flexible, dealing with various combinations of people at different times, including new extended family members (ex-spouses, stepparents). Finally, this case demonstrates that brief therapy at different phases of stress within a family can be helpful and effective.

Traditionally, each of the young people just described might be viewed as isolated individuals with intrapsychic conflicts independent of their family relationships. With the locus of pathology thus defined as internal, clinical intervention by a therapist is likely to be, correspondingly, individually focused.

On the other hand, family therapy, as Haley (1971b) has noted, represents a radical change in our thinking about human dilemmas and what to do about them. He sees this **paradigm** shift as representing a discontinuous break with past ideas; it calls for a new set of premises rather than merely offering a new method of treatment. No longer do we see problems or symptoms emanating from a single "sick" individual. Instead, we conceptualize the dysfunctional behavior as the product of a dyadic (for example, mother/child) or triadic (for example, mother/father/child) relationship. The symptom-bearer (for example, the schizophrenic adolescent in the first case or the child with behavior problems in the second case) is simply the family mem-

ber who manifests the disturbed behavior—the **identified patient**—
expressing the family's disequilibrium. As Satir (1967) points out, a
disturbed person's "symptoms" may in reality be a message that he or
she is distorting self-growth as a result of trying to alleviate "family
pain."

Family therapy offers a broader view of human behavior than
does individual therapy. The "identified patient," the person sent initially for help, does not remain the central focus of therapy for long.
Rather, the family begins to understand that his or her problems or
symptoms are an expression of the entire family system. Problems get
restated within a family framework as relationship difficulties. Within
such a systems viewpoint, the locus of pathology is not the individual
but rather the individual in context (Minuchin, et al., 1978). Change
the family environment, the context, and the individual's experiences
and subsequent behavior patterns begin to change. The focus of family
therapy is on changing the system—the family's characteristic pattern
of interacting with one another, their style and manner of communication, the structure of their relationships—so that each member experiences a sense of independence, uniqueness, and wholeness while remaining within the context and security of the family relationship.

CHANGING AMERICAN FAMILIES

There is no typical American "family" today. It is more accurate
to speak of types of "families"—with diverse organizational patterns,
diverse styles of living, diverse living arrangements. The traditional
family structure, the conventional **nuclear family** consisting of a
homemaker mother, breadwinner father, and children is now in the
minority (Skolnick & Skolnick, 1977). The birth rate is the lowest in
our history, the divorce rate the highest ever and the highest rate of
any industrialized country. Parenting without marriage has risen
sharply in recent years; 15% of all births are now illegitimate (50%
among Black women). Of the nation's 56.7 million families, 9.2 million, or fully one-sixth of the total, are single-parent families ("Saving
the Family," 1978). Table 1-1 summarizes some common current family living patterns.

Even the nuclear family is undergoing dramatic changes. American women working at paying jobs, even when young children are in
the home, already outnumber those who stay at home. Two-income
families are becoming more commonplace, resulting in many changes
in role-sharing, child-rearing, use of day care facilities and domestic
help, and relationship changes between husband and wife. A "career
woman" in the past was likely to be defensive about not devoting her

TABLE 1-1. Common Variations in Family Organization and Structure

Family Type	Composition of Family Unit
Nuclear family	Husband, wife, children
Extended family	Nuclear family plus grandparents, uncles, aunts, and so on
Blended family	Husband, wife, plus children from previous marriage(s)
Common law family	Man, woman, and possibly children living together as a family, although the former two have not gone through a formal legal marriage ceremony
Single-parent family	Household led by one parent (man or woman), possibly due to divorce, death, desertion, or to never having married
Commune family	Men, women, and children living together, sharing rights and responsibilities, and collectively owning and/or using property, sometimes abandoning traditional monogamous marriages
Serial family	Man or woman has a succession of marriages, thus acquiring several spouses and different families over a lifetime but one nuclear family at a time
Composite family	A form of polygamous marriage in which two or more nuclear families share a common husband (polygyny) or wife (polyandry), the former being more prevalent
Cohabitation	A more or less permanent relationship between two unmarried persons of the opposite sex who share a nonlegally binding living arrangement

time and energies to her home, husband, and children. Today she probably is either a working wife trying to attend to her job and home (with assistance from her husband and others), a single woman who may or may not marry, a married woman who has chosen to delay or forego having children, or the head of a **single-parent household**. Today, it is the woman who describes herself as "only a housewife" who may feel on the defensive. A 1977 survey ("Who is the Real Family?", 1978) found that one-third of all full-time homemakers planned to enter the salaried field later in their lives.

One major reason for changing family patterns today is the fact that divorce has become more commonplace than ever before. Nowadays, almost four out of ten marriages end in divorce, as people with marital problems are less willing to maintain an unhappy marriage than their counterparts were in the past. Greater public acceptance of divorce, liberalized divorce laws, and the increased economic independence of women making them less likely to stay in a marriage for reasons of financial security have all contributed to this phenomenon and made divorce a realistic alternative to an unhappy marriage.

The rising divorce rate has contributed greatly to the diversity of family life, as some persons, following the dissolution of their marriage, choose to live alone or become heads of single-parent households. The number of such families headed by women is growing rapidly; in 1975, 11% of White families and 35% of Black families lived in female-headed households (Nass, 1978). Remarriage is also on the increase (79% of those who get divorced remarry), especially for divorced men, suggesting a commitment to a family life even if a previous marriage was an unhappy experience. Glick (1976) has reported from census data that only about 70% of all children under 18 years of age in 1970 lived with their two natural parents who themselves had been married only once; among Black children the corresponding figure was 45%. As a result, **blended families** have become common, as divorced people remarry and the children from the previous marriages of each are blended into one family. Remarriage today blends about 18 million stepchildren from what used to be called "broken homes" into new family units ("Saving the Family," 1978). Television situation comedies such as *The Brady Bunch* to the contrary, the result of such blending has often been new complications and stresses on the family's ability to establish and redefine relationships. Stepparenting has created new **extended families** made up of ex-spouses, new spouses, and assorted grandparents as well as the children and their stepsiblings, making it difficult to keep track of so many new relationships ("In Her Own Words," 1978). As Nass (1978) illustrates in a rather overwhelming example:

> If a divorced woman with children, for instance, marries a divorced man whose children from his former marriage visit him occasionally, the new relationships include those between the new husband and wife, the wife and the husband's children, the husband and the wife's children, the two sets of children who must at least sometimes live together, the husband and the wife's ex-husband, the wife and the husband's ex-wife, the new couple and the new in-laws on either side, the spouses' parents and their stepgrandchildren, and everybody with any new children conceived within the remarriage [p. 439].

Ninety-six out of every 100 American adults marry; nearly two-thirds of these people remain married until separated by death (see Figure 1-1 for a typical pattern). Of the 38% who get divorced, 75% of the women and 83% of the men remarry within three years. Clearly, marriage remains the preferred state for the majority of our population. Even those who know from bitter experience that marriage is not all harmony and satisfactions are willing to try again, accepting the fact, as Skolnick and Skolnick (1977) point out, that intimacy provides not only love and care but often tension and conflict as well. Both as-

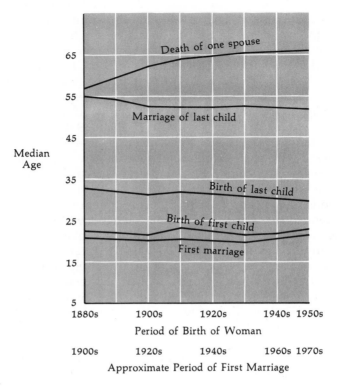

FIGURE 1-1. Historical trends in the timing of five significant life events for women. The latest census data project that women born in the 1950s—most of whom will have married in the 1970s—were likely to be 21.1 years old (on the average) at the time of their first marriage, delaying marriage somewhat longer than their counterparts of a decade or two earlier. They averaged about 22.7 years old at the birth of their first child and can expect to be about 29.6 years old when their last child is born. This trend is expected to continue in the 1980s. Thus, women currently entering marriage can expect to complete childbearing earlier than ever before and can expect to have a smaller number of children (average: 2 to 3) than previously. By their early fifties (average: 52.3 years) most women will have seen their last child married and out of the house (if indeed that child, following the current trend, has not left home before marriage). The much longer empty nest period now than formerly is probably the most dramatic change that has occurred in the pattern of a family's life. (From "Updating the Life Cycle of the Family," by P. C. Glick, *Journal of Marriage and the Family*, 1977, *39*, 5-13. Copyright 1977 by The National Council on Family Relations. Reprinted by permission of the author and publisher.)

pects of marriage are inseparable parts of intimate relationships. All of the changing patterns described above do not mean we are experiencing the death of the family, according to these authors, but rather the demystification of family life, the erosion of sentimental myths portraying family life as utopian. The various alternative family styles (see Table 1-1) existing today do not mean the traditional family is obsolete, but rather that it is not the only possible living arrangement. Our society is likely to continue to experiment with unconventional family patterns and nonfamilial living arrangements.

THE DEVELOPMENTAL APPROACH TO FAMILY LIFE

One useful way to conceptualize a family system is to study it longitudinally, along its time dimension or developmental stages. Frequently, family behavior patterns or perhaps family crises become more understandable when seen within the context of the phase of development the family is in. A recently married couple must reconcile the different expectations each partner brings to the marriage, learning new transactional patterns that will be mutually satisfying. Middle-aged parents must deal with their adolescent's struggles to forge an identity, especially difficult when the parents themselves must deal with their own "midlife" crises. The transformations brought about by old age bring additional sources of crises. In each case, placing the problem within the phase of the developmental process the family is in helps the family therapist to better conceptualize each member's part in the problem or crisis and how intervention into the family system can be most effective.

Family Life Cycle²

Each intact family goes through more or less the same developmental process over time, passing through the same sequences or phases, each usually marked by a critical transition point—marriage, birth of the first child, last adolescent leaving the home, retirement,

---

²The reader might assume from the following discussion that we believe all families remain intact over the lifetimes of the parents, all families have children, and so on. Of course that is not the case. As we have indicated in our previous discussion, in recent years there has been a dramatic increase in divorce rates, one-parent families, communal families, young men and women who live together without being married or who marry later and thus have a shorter "married" life together, as well as couples who marry but decide to remain childless. While most family life cycle research pertains primarily to conventional middle-class family arrangements, we will endeavor to focus on the relationships between family members as the family matures, assuming such observations have broader applicability.

and so on. Much like an individual, a family can be viewed as going through a **life cycle**—successive patterns within the continuity of family living over the years of its existence—with members aging and passing through a succession of family roles. To be sure, each family has its unique and peculiar rhythms and tempos, hazards and rewards, harmonies and dissonances, but by and large it is useful to adopt such a longitudinal frame of reference in looking at family life (Duvall, 1977). From a family therapy perspective, psychiatric symptoms (for example, **anxiety,** depression, schizophrenia, delinquency) appear in a family member when there is a dislocation or interruption in the naturally unfolding family life cycle. The symptom is a signal that the family is having problems mastering the tasks inherent in that stage of the life cycle (Haley, 1973). For example, a woman who suffers a postpartum depression following the birth of a child is commonly thought to be undergoing some intense, personal, intrapsychic conflict, possibly involving guilt and hostility turned in upon herself. The family view, on the other hand, is that the entire family is having difficulty dealing with this new phase in its development brought about by the introduction of a new member. The signs of that family disturbance may be most obvious in the mother in this case, but a closer look would reveal a number of role shifts and realignments in the family brought about by the baby's birth. Haley argues that human distress and psychiatric symptoms appear when the family's normal unfolding life cycle is disrupted. The task for the family therapist is to help the members resolve the crisis, achieve a new balance, and get the family's developmental processes moving again.

Traditional middle-class American families generally proceed through the life cycle in a fixed sequence: families form when two people marry, separate from their families of origin, learn to accommodate to each other as husbands and wives, and assume new roles of fathers and mothers with the arrival of their first child. Each addition to the family not only increases the number of family members, but significantly reorganizes the family structure and way of living. No two children are ever born into the identical family situation. As families mature, new parent/children relationships develop; the mother and father's relationship may undergo change in the process. Families that once expanded to accommodate the requirements of growing children must later contract as these children launch their own families. Duvall (1977), a family life consultant, describes the typical life cycle of an intact family in terms of a circle with eight sectors (Figure 1-2). These are averages, of course, and do not resemble any one family in all particulars. However, we can plot generalized family expectancies, stages through which families typically pass, and the approximate times in the family's lifetime history when each stage is reached. Note

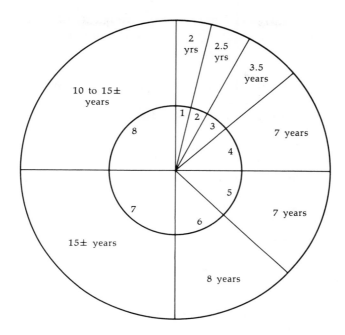

1. Married couples
   (without children)
2. Childbearing families
   (oldest child, birth—30 months)
3. Families with preschool children
   (oldest child 30 months—6 years)
4. Families with schoolchildren
   (oldest child 6—13 years)

5. Families with teenagers
   (oldest child 13—20 years)
6. Families as launching centers (first
   child gone to last child leaving home)
7. Middle-aged parents
   (empty nest to retirement)
8. Aging family members
   (retirement to death of both spouses)

FIGURE 1-2. The traditional family life cycle by length of time in each of the eight stages of life as proposed by Duvall (1977). The duration of each stage has implications for budgeting, housing needs, health care, recreation, education, home management, and various other family resources and services. Note especially that one-half of the marriage typically is spent as a couple after the children have grown and left the home. (Figure 7–2, p. 148, from *Marriage and Family Development* [5th Ed.], by Evelyn Millis Duvall. Copyright © 1957, 1962, 1967, 1971, 1977 by J. B. Lippincott Company. By permission of Harper & Row, Publishers, Inc. Based on data from the U.S. Bureau of Census and from the National Center for Health Statistics, Washington, D.C.)

especially that about half of an average family's life is spent with children at home, half with husband and wife alone.

This outline of the historical course of a nuclear family is often described as extending from courtship to the death of the last parent of a given family. As the family moves through various phases in this ongoing process (see Figure 1-3) different family tasks need to be ac-

Phase of courtship (informal partnership)
↓
Phase of early marriage (legal partnership)
↓
Phase of expansion
↓
Phase of consolidation
↓
Phase of contraction
↓
Phase of final partnership
↓
Phase of disappearance

FIGURE 1-3. Diagram of the historical course of a family. (Adapted from *Principles of Family Psychiatry,* by J. G. Howells. Copyright 1975 by Brunner/Mazel, Inc. Reprinted by permission.)

complished, as we will see in the following section, in order for the family to move on to its next stage of development. All creatures, humans as well as other animals, share the following developmental process: courting, mating, nest building, child rearing, and the dislodging of offspring into a life of their own. The more complex social organization of humans, however, causes certain unique problems in this family life cycle, as we are about to see.

Family Developmental Tasks

Each developmental phase provides the family with new tasks, the necessity to learn new adaptational techniques, and correspondingly, new risks of family dysfunction. The successful adaptation at any one phase depends heavily on the family's ability to master the tasks required at the previous phase. Thus, a young couple who themselves have not separated completely from their parents and been able to establish their own independent unit may experience considerable distress, conflict, and confusion at the family's next phase—dealing with the birth and rearing of their own children.

Marriage involves more than two people. Rather, it is a coming together of two families who exert their influences by becoming part of the decision-making process regarding marriage. (Even when young people select mates in order, consciously or unconsciously, to spite their parents, they are still responding to their parents, and are not making an independent choice.) Not uncommonly, there may be a premature rush to get married in order to disengage from an enmeshing family system. The problem with this is that once a couple marries, the reason for their marriage disappears and they must find some more sound basis for their relationship (Haley, 1973).

The initial task early in marriage is to adapt to one another and to develop new transactional patterns that satisfy both partners. Because each mate grows up in his or her own family, each acquires a set of expectations or rules for marital interaction. As Minuchin and associates (1978) put it, both partners' paradigms, brought into the marriage, must be retained, so that each person may retain a sense of self. However, the two paradigms must also be reconciled for them to have a life in common. In the process of reconciling their paradigms, the spouses develop new transactional patterns—compromises or embodied unresolved differences—that become familiar and ultimately the preferred way of dealing with each other.

A newly married couple also has the **developmental task** of separating from their families of origin. New relationships must be negotiated with each set of parents, siblings, and in-laws. Loyalties must shift as the primary commitment is to the marriage, and the family of origin must accept and support this break (Minuchin, 1974a). In the same way, each spouse must meet the other's friends and select those who will be the couple's friends. Together they gain new friends and lose touch with old ones.

When first married, their roles can be flexible and interchangeable. Without children, the structure of the family allows for a wide variety of solutions to immediate problems. For example, either or both may prepare dinner, they may choose to go out to eat, they may drop in at a friend's or parents' for a meal, or they may eat separately. With children, however, a more formal and specific solution has to be formulated in advance of dinnertime. The distribution of duties, the division of labor, must now be more clearcut. Who shops, cooks, picks up the child at a child-care center, washes dishes, and does many other tasks needs to be assigned. The physical and emotional commitment to the child usually changes the transactional patterns between spouses. The risk here is that roles between husband and wife may become too fixed, too rigid, without room for the previous flexibility.

Notice how the following couple has worked out a transactional pattern in the course of their four-year marriage. They see themselves as a normal family and are proud of having reached a point in their development where there is mutual support and growth.

FIGURE 1-4. Salvador Minuchin, M.D. (Photo by Anthony A. Bottone.)

MINUCHIN: The first thing that I want to know is why are you here? How
did you resolve to do it? What was the process?

MR. WAGNER: Saturday, as far as I'm concerned, is our free day, so to speak.
Whatever she would like to do, well then, we should do. I'm willing to
go along with it. Sunday, then, is more or less my day.

MINUCHIN: That's an interesting thing; that means that you decide to divide
the weekend in terms of days in which you make the major decisions
and days in which your wife does?

MR. WAGNER: Not quite, it's sort of a—

MINUCHIN: It just happens. How did that happen? That's interesting historically; how did you come to this kind of division of decision making? Do
you remember?

MR. WAGNER: I will hazard to venture a guess. I used to work Mondays
through Saturdays, in the hospital business; Saturday was sort of bat-
around. I felt Sunday was my day off, as far as I was concerned. So as
soon as Saturday was available, she jumped at it, so to speak. I wouldn't
let her have her preference on Sunday, because Sunday was sort of my
day.

MINUCHIN: So, you evolved that kind of implicit rule without ever having it
stated that this is the way you function.

MRS. WAGNER: As a rule, on Sunday he goes fishing or something, and I go
my way. It's always been that way; well, it's been that way for about a
year.

MINUCHIN: He goes fishing Sunday. Saturday is the day on which both of
you do things together, and you are the one that decides.

MR. WAGNER: It's not, it's not that hard and fast, really. I would say that on Saturday there is a better chance that my wife would decide what we are going to do.

MRS. WAGNER: I usually have something planned, you know, that I want to do, and we usually do it [Minuchin, 1974a, pp. 18-19].[3]

While this couple may not be able to reconstruct the development of this pattern, it has become part of the arrangement of their life in common.

Child-rearing often cuts the woman off from adult life for a time, and this may be personally frustrating. The most common period of crisis, according to Haley (1973), occurs when children start school; this represents the first experience of the fact that the children will ultimately leave home. If a grandparent is present, particularly in single-parent households, the triangle often involves that grandparent/parent/child, and there is frequently increased conflict in the home over how best to deal with the growing child.

The middle years of marriage often reveal a husband who begins to realize he will not fulfill his youthful ambitions, or conversely, he may be more successful than he anticipated. In the former case, his depression may permeate the entire family, while in the latter, his wife may still relate to him as he was before, with consequent resentment and family conflict. The wife, similarly, may realize that she has not fulfilled certain earlier ambitions for a career or for a particular kind of marriage relationship. With increased free time, she may feel forced to consider earlier career plans, about which she may now be insecure regarding her abilities. But life at home may seem without purpose, especially with her declining status now that the children are grown and need her less.

The problems of retirement are well chronicled; interpersonally, such problems typically revolve around 24-hour per day togetherness and, usually, a significant reduction in income. A man must detach himself from his familiar occupational role and both he and his wife must work out new arrangements with each other and new non-work-related involvements outside the home (Rapoport & Rapoport, 1965).

With the death of one partner, the family must care for the remaining parent, often bringing about a new crisis, as the family cycle begins to be drawn to a close.

In Table 1-2, we present Howells's (1975) phases of a family's life cycle once more, along with common developmental tasks that require mastery at various points along the way.

---

[3] This and all other quotations from this source are reprinted by permission of the publishers from *Families and Family Therapy*, by Salvador Minuchin, Cambridge, Mass.: Harvard University Press. Copyright © 1974 by the President and Fellows of Harvard College.

TABLE 1-2. Developmental Phases in the Family's Life Cycle, with Typical Tasks to Be Mastered at Each Phase

Phase	Developmental Tasks
Courtship	Contending with partner-selection pressures from parents; giving over autonomy while retaining some independence, preparing for marriage, including mutually satisfying sex life; becoming free of parents.
Early marriage	Sexual compatibility; sporadic contact with a partner becomes permanent; dealing with relatives; preparation for children; increased living standard with both partners working; interdependence.
Expansion	Children—new roles as parents, reduced income if wife loses earning power; agreements between spouses re: birth control, pregnancy, child care; greater interdependence; dealing with rivalries between children; dealing with one or the other parent's overinvolvement with the children.
Consolidation	Family has no new additions but problems of school, adolescence. Sexuality in children must be dealt with; high earning power required of one or both parents; greater independence in children; generation clashes between parents and children.
Contraction	As children leave, the major activity of the couple—being parents—is gone; need for new interests; loss of involvement with children; increased economic prosperity.
Final partnership	Wife's return to work if she has not done so previously, new roles as spouses, alone with each other; height of husband's career; high economic status.
Disappearance of family	Retirement with lower economic status and reduced prestige; increased dependency on others; maximum contact time between partners; problems of death—loss of partner, bereavement, loneliness.

Adapted from *Principles of Family Psychiatry*, by J. G. Howells. Copyright 1975 by Brunner/Mazel, Inc. Reprinted by permission.

Changing Family Roles

A family member's role, based on that person's age and sex, defines certain expected, permitted, as well as forbidden patterns of behavior. On the surface, such roles may appear to be biologically based and sexually stereotyped (although they need not be unchangeable). That is, in almost all societies, men are likely to be perceived as more aggressive than women, while women are more apt to be viewed as nurturant, cooperative, emotional, and tender (D'Andrade, 1974). According to traditional social theory, men are believed to be concerned with *instrumental* activities (making decisions, earning money, solving problems rationally) while women concern themselves with *expressive* activities (forming and maintaining emotional bonds, caring for children, creating a warm and supportive home atmosphere). Today, social scientists are beginning to question whether such role distinctions really are biologically determined and fixed. According to Hoffman (1977), a psychologist, sex differences in personality and behavior are not inborn but instead reflect adult role expectations that females will be mothers and males will be workers. Until recently, women have spent much of their lives pregnant, nursing, and caring for children. Hoffman argues that the reproductive role has been a major factor in determining the status and behavior patterns of women in all societies.

Role-playing differences between adult males and females stem from their differences in socialization experiences in childhood. Males prepare for adult occupational roles from their earliest years, while much of the socialization experience of females is geared toward motherhood. Yet these fixed or stereotyped sex roles are now being increasingly challenged. Hoffman (1977) notes that the sex-linked differences in early experiences may be expected to diminish in the future, largely due to two factors: (1) motherhood is no longer the major role of a woman in society, with mothering now occupying only a small portion of her adult years, and (2) increased maternal employment has led to a sharing of the traditional breadwinner role with the husband, who in turn may participate more in child-rearing functions than previously. According to Hoffman's thesis, smaller family size today than in the past, higher employment rates for women (half of all mothers with children under age 18 now work outside the home), and a longer life expectancy together are bringing about changes in family roles that tend to blur differences between the sexes.

During the past decade, American society has undergone both a sexual revolution and a sex-role revolution (Skolnick & Skolnick, 1977). The former has liberalized attitudes toward erotic behavior and its expression. The latter has changed the roles and statuses of both men and women in the direction of greater equality. Today, with greater egalitarian relations between many husbands and wives, there is a greater sharing and interchanging of the parenting roles. To a large extent this involves a joint effort to "humanize the young" to use Fleck's (1976) words—by teaching them about themselves, what is involved in living within a family, and especially the mores and cultural values of the society.

Women's traditional role sequence—daughter, wife, mother, grandmother, widow—is becoming more highly individualized. Changes are especially noteworthy during what has been considered the main portion of a woman's life cycle—marriage and childbearing. As we have seen, women are postponing marriage, postponing childbearing within marriage, and reducing family size. The percentage of women under 35 remaining single is rising; in 1960, 28% of all women aged 20-24, the age group in which most women traditionally marry, remained single, while in 1974 the figure had jumped to 39% (Van Dusen & Sheldon, 1976). In part because of postponed marriage, in part to pursue their education or career, women are postponing childbearing, having fewer children, or choosing to remain childless. Women now enter this phase of their traditional life cycle more slowly, and, because they are having smaller families, spend less time in child-rearing activities.

Today, most working women are married and middle-aged. The two-career family characterizes a growing portion of all American families. In what Rapoport and Rapoport (1969) call **role overload** in a dual-career family, various stresses are likely to appear when two people try to play too many roles at work and at home for the time and energy they have available. Conflict, fatigue, and guilt feelings in women over not fulfilling customary role expectations at home often increase the strain between husband and wife, especially if no domestic help or adequate child-care facilities are available. Children in such situations are often given increased responsibilities for domestic chores. Despite these obstacles, there are the benefits of personal stimulation and fulfillment, increased income, and possibly a closer relationship between the father and his children as a result of his greater participation in their upbringing. However, despite the egalitarian marriage, women are more likely to retain the major responsibilities for the home and the children. The working mother, with more role opportunities, may try to take advantage of the opportunity to utilize her talents and skills, but not without a significant shift in the roles played at home by other family members.

The Socialization Process

Teaching children skills and coping techniques that make for successful adaptation to the culture is a key task for parents in every society. Fleck (1976) sees the central mission of a modern nuclear family as the nurturance, enculturation, and guidance of the younger generation into adulthood. He contends that every family needs to accomplish specific evolutionary tasks: effecting a **coalition** between husband and wife capable later of forming a triad of parents and infants; nurturing and then weaning the infant in order that he or she exist apart from the mother; imparting language; introducing the child into society through school and through peer relationships; helping the child develop communications skills and competence in thinking and self-expression; and aiding the adolescent in establishing his or her sexual identity and also in undertaking more lasting relationships with peers outside the family. Finally, the young adult must be helped in the process of emancipation from the family in order to become a full-fledged adult member of society ready to begin his or her own family. At any of these stages, any malfunction may burden or handicap the offspring (as well as the family) severely.

Harmonious dyadic (two-person) relationships do not necessarily assure that the happy couple will make involved and caring parents. Sometimes, in fact, unless they develop a parental coalition, the opposite is the case: the arrival of a child is seen as a threat to the closeness between man and wife (one or both of whom are immature and self-centered), an intrusion that upsets the dependency gratification sought by one or the other (or both). On the other hand, it is sometimes possible to be good parents but have a poor marriage. Here there is greater risk for the children, however. As Glick and Kessler (1974) point out, instead of forming a workable parental coalition, each parent may openly deprecate the other or become a rival for the child's attention and affection. In severe cases, loyalty to the other parent is equated with rejection of themselves. Such parents frequently point out to the child that some undesirable behavior is "just like your mother" or "just like your father" and is unacceptable. Inevitably, destructive parent/child coalitions develop.

The manner in which families deal with the separation of children from their parents often produces a family crisis. In the following case, the ostensible reason for a woman seeking psychotherapy—a desire to obtain relief from her acute depression—turned out on closer examination to be secondary to a basic family entanglement or **enmeshment.** Contrary to appearances, it is the woman's adolescent son, and not his mother, who is most at risk.

Helen Turner, a 48-year-old housewife, was seriously depressed following the death of her eldest child, a daughter of 22. Her depression persisted beyond the expected bereavement period, and reached the point where she had difficulty eating and sleeping. Her waking hours were filled with gloomy thoughts, frequent crying spells, and a sense of hopelessness regarding the future.

Helen's husband as well as her remaining three children (2 daughters and a son) seemed unable to console her, no matter how hard they tried. Her family physician thought that perhaps the lingering depression might be related to hormonal changes during the menopause, which she was undergoing, but that proved to be a false lead. The antidepressant medication he prescribed helped some, but Helen's symptoms of depression continued.

Mrs. Turner finally decided to seek help at a neuropsychiatric hospital outpatient clinic. It had been five weeks since her daughter's death; sad as it was, it may have triggered some deeper family disturbance, and the intake worker, after interviewing Mrs. Turner, concluded that her depression was related primarily to that family's difficulty in resuming their life cycle. Family therapy was decided upon on a weekly basis; thereafter, Mr. and Mrs. Turner, their son Barry, and their daughters Barbara and Tracy, all the children in their late adolescence (18-21), were seen together by co-therapists over a six month period.

During the first family session, all of the family members expressed their grief over Katherine's strange death. What seemed to emerge, heretofore covered over, was the suspicion each had in varying degrees that Katherine had committed suicide, if not intentionally then subintentionally (i.e. by excessive risk-taking). (Katherine had actually fallen from the rooftop of their house, although it was never clear why she had climbed onto the roof in the first place.) This, and data accumulated over subsequent sessions, led the therapists to speculate: first, that Katherine may have seen death as her only way to separate from her parents and family; and second, that this same pattern is being reenacted with Barry, who is now the oldest child. A straight A student, president of his student body and a tennis champ in high school, Barry never went to college or work, but was at home unable to make a decision about the *right* school to attend.

(In an enmeshed family, such as the Turners, a member may view suicide as the only way to make a statement that will finally be heard. To such a desperate and despairing person, the suicidal act may be attempted as the only way to separate from the family. Ironically, the successful suicide may leave the family even more enmeshed than before. Moreover, the act may increase the likelihood of further suicides among the surviving family members. Working with such a post-suicidal family, therapists must help its members to develop alternate methods for gaining autonomy.)

Apparently, for some time prior to her death, Katherine served as a bridge between her parents. Because of their widening marital rift, it was her family function to keep them together. One consequence of that family role, however, was her own inability to leave the home to form an identity of her own. Unable to resolve the conflicts that the parents had and unable to leave, as she felt her mother could not manage without her, she became more and more confused about her own competency and identity and increasingly desperate about her own feelings of powerlessness and inadequacy, ultimately killing herself. Piecing the story together, the two therapists helped the family accept the reality of the suicide, along with its attendant rush of anger, blame, and guilt. At the same time, the therapists helped each member work through the usual grief process at the loss of a loved one. Barry, in particular, needed to understand his own behavior, especially the danger that he might follow in Katherine's footsteps unless he could emancipate himself from the family without excessive guilt. While the conflict between mother and father did not prevent the children from growing up and becoming individuals, it did make it extremely difficult for the children to separate from the parents. As the marital discord was brought into the open and slowly resolved, the children, and especially Barry, felt free to step out into the world [Goldenberg & Goldenberg, 1977].

We learn from this case that children may play a variety of roles and serve a variety of functions within a family; sometimes they become so caught up in the family vise that they become immobilized or can escape only through suicide.

Children inevitably acquire labels in the process of growing up. Billy is lazy, Joey is handsome, Elizabeth is bright, Amy tells lies. Some children make a determined effort to play the "good child"; their rooms are neat, their homework turned in on time, their library books never overdue. Others, more defiant, may be scapegoated as the "bad child"—incorrigible, destructive, unmanageable. For every child who pays the price of being a "bad" child, there is probably a sibling who pays the price of posing as a "good" child. We saw just such a situation in the case of Eric and his sisters earlier in this chapter.

In **pathogenic** families, families that produce dysfunctional behavior, one or both adults and all the children may be assigned roles inappropriate to their age, sex, or full range of personality characteristics. As indicated in the previous paragraph, they may be treated as if they had only a single characteristic—as stupid or lazy or selfish or a liar, for example—instead of a wide human range of feelings and attitudes. In some such families, parents who are uncomfortable in accepting the dependence of their child (possibly because they themselves are immature and needy) may reverse roles with that child; in extreme cases, the child may become overburdened with demands that he or she take care of infantile parents (to say nothing of younger siblings) and thus may never be given a chance to be a child in his or her own right. Boszormenyi-Nagy and Spark (1973) refer to this process as the **parentification** of the child. They believe such a child—usually the one who is quiet, conforming, and good—frequently is part of a family in which there is depression, despair, and rage, although these feelings may not get expressed. Sometimes childlike adults, abdicating their leadership responsibilities to the child, may try to justify their inadequacies under the guise of permissiveness or being democratic and nonauthoritative, thus "allowing" the child adult responsibilities.[4]

In some families, children are assigned the **scapegoat** role—bad, always in trouble, uncontrollable, the cause of the mess the family is in. Usually such a role assignment occurs through the collusive action of several family members, who validate each other's impression that the family must punish, restrain, or in some way get rid of this bad influence. Closer observation of the family reveals that they have no intention of letting the scapegoat leave, because they need that person to blame for any signs of family disharmony or dysfunction. (A fuller discussion of scapegoating, together with a case study, is presented in Chapter 3.)

Some pathogenic families maneuver their children into playing out *sexualized roles*. Seductive, incestuous-like relationships, or overt incest may be found in many severely disturbed families. Sexual relations between the parents may occur infrequently or have stopped completely in these cases. As a consequence, the angry or rejected parent may seek gratification with his or her child. This may result in incest, but more likely it means showering special attention or gifts on the child, overinvolving oneself in the child's social life, perhaps going places—restaurants, the theater, parties—regularly with the child where one would normally attend with a spouse. Boszormenyi-Nagy and Spark (1973) point out that such a child is not seen by the offending parent as a child but as an object, to be used for satisfying parental dependency needs or to retaliate and gain revenge against the rejecting or indifferent marital partner.

Finally, these authors describe the *family pet*, a role assignment in which families cast one of their children as perfect or ideal. Such children rarely cause overt trouble, being allowed to act silly or clownlike. If the parentified child is the family "healer" or caretaker, and the scapegoated child is the family trouble-maker, the family pet is the good, carefree, affectionate, undemanding model child. Unfortunately, "pets" are rarely taken seriously; it is as if they existed merely to bring laughter and lightness to the family. Yet there may be considerable sadness and depression underneath the surface playfulness and good

---

[4]Parentification of a child may occur under a variety of circumstances. More and more commonly we see the phenomenon today when a parent deserts the family, becomes ill or incapacitated, dies, drinks too heavily, and so on. In each case, the parent is unavailable and the child is expected to fill the parent role, physically as well as psychologically.

citizenship. One reason is that the family pet, frequently the baby or youngest child, is treated in a sense as a nonperson, without position or status in the family, with a resulting loss of self-esteem. The cute, adorable, "darling" facade may hide inner feelings of emptiness.

SUMMARY

A family is a natural social system. The way it functions—establishes roles, communicates, negotiates differences between members—has numerous implications for the development and well being of its individual members. Adopting a family perspective, a member's dysfunctional behavior may represent a system that is in disequilibrium; he or she may simply be the "identified patient," a representative of a troubled family. From this viewpoint, the locus of pathology can be found in family relationships and clinical intervention involves the entire family unit.

A family may be studied developmentally, in terms of how it deals with the problems or crises that arise at various phases of its life cycle. In each phase, the family must learn new adaptational techniques and run the risk of family dysfunction.

American families today show a variety of living styles and living arrangements in addition to the traditional nuclear family. Single-parent households, blended families, communes, and cohabitation between unmarried persons are providing alternative choices to the nuclear family organization. Within the nuclear family, working women have brought about changes in role-sharing and child-rearing with their husbands, as well as demanding better child-care facilities. The major reason for these changing family patterns today is the large increase in the divorce rate in recent years.

Changing views of a woman's role in society, once believed to be biologically fixed, but now thought to reflect society's adult role expectations for them, have led to many women breaking out of their traditional roles of wife and mother to pursue their education and careers. As a consequence, they are postponing marriage more than in the past, postponing childbearing, having fewer children or remaining childless. **Dual-career marriages,** for all of their personal benefits to both husband and wife, often cause stresses due to role overload.

Parents need to teach children coping skills so that they can adapt successfully to society. In pathogenic families, adults and children alike may be assigned roles inappropriate to their age, sex, or personality characteristics. Parentification of a child, scapegoating a child, or casting the child in sexualized roles or as family pet sometimes occurs in such families.

2

FUNCTIONAL AND DYSFUNCTIONAL FAMILY SYSTEMS

We have described the family as a natural social system in the previous chapter, and we must now elaborate on just what is meant by this concept. What is a system? What are its characteristics? What is the relationship between an individual family member and the family system of which he or she is a part? Are there different **subsystems** within a family, and, if so, what bearing do they have on one another and on the family as a whole?

In system terms, families are rarely if ever "normal" or "abnormal." However, some function more effectively and with greater competence and resiliency than others; in so-called dysfunctional families, there may be a breakdown, perhaps temporarily, in the system's ability to cope with **stresses** and strains. Much of the behavior patterns and forms of interactions in families are similar and overlap with each other. Every family faces a number of crises as they evolve through the family life cycle. Napier and Whitaker (1978) distinguish between **acute** situational stress, interpersonal stress, and intrapersonal stress; all three add to the wear and tear of family living. *Acute situational stresses* (a serious illness, a job change, the birth of a baby, a move to a new city, the death of a family member) are predictable crises for almost every family sometime during its life cycle, and call for coping with a life suddenly altered by new circumstances. *Interpersonal stresses* involve conflict and disunity within a group such as a family, schisms that keep the group perpetuating patterns of disharmony. *Intrapersonal* *stresses*—conflicts within an individual—are the product of external pressures, including those that result from growing up in a particular family, that the individual internalizes. Family therapists are interested especially in those interpersonal stresses that cause patterns of conflict and tension within a family.

Jackson (1967) argues that "there is no such thing as a normal family" and that when a casual observer refers to a family as "normal," that person probably is referring to some single facet of family living and not to the total family interaction. Later in this chapter we will examine some of the findings of recent research comparing optimally functional, midrange, and severely dysfunctional families.

SOME CHARACTERISTICS OF A FAMILY SYSTEM

A system may be defined as a set of interacting units with relationships among them (Miller, 1978) or as sets of elements standing in interaction (Bertalanffy, 1968). That is, a system is an entity with component parts or units that co-vary, with each unit constrained by or dependent on the state of other units. There are solar systems, ecosystems, systems of law, electronic systems, and so on. In each case, there are components that have some common properties. These components interact with one another so that each influences and in turn is influenced by other component parts, together producing a whole—a system—that is larger than the sum of its interdependent parts. A system is characterized by *wholeness* or unity and must take into account the ongoing interaction between parts. It exists as part of some *hierarchical order* of systems; each higher or more advanced level is made up of systems of lower levels. All systems are organized and strive to maintain some kind of balance or **homeostasis.** A system may reach the same final state from different initial conditions and in different manners; this is the concept of **equifinality.** The family qualifies as such a system. The following are its major characteristics:

Family Rules

A family is a rule-governed system; its members behave in an organized, repetitive pattern of interactions with one another. This idea was first proposed by Don Jackson (1965a), a psychiatrist who, as a member of the Mental Research Institute in Palo Alto, California, contributed many of the conceptualizations of family life that we now subsume under communications theory (see Chapter 5). Jackson observed that in marriage the partners are faced with the challenge of collaboration on a wide variety of tasks—money-making, housekeeping, social life, love-making, parenting. At the start of their relationship, they immediately exchange views as to how they are defining the nature of that relationship. Together, they define the rights and duties of the spouses. "You can depend on me to be logical, practical, realistic." "In return, you can depend upon me to be a feeling, sensitive, social person." (Commonly, these patterns are tied to culturally linked sex roles—in this case, male and female, respectively—but variations are frequent.) Appropriate for the individuals involved, and not rigidly set, such a division of labor helps a couple work out the sort of life they choose to lead.

Trained as a psychoanalyst and committed to the study of an individual's intrapsychic stresses, Jackson became intrigued with the influence of family interactive patterns on individual functioning. Family rules, he observed, determine the patterning of behaviors between people, which become the governing principles of family life. Each person's behavior within the family is related to and dependent on the behavior of all the other members.

A redundancy principle operates in family life, in that a family will interact in repetitive sequences in all areas of its life. That is, the entire system can be run by a relatively small set of rules governing relationships. Understand these rules, and you understand how together they define that relationship. These rules determine behavior among its participants rather than individual needs, drives, or personality traits, according to Jackson.

Observe the rules that define the following relationship between husband (H) and wife (W), as they are getting dressed to go out to dinner with another couple:

W: I wish you would dress better. I'd like you to pay more attention to your clothes. Why don't you take your Christmas bonus and buy yourself a new suit?
H: I just can't spend the money on myself when you and the children need so many things.
W: But we want you to have something, too.
H: I just can't put myself first.

Notice how, contrary to appearances, the one-down behavior of the husband (whereby he humbly places his needs "one down" from those of the rest of the family) is quite controlling. What sort of relationship have they worked out? The wife is allowed to complain about her husband's appearance, but he retains control over the family's expenditure of money. He apparently does not intend to follow her suggestions, and, moreover, cannot be faulted because he is the good person sacrificing for his family (and probably making them feel guilty). This couple, caught up in a repetitive exchange that defines and redefines the nature of their relationship, in fact executes no action and eliminates the possibility of finding new solutions to their differences.

All families follow rules for dividing labor, power, and so on, in order to carry out the tasks of daily living.[1] Sometimes these rules are stated overtly: children shouldn't interrupt an adult who is speaking, children should hang up their clothes, parents decide on bedtime, father should not be interrupted while watching Monday night football on television, mother makes the decisions regarding purchases of new clothes.

Most family rules are unwritten and covertly stated. That is, they are inferences that all family members make to cover the redundancies or repetitive patterns in the relationships they observe around the house. "Go to father when you have a problem; he's more understanding." "It's best to ask mother for money after dinner when she's in a good mood." "Stay away from their bedroom on Sunday morning, they like to be alone." Sometimes a family rule, unstated but understood by all, is that decisions are made by the parents and handed down to the children; in other cases, all learn they may state their own opinions freely. Parents also learn and adhere to covert rules: daughters help with dishes, but it isn't right to ask a son; child A can be depended on to tell the truth, but child B cannot; child C is a spendthrift and cannot be trusted with money, and so on.

Family therapists such as Satir (1972) often try to help a family recognize its unwritten rules, especially those that involve the exchange of feelings or that cause family pain. For example, some families forbid discussion of certain topics ("Mother is becoming an alcoholic." "Father does not come home some nights." "Brother does not know how to read." "Sister should be talked to about sex and contraception.") and as a consequence, fail to take realistic steps to alleviate the problems. Other families forbid overt expressions of anger or irritation with each other (parents, as models, refusing to fight in front of the children). Still others foster dependence ("Never trust anyone but your mother and father."), keeping children from entering the outside world. Satir argues that dysfunctional families follow dysfunctional rules. She attempts to help them become aware of these unwritten

---

[1]A small child visiting a friend for the first time is apt to be bewildered by observing a family operating under an alien set of rules. Thus, he or she may notice, that, contrary to his own family's operations, mothers and fathers may greet each other with a kiss, may not get into a quarrel over the dinner table, may include the children in the conversation. Sometimes, visiting children are startled to learn that according to the rules of some families, it is not necessary to finish all the food on your plate before you are allowed to have dessert!

FIGURE 2-1. Virginia Satir, M.S.W. (Photo by John Nakles.)

rules that retard growth and maturity, and to change them. Changing outmoded or irrelevant and growth-retarding rules helps modify the operation of the family system.

Family Homeostasis

Psychologists have long been aware of the body's ability to operate as a self-regulating system, maintaining a steady state in the presence of drastic changes in the environment. Despite outside temperatures, body temperature varies little from its customary 98.6°; various body-regulating mechanisms (perspiration, change in water retention, "goose pimples," shivering) ordinarily are called into play to maintain the constancy of body temperature should a sudden change in outside temperature occur. This automatic tendency of the body to maintain balance or equilibrium is called homeostasis.

In family terms, homeostasis refers to the inclination of a system to maintain a dynamic equilibrium around some central tendency, and to undertake operations to restore that equilibrium whenever it is threatened (Bloch & LaPerriere, 1973). Thus, a family's homeostatic mechanisms usually restrict behavior to a narrow range—for example, not allowing a quarrel between two children to escalate beyond a certain point, say to physically assaulting each other. In such a situation, parents are likely to do one or more of the following: separate the children, scold them, lecture one or both, remind them of their family ties and responsibilities, punish one or both, hug them both and urge them to settle the argument, act as referee, or send each out of the way of the other until tempers cool. Whatever the solution, the effort is directed, at least in part, to returning the system to its previous balance or equilibrium.

Jackson (1965b) reminds us that during a courting period, couples may engage in endless and wondrously varied behavioral ploys with each other. Upon marriage or after a long-term relationship, however, most of these are excluded from their interactional repertoire and are no longer used. What remains is a narrower range of behavior that may require balancing from time to time. Usually a private code develops, each one learning to cue the other homeostatically, perhaps with a glance or gesture (saying, in effect, for instance, "I'm hurt by what you've just said and want you to reassure me that you don't mean it and that you still love me.") that communicates to the other that disequilibrium has just been created and requires some corrective reaction in order to return the interaction to its previous balanced state. Sometimes the analogy is made to a heating system in a house, with the thermostat set to cause the furnace to respond if the temperature dips below the desired level of warmth. Figure 2-2 demonstrates such a situation.

Homeostatic mechanisms, in an ongoing relationship between two people, help maintain their arrangement by restoring the rules that define their relationship. If a family rule is that no disagreement ever gets aired, then if trouble arises, family members may start to show uneasiness, change the topic, or become physically ill. In the case of Jerry M., cited in the previous chapter, he developed severely dysfunctional behavior just before the family had to deal with separating. The parents are thus distracted, they again function as a unit in their concern over their emotionally disturbed child, and the family homeostatic balance is returned, at least for the time being.

What happens when a family must change or modify its rules? As children grow up, they press for redefinitions of family relationships. They no longer wish to accompany their parents on weekends, preferring to be with friends. They expect to be given allowances to spend as they wish, to decide themselves on a suitable bedtime, to listen to music that may be repellent to their parents' ears. They want to borrow the family car, sleep over at a friend's, pursue interests alien to

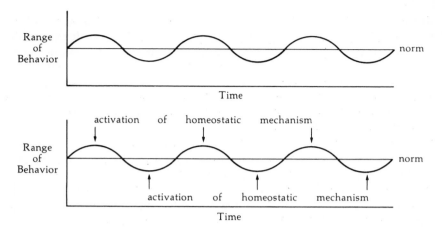

FIGURE 2-2. This figure demonstrates the operation of homeostatic mechanisms in the family. As in a home heating system, when the temperature deviates from a preset norm, the deviation is registered and counteracted by the homeostatic mechanisms of the thermostat system. Families utilize similar cues for achieving balance and equilibrium. (From "The Study of the Family," by D. D. Jackson, *Family Process,* 1965, *4,* 1-20. Reprinted by permission.)

those traditionally cared about in the family. They challenge family values and traditions; they no longer share their innermost secrets with parents; they insist on being treated as equals. All of this causes disequilibrium within the family system, a sense of loss, and perhaps a feeling of strangeness until new transactional patterns restore family balance. As Minuchin and associates (1978) point out, the system tends to maintain itself within preferred ranges; a demand for deviation or change that is too great or too sudden, beyond the system's threshold of tolerance, is likely to elicit counter-deviation responses. In pathogenic families, demands for even the most necessary changes may be met with increased rigidity as the family stubbornly attempts to retain familiar patterns. Unless the family is helped to remain flexible and open to change, some family members will inevitably feel trapped within a family system that allows no alternatives.

Feedback and Information Processing

From the field of cybernetics (the study of methods of feedback control) that underlies automation and computer technology comes an understanding of how a system maintains activity in a constant direction while maintaining a steady state. Through the process of **feedback,** information about the state of the system can be fed back through that system, automatically triggering any necessary changes to keep that system "on track." A part of a system can alter its communications or behavior (output) based on information it receives regarding the effects of its previous outputs on other parts of the system. That is, through feedback mechanisms, part of any system's output is reintroduced into the system as information about the original output. Setting a home thermostat at 70°F programs the heating system so that it will receive instructions to activate when the temperature drops below that point. When the desired temperature is reached, feedback information will alter the ongoing state and the system will deactivate until such time as reactivation is needed to again warm up the house and keep the temperature stable.

What has all this to do with families? Family members also exchange information—sensations and behavior—in an effort to keep the family system operating smoothly. Feedback may be either positive or negative. Positive feedback increases deviation from a steady state (in the analogy above, the furnace gets hotter and hotter). Negative feedback is corrective, adjusting the input so that the system may adjust homeostatically to its environment and return to its steady state (see Figure 2-3). Observe how the husband and wife in the following

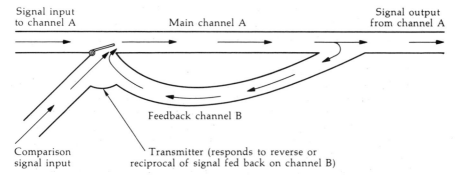

Signal input to channel A   Main channel A   Signal output from channel A

Feedback channel B

Comparison signal input   Transmitter (responds to reverse or reciprocal of signal fed back on channel B)

FIGURE 2-3. In this illustration of negative feedback, part of a system's output is reintroduced into the system as information about the output, thus governing and correcting the process. A negative signal from channel A, fed back to the sender through channel B, alters the signal in A. Feedback loops characterize all interpersonal relationships. (From "The Nature of Living Systems," by J. G. Miller, *Behavioral Science,* 1971, *16,* 277-301. Reprinted by permission.)

condensed exchange of information, under the guidance of a family therapist, provide the negative feedback to one another needed to modify the original position each takes. The husband, six months previous to this session, left his wife to move in with a younger woman from his office. He now lives alone in a furnished room and wants to return home, but his wife resists the idea at first.

H: I don't want to move back in if you're never going to let me forget what happened earlier this year.
W: I'm afraid to let you move back. I don't trust you not to do the same thing again.
H: We can't work out anything while we're apart.
W: I wish I could believe it was me you were coming home to, and not so that you could have your meals served when you arrived home and your laundry done for you.
H: How can I prove I want to try again?
W: You could love me . . . You could want to make love to me, which you don't seem to want to do anymore.
H: You could be more friendly yourself, not so angry at me all the time.
W: I want this to work out. It would be awful if you left again. I just don't know.
H: Let's try. I can't promise, but let's try.
W: Okay . . . but I'm still not sure.

All interactions between people may be viewed as **feedback loops,** because the behavior of each person involved affects and is affected by each other person's behavior (Watzlawick, Beavin, & Jackson, 1967). Thus, it becomes meaningless to speak of causality in linear terms of A leads to B (for example, she feels hurt and rejected and wants to punish him) as though the trouble resides in one person and is imposed on the other. The systems approach emphasizes the behavior of an individual within a context in which another person or persons is present and exchanges information with that individual, each influencing the other. Within a system, a single event such as the husband leaving is both effect and cause. There is a circular movement of parts that affect each other, but no beginning or end to the circle. Each person's behavior is simultaneously caused by and causative of behavior in another part of the system. It is that system that the family therapist tries to help overhaul and change.

A system is constantly changing as new input information is fed back into the system and alterations are made in response to the new input. Anthropologist Gregory Bateson (1972) has offered an elegant definition of information: "a difference that makes a difference." A word, a gesture, a smile, a scowl—these are differences or changes in the environment, much as a temperature drop is an environmental difference or change in the heating system. These differences in turn make a difference, as the receiver of the information alters perceptions of the environment and modifies behavior. **Information processing** is basic to understanding how any system operates. If information processing is faulty, the system is likely to malfunction.

Subsystems and Boundaries

All systems have structure, function, and evolution. They are organized into a more or less stable set of relationships; they behave in ways that carry out certain actions; and they are continuously in the process of change. Here we are especially concerned with the structure of a system, the arrangement of its subsystems or components in a particular geographic space and at a given moment in time. Subsystems are organized units within the overall system that carry out distinct functions in an effort to maintain themselves.

Every family system contains a number of coexisting subsystems. Husbands and wives form one **dyad,** mothers and children form another, siblings form still another subsystem, and so on. Subsystems can be formed by generation, by sex, by interest, or by function (Minuchin, 1974a). Each family member belongs to different subsystems simultaneously; in each, different levels of power are exercised and different skills learned. For example, the oldest child may have power within the sibling subsystem, but must cede that power when interacting with his or her parents.

The family system carries out its functions through subsystems. Because each member belongs to several subsystems simultaneously, he or she enters into different complementary relationships with other family members in each, depending on the subsystem they belong to in common. A woman can be wife, mother, daughter, younger sister, older sister, niece, granddaughter, and so on, depending on the nature of the relationship with another family member. In each relationship she plays a separate role and can expect to engage in different transactional patterns. Giving her younger sister advice about finding a job, she may be told by her husband to get off the phone and hurry up with dinner. She has to remember not to be hurt if the children do not eat what she has cooked or if her mother, a dinner guest, gives her advice on how to improve the table setting. Various coalitions are also possible. The husband and wife vow to remain united on the issue of buying new clothes, even if their adolescent daughter tries to divide them, and the grandparents ally themselves with their grandchildren against the parents. Such passing alliances are characteristic of temporary subsystems.

More enduring subsystems are the spouse, the parental, and the sibling subsystems (Minuchin, et al., 1978). The husband/wife subsystem is basic; any dysfunction in this subsystem reverberates through the family as children are scapegoated or co-opted into an alliance with one parent against the other because the couple are in conflict. The spouse subsystem also provides a model to the child about the nature of intimate relationships or the transactions between a man and a woman in general, all likely to affect the child's relationships later in life. The parental subsystem (which may include grandparents or older children assigned to parental roles) is involved with child-rearing and functions such as nurturance, guidance, and control. The child learns to deal with authority, with people of greater power, before increasing his or her own capacity for decision making and self-control. The sibling subsystem contains the child's first peer group. Through participation in this subsystem, patterns of negotiating, cooperating, or competing develop. The interpersonal skills developed by a child will be significant as he or she moves beyond the family into school and later the world of work.

Boundaries are delineations between subsystems. The boundaries of a particular subsystem are the rules governing who participates in its transactions and in what way. They must be clear and well defined for proper family functioning, allowing subsystem members to carry out their differentiated functions without too much interference. At the same time, they must be **open systems** to allow contact between members of the subsystem and others.[2] That is, they must be both limiting and permeable. If parents and children have different and nonoverlapping roles and responsibilities, the function of the boundaries is to protect that necessary differentiation. A mother defines the boundary of the parental subsystem when she tells her 15-year-old son, the oldest of three children: "Don't you decide whether your sisters are old enough to stay up to see that TV program. Your father and I will decide that." However, she may redefine that boundary to include the parental child when she announces: "I want all of you to listen to your older brother. He will be in charge while your father and I attend an all-day meeting tomorrow." What should be clear from these examples is that it is the clarity of the subsystem boundaries that is far more significant in the effectiveness of family functioning than the composition of the family's subsystems (see Figure 2-4).

OPTIMAL FAMILY FUNCTIONING

Up to this point we have described and illustrated a number of interactional patterns within a family system that may lead to disorganized or dysfunctional behavior in one or more of its members or in the family in general. Before proceeding further, it might be well to

---

[2]A **closed system** such as the solar system operates only within its own boundaries. Living systems are open; they receive inputs from their environments and discharge outputs into these environments. In a living system, a boundary must be semipermeable; it must be open enough to interact with the outside world but not so blurred as to lose its integrity and identity.

FIGURE 2-4. The effect of stress on the subsystem boundaries of a family. In the top diagram, a father (F) and mother (M), both stressed at work, come home and criticize each other, but then detour their conflict by attacking a child. This results in less danger to the spouse subsystem, but stresses the child (C). In the lower figure, the husband criticizes the wife, who seeks a coalition with the child against the father. Note the inappropriately rigid cross-generational subsystem of mother and child in the latter case as well as the diffuse boundary between mother and child; both have the effect of excluding the father. Minuchin refers to this result as a cross-generational dysfunctional pattern. (Reprinted by permission of the publishers from *Families and Family Therapy,* by Salvador Minuchin. Cambridge, Mass.: Harvard University Press. Copyright © 1974 by the President and Fellows of Harvard College.)

pause to indicate what we know of the day to day operation of competent families, families with parental relationships that presumably help develop capable, adaptive, healthy individuals. Are such families really unique or do they in some ways and to some degree resemble what takes place in inadequately functioning families? Actually, such information is vital if we are to establish some interactional baseline against which to measure transactions within other families. Such findings also have therapeutic and preventive implications. Unfortunately, data on so-called "normal" family operations are slim indeed, especially when compared to the growing literature on pathogenic families.

Perhaps the most authoritative word to date on how "healthy" families function comes from the research of Lewis, Beavers, Gossett, and Phillips (1976). These clinicians looked beyond the strengths and weaknesses of individual family members in order to search out those interactions within a family system that make for optimal functioning. Working with intact families, with at least one adolescent but with no family member identified as a psychiatric patient or receiving psychiatric treatment, volunteer families were interviewed and their interactions on a variety of tasks videotaped. Ratings by various judges of their videotaped behavior were made along five major dimensions, with various subdimensions contained within these major headings:

I. Structure of the Family
   A. Overt power (how family dealt with influence and dominance)
   B. Parental coalitions (strength of husband/wife alliance; see Figure 2-4)
   C. Closeness (presence or absence of distinct boundaries and degree of interpersonal distance; see Figure 2-4)
   D. Power structure (ease in determining family "pecking order")
II. Mythology (degree to which a family's concept of itself was congruent with rater's appraisal of family behavior)
III. Goal-Directed Negotiation (the effectiveness of the family's negotiations)
IV. Autonomy
   A. Communication of self-concept (degree to which family nourished or discouraged clear communication of feelings and thoughts)
   B. Responsibility (degree to which the family system reflected family members' acceptance of responsibility for their own feelings, thoughts, and actions)
   C. Invasiveness (extent to which the family system tolerated or encouraged family members to speak for one another)
   D. Permeability (degree to which the family system encouraged the acknowledgment of the stated feelings, thoughts, and behavior of its members)
V. Family Affect
   A. Expressiveness (extent to which the open communication of affect is encouraged within the family system; see Figure 2-5)
   B. Mood and tone (the family system's mood, ranging from warm and affectionate to cynical and hopeless; see Figure 2-5)
   C. Conflict (degree of family conflict and its effect on family functioning)
   D. Empathy (degree to which the family system encourages members to be sensitive to each other's feelings and to communicate this awareness)

On the basis of these ratings, each family received a score in a Global Health-Pathology Scale. Thirty-three "healthy" families were distinguished from 70 families with a hospitalized adolescent, and 12 families in the former group were studied intensively.

Results indicated that no single quality was unique to optimally functioning or competent families compared to those more poorly functioning families. Rather, the mixture of a number of variables accounted for their special style of relating to one another. Thus, family "health" was considered not as a "single thread," but rather a tapestry reflecting differences in degree along many dimensions. The capacity of families to communicate thoughts and feelings and the cardinal role of the parental coalition in establishing the level of functioning of the

A. Expressiveness: Rate the degree to which this family system is characterized by open expression of feelings.

1	1.5	2	2.5	3	3.5	4	4.5	5
Open, direct expression of feelings		Direct expression of feelings despite some discomfort		Obvious restriction in the expression of some feelings		Although some feelings are expressed, there is masking of most feelings		No expression of feelings

B. Mood and Tone: Rate the feeling tone of this family's interaction.

1	1.5	2	2.5	3	3.5	4	4.5	5
Unusually warm, affectionate, humorous and optimistic		Polite, without impressive warmth or affection; or frequently hostile with times of pleasure		Overtly hostile		Depressed		Cynical, hopeless and pessimistic

FIGURE 2-5. Two of 13 rating scales used by judges to score family interaction patterns following the viewing of the videotape of a family carrying out a variety of tasks together. The upper scale measures the degree to which the family system encourages the open communication of feelings. The lower scale asks the judge to rate the mood or feeling tone of the family interaction. (From *No Single Thread: Psychological Health in Family Systems,* by J. M. Lewis, W. R. Beavers, J. T. Gossett, and V. A. Phillips. Copyright 1976 by Brunner/Mazel, Inc. Reprinted by permission.)

total family stand out as the key factors. Parental coalitions offer family leadership as well as providing models of relating to other persons.

Optimally functioning families demonstrate strikingly affiliative attitudes about human encounter. That is, they expect transactions with one another to be caring, open, empathic, and trusting. By contrast, responses in dysfunctional families are often guarded, painful if somehow necessary, distant, or hostile. In optimally functioning families, there is basic respect for one's own views and those of others rather than one member dominating and insisting the others submit; thus each member feels free to be honest in agreement or disagreement with others, even when this leads to conflict or angry exchanges. They do things together, actively and with initiative. Members of dysfunctional families are apt to feel isolated and to respond to one another in a passive, powerless, controlled fashion. While power resides in the parental coalition in optimally functioning families, it is not exercised in an authoritarian way; children have opinions and negotiations are common, so that competing parent/child coalitions do not form and defensive power struggles are not necessary.

Successful, effective, well-functioning families, while close, respect personal **autonomy** and tolerate individuality and separateness between their members. There is no tidal pull toward family oneness that obliterates individual differences. Actually, in healthy families boundaries exist between members and each person knows a sense of "I-ness" and therefore accepts whatever he or she thinks or feels. Separation and loss are accepted realistically, so that family members are able to adapt to changes brought about by growth and development, aging and death. The most capable families demonstrate open, direct expression of humor, tenderness, warmth, and hopefulness.

MODERATELY AND SEVERELY
DYSFUNCTIONAL FAMILIES

We have seen that all families face common developmental tasks and evolve ways of organizing themselves to meet and cope with such tasks. We have seen too that certain families—we referred to them as optimally functioning—develop ways of interacting that are efficient, effective, and that help produce competent, adaptive children, themselves capable of forming and engaging in meaningful and mutually rewarding relationships with others. Well-functioning families typically have a structure that allows for shared power, an appreciation of individuality among their members, and the ability to deal realistically with separation and loss. Such families are more likely than others to manifest a warm, expressive feeling tone and to accept the passage of time and inevitably of change (children growing up and becoming more powerful than their parents, the parents' waning abilities, the inevitability of death) (Lewis, Beavers, Gossett, & Phillips, 1976).

What of those families who function less well (for example, those who fail miserably at child rearing)? Are they different in degree or kind from the families we have just described? Beavers (1977) presents convincing evidence that families can be ordered along a continuum with respect to their effectiveness. At one end of the continuum are the most flexible, adaptable, goal-achieving systems, while the other end of this continuum contains the most inflexible, undifferentiated, and ineffective systems. Beavers uses the systems concept of **entropy** as an orienting framework in understanding the effectiveness of family functioning. Entropy is a term used to describe the tendency of things to go into disorder; thus a family with low entropy implies a high degree of orderliness. Systems, including family systems, can be thought of as having degrees of entropy, as being in states of greater or lesser disorder. Beavers contends that the more closed family systems are doomed to increase in entropy because, without access to the world outside their boundaries, they cannot avoid the downhill pull toward greater disorder. Only open systems are able to receive energy by interacting with the environment, in order to build increasingly ordered structures, low in entropy, within their boundaries. By utilizing such energy, they can develop a structure that fights the inexorable downhill pull found in any closed system.

According to Beavers (1977), there is a relationship between the level of family system competence and the level of functioning of the children of those families. (This relationship is diagrammed in Figure 2-6, although the reader should be aware that a correlation is suggest-

Family	Severely disturbed		Borderline		Midrange		Adequate		Optimal	
	10	9	8	7	6	5	4	3	2	1
Children	Process schizophrenic, severe behavior disorder, "sociopathic"		Borderline patients		Neuroses and behavior disorders (the sane but limited)		No obvious pathology		Unusual individual competence	

FIGURE 2-6. A schematic relationship between family competence and individual functioning among adolescent children. (From *Psychotherapy and Growth: Family Systems Perspective,* by W. R. Beavers. Copyright 1977 by Brunner/Mazel, Inc. Reprinted by permission.)

ed only, and that in actuality family and individual competence both fluctuate, depending largely on their ability to solve problems presented by the internal and external stresses that occur at particular developmental phases. However, family and individual competencies probably have limited ranges of fluctuation.) While Beavers distinguishes five levels of family functioning (optimal, adequate, midrange, borderline, and severely disturbed), he points out that he really is dealing with a continuum, not different kinds of families. Thus, as we shall see, characteristics of severely disturbed families blend subtly into those only moderately disturbed, and these in turn blend into those likely to be labeled as adequate or even optimal in their level of functioning.

Moderately dysfunctional (or midrange) families, more entropic than those labeled as optimal or even adequate, tend to experience greater pain and difficulty in their day-to-day functioning. Offspring, while not as seriously disturbed as children from severely dysfunctional families (who often are schizophrenic), are nevertheless limited, such as being diagnosed as neurotic or having a behavior disorder. (The former usually experience marked feelings of anxiety or depression, as well as inadequate coping devices; the latter show difficulty in following the rules of behavior expected in the world beyond the family.) In terms of relative size in the population, Beavers contends that moderately dysfunctional families probably comprise the largest group, greater than the family groups at either end of the continuum.

These midrange families, according to Beavers (1977), show parental coalitions, but they are shaky. Just as in optimal families, there are generational boundaries; parents and children have accepted their separate roles within the family. However, power issues persist unresolved and family rules are riddled with "shoulds" and "oughts," encouraging intimidation rather than negotiation when the family interacts. While such families do attempt to communicate, they somehow avoid responsibility for feelings, thoughts, or actions ("You shouldn't talk that way about your teacher." rather than "I'm upset that you're unhappy about your teacher.") Family myths—shared distortions—also persist: father is only interested in his business, mother is a saint, one child is always seen as mean while another is always seen as kind.

Unlike optimally functioning families, those Beavers calls moderately dysfunctional do not accept changes brought about by time (for example, mothers may insist on competing with teenage daughters for who is more sexually attractive).

Competition and hidden conflicts between members suggest that while such families are able to get by, frustration is common and may even be a constant underlying factor in their transactions with one another. One frequent consequence is that children grow up learning stereotyped roles and developing constricted identities. For example, in midrange families it may be assumed as inevitable that men are powerful, stupid when it comes to feelings or understanding relationships between people, action-oriented, aggressive, and monetarily successful. By the same token, it may be assumed without question that the female role is ordained to be weak, emotional, intuitive about feelings and people, and dependent. Such stereotyped role definitions, along with family myths, if unchallenged, may fix behavior patterns early in life, frequently allowing no room for developing individual capabilities or loosening boundaries in order to increase contact with the outside world.

The pattern adolescents adopt when the time comes to separate from the family has been characterized by Stierlin (1972) as either **centripetal** or **centrifugal.** In the former, the style is related to the degree that family members cling together; the latter refers to the degree of ease with which they have left the family nest. These differences in style exist in all families, regardless of competence level. However, in families that show competence in their functioning, the style is softened and modified by the various patterns present, and therefore is rarely dramatic or noteworthy. In centripetal families where dysfunction exists, according to Beavers (1977), the children view the family as holding greater promise of fulfillment of their needs than does the outside world. Separation appears threatening and difficult because the family's style is binding and discouraging of experiences in the world outside the family. Midrange families with a centripetal style usually produce neurotic children.

On the other hand, members of centrifugal families view sources of gratification as coming from outside the family. They tend to distance themselves from the family conflict and to seek solace from peers. Rather than binding children, centrifugal families expel children, often before they are mature enough to develop anything but shallow relationships with others. Midrange families with a centrifugal style thus are apt to produce offspring with behavior disorders.

Even more than midrange families, those families who are seriously disturbed represent closed systems—chaotic, rigid, with little vital interaction with the outside world. Beavers believes that in severely dysfunctional families with a centripetal style, there is a good chance that one or more offspring will become a process schizophrenic. (A *process schizophrenic* usually shows social isolation and a lack of emotional responsiveness to others early in life, becoming progressively withdrawn and disorganized as an adult. A *reactive schizophrenic,* on the other hand, usually has a history of adaptive behavior, but due to sudden precipitating external stresses, shows an acute onset of symptoms, possibly occurring as an adult. Of the two, the **prognosis** for the former is much poorer.) Children of centrifugal families are prone to sociopathic behavior. (A *sociopath* is an antisocial person who is callous, irresponsible, egocentric, impulsive, fails to learn from experience or punishment, and is without remorse or shame. Many criminals probably come under this heading.)

Centripetal families who are severely dysfunctional have fragile parental coalitions, so that leadership is absent, no one exercises personal power, and it is often difficult to tell who is the parent and who is the child. Children are not helped to become autonomous, since individuality is discouraged and family closeness is defined as everyone thinking and feeling alike. As a consequence, offspring often fail to establish a coherent identity or to develop a clear sense of their own boundaries (as distinct from other family members). At the same time, the impermeability of the family boundary handicaps them from engaging in relationships outside the family. Needless to say, communication within the family is poor and confusing, making the negotiation of differences between members all but impossible. The absence of warmth is striking, with each encounter within the family seen by the participants as inevitably destructive. The passage of time is denied, so that the myth persists that everything and everyone will always remain the same. Any rival thought of change (increased competence in children or failing abilities in parents, for example) is too upsetting to consider. It is hardly surprising that Beavers labels the process schizophrenic as someone who has suffered a profound deficiency of human relationships.

Those families with centrifugal styles who are severely dysfunctional often show open discord and teasing manipulation when the family interacts. Because the family organization is so unstable, no one (including the parents) has a clear idea of what his or her role should be, leadership may be shifting from moment to moment or be nonexistent, and each person within the family is off on an individual tangent. Bickering, blaming one another, attempting to gain control through intimidation—all of these make for chaos and incoherent communication. Frequently, it is as if no two people are talking on the same topic or responding to what has just been said. Children are apt to move away from such family settings as soon as they can, sometimes by running away or engaging in antisocial behavior that brings them in conflict with the law and placement in a detention home.

The lack of warmth or tenderness in such entropic families, the confusion over trying to follow inconsistent family rules, the shifting power structure, the disjointed pattern of communication, all these factors offer few, if any, rewards for closeness or caring. A facade of indifference may develop, thus making the child appear to be without guilt, but actually, according to Beavers (1977), he or she is feeling hopeless. Experiences in such families lead to the conclusion that one's feelings, impulses, and needs are unacceptable. The antisocial person's self-defeating behavior, seen in a family light, may be an expression of rage at an uncaring world.

SUMMARY

Much of the behavior patterns and forms of interaction in all families overlap as they face various crises during the family life cycle. Acute situational stresses call for coping suddenly with new life circumstances, interpersonal stresses involve disunity within the family, and intrapersonal stresses arise from internalizing the pressures that come from growing up in a particular family. Rather than view a family as normal or abnormal, it is best to judge its degree of competent functioning in family system terms.

A system is a set of interacting components that co-vary, with each element dependent on the state of functioning of each other element with whom it has a relationship. A family system is governed by rules, which may or may not be overtly stated but which are understood by all family members. These rules determine the patterning of behavior within the family. Each family develops its own set of homeostatic mechanisms, which keep the system in balance. When problems arise or escalate to the point of endangering the system's normal functioning, these mechanisms attempt to return the system to its previous equilibrium. Feedback—particularly negative feedback—of feelings, sensations, thoughts and behavior provides information that keeps family functioning "on track." Subsystems within families (a member usually belongs to more than one) are organized sections of families charged with carrying out separate functions to maintain the family system. Boundaries delineate the subsystems and need to remain clear and to some extent permeable for effective family functioning.

Optimally functioning, competent families relate to each other in a number of ways that distinguish them from those less well functioning. Better communication patterns and consistent parental coalitions stand out as especially significant. Moderately and severely dysfunctional families tend to be less flexible, their members more undifferentiated, their systems less efficient. The more severely dysfunctional, the higher the entropy or tendency, particularly within a closed system, to go into disorder. Moderately dysfunctional families tend to produce children more likely to be neurotic or having behavior disorders than do more stable families. Compared to the latter, their parental coalitions are weaker, intimidation rather than negotiation is common between members, and hidden conflicts inevitably play a part in their transactions with each other. Severely dysfunctional families are more apt to have parental coalitions that are fragile, leadership by parents that is weak or shifts or is nonexistent, and either a binding relationship to the family (a centripetal style) or one in which offspring leave the family as soon as they can (centrifugal style). The former pattern is likely to produce schizophrenic children, the latter those considered to have antisocial personalities.

3

EXPRESSIONS OF
FAMILY DYSFUNCTION

Having looked at some principles of family living and causes of dysfunction within a family, we are ready to be more specific about just how dysfunction manifests itself within a family's transactional patterns. Once again, it should be noted that while such interactive patterns occur in all families at one time or another, one or more patterns is most likely to persist in dysfunctional families and often to be their characteristic way of dealing with each other.

In this chapter we shall look first at the ways in which families cope with various crises during their life cycles. Such crisis points often provide an opportunity for growth, as the family emerges better equipped to cope with future developmental tasks. On the other hand, some families fail to change or gain a sense of competence, their members continuing to deal with one another in dysfunctional, growth-retarding ways. We shall examine four common expressions of such dysfunctional behavior within a family: pathological communication, enmeshment and **disengagement,** scapegoating, and, finally, the persistence of family myths.

DEVELOPMENTAL SEQUENCES AND FAMILY CRISES

The most reasonable approach to the understanding of a family's functioning would seem to be one that focuses on how that family carries out its various tasks. While there are some families whose entire life cycles seem to be an uninterrupted series of disasters, they are, mercifully, relatively rare. More likely, family crises are tied rather specifically to the tasks current to the family's developmental phase. Thus, as we have previously indicated, a childless couple who appear content may face considerable marital stress with the birth of a baby, resulting in changes in roles, freedom of movement, economic status, and so on. Another set of parents may do an excellent job when nurturing behavior is needed, but fail miserably and disrupt a smoothly functioning family system when the child needs to break out of the confining boundaries of the family unit, as when he or she enters school. Another crucial boundary within the family is generational; the husband/wife dyad composes one subsystem, the children another subsystem. In such a case, one or both parents may enjoy being playful with a child, being a pal, but cannot behave like an adult model or offer leadership and guidance when the child reaches adolescence and such new parental behavior becomes mandatory.

Similarly, late adolescents may provoke a family crises as a result of their first prolonged separation from their family when entering a university away from their home city or town. Shapiro (1967), who has studied such young people and their families in both individual and family therapy, found that earlier parent/child relationships contributed to the adolescent's consolidated or confused sense of identity, and in turn this constituted an important determinant of the adolescent's (and consequently the family's) disturbance. Specifically, he found that in families where there is evidence of striking distortions, inconsistencies, and contradictions in how the parents view and treat the adolescent, then he or she is likely to react by showing serious psychological disturbance. In such families, Shapiro found repeated evidence of anxiety in the parents over an adolescent's expression of his or her new developmental potentialities.

Each crisis calls for developing new styles of coping by all family members. While **regression** to less effective interaction patterns is always a possible danger under the current stress, the crisis also presents the family with an opportunity to grow by learning more effective coping strategies. In the following case, we see a subsystem, operating within the overall family system, that takes the form of an alliance between the father and his adolescent daughter. Although such a union need not necessarily be damaging to overall family functioning, in this case it is. (In dysfunctional families, there often exist such subsystems, with one parent outside the inner circle and unable to communicate with the marital partner, who in turn has formed a close emotional alliance with one or more of the children.) Notice how the crisis situation provides an opportunity for positive change, as the mother challenges the father/daughter subsystem.

A domineering, stubborn husband; his meek, childlike wife; and their 16-year-old daughter Joyce were approaching the point in Joyce's therapy where they were becoming aware that the 16-year-old's repeated behavior of running away and sexually acting-out often occurred after father and daughter had had a particularly intense encounter with one another. In their encounters each usually tried to convince the other of the "rightness" of his or her point of view by means of shouting arguments. When all three came to the therapist's office after a crisis phone call, they began by relating that two days ago Joyce had met a former boyfriend and spent the night with him at the beach without letting her parents know where she was, and had been "raped" by him. The next morning, i.e., yesterday, Joyce had come home sobbing to tell her parents of the outrage that had befallen her. The father was incensed. He didn't believe Joyce's cry of rape; he accused her of being a slut. Predictably, this triggered Joyce, and the father and daughter were into a shouting match. The meek wife spoke up, addressing her husband, "Why object now, it's happened many times before. I don't like it either; but I like it even less that she is getting between you and me again. I had begun to think recently that maybe I was more to you than just the 'child-mother' of your daughter. I don't want her to ruin that" [McPherson, Brackelmanns & Newman, 1974, p. 83].[1]

Crises occur throughout the family life cycle, often unsettling family stability. For example, several generations of a family, and not just the aging individuals alone, must accommodate to retirement, grandparenthood, illness, the process of dying, and widowhood. The death of a grandparent may be the young child's first encounter with separation and human mortality. It may, at the same time, make the parents more aware of their inevitable mortality, as generational shifts occur within the total family constellation. How the family manages to cope with the dying process has implications for several generations as all move inevitably toward the aging phase of the family life cycle (Brody, 1974).

PATHOLOGICAL COMMUNICATION

For a family to function effectively, it must develop ways and means of establishing and maintaining clear communications channels (Stachowiak, 1975). Language is the most effective means for exchanging factual information, but a great deal of the emotional interaction

---

[1]From "Stages in the Family Therapy of Adolescents," by S. R. McPherson, W. E. Brackelmanns, and L. E. Newman, *Family Process*, 1974, 13, 77-94. Reprinted by permission of the author and publisher.

between people is expressed through nonverbal messages—gestures, tone of voice, facial expression, even the amount of physical space between the communicants. Sometimes silence is a powerful message, as when one marital partner, hurt and angry, stops talking to the other for a period of time. As we have seen, from a systems viewpoint each participant contributes to the behavior of the other; their interaction reflects this joint influence. According to a survey conducted by Beck and Jones (1973), poor communication is by far the major problem reported by couples seeking family counseling (see Figure 3-1).

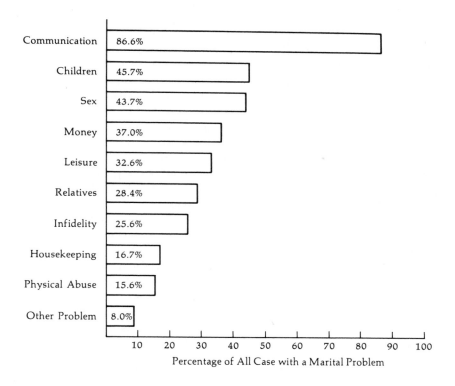

FIGURE 3-1. Ranking of marital problems reported in the case loads of 266 U.S. family counseling agencies who participated in this survey. Note that almost nine out of ten couples complained of difficulties communicating with each other. Communication problems in this sample are almost twice as common as the next highest set of family problems involving relationships with children. (Reprinted from *Progress on Family Problems*, by Dorothy Fahs Beck and Mary Ann Jones, by permission of the publisher. Copyright 1973 by *Family Service Association of America*, New York.)

The Double-Bind and Mystification

In dysfunctional families, it is common to see members substitute speeches at each other in place of conversation, or perhaps turn away and avoid eye contact when someone is speaking. Some families engage in other activities (for example, watching TV, walking in and out of the room) while allegedly conversing, once again interfering with clear and direct communication. Others exchange **double-bind messages**; in such situations, one person issues a statement to another that contains at least two messages or demands, one of which contradicts the other. The person receiving the message is called on to make a response but is doomed to failure whatever response he or she makes, since to respond positively to one is automatically to respond negatively to the other (Bateson, Jackson, Haley & Weakland, 1956). Either way, that person is in a no-win situation. A young woman, having been taught by her parents to be careful of men's advances, becomes anxious whenever her husband gets physically close to her. Whenever he approaches her affectionately, she stiffens and recoils. However, she finds the image of herself as "frigid" or a prude to be repugnant, so as he begins to withdraw in response to her withdrawal from him, she simulates affectionate and seductive behavior, asking in a hurt manner why he is so unresponsive tonight. The husband is caught in a double-bind, a situation without alternatives. Whichever message he obeys— "go away" or "come closer"—he is disobeying the other. His dilemma becomes: "If I like her, I must not show her affection, but if I do not show her affection then I will lose her." Several examples of the double-bind situation, especially as a causative factor in the development of schizophrenia in a family member, are presented in Chapter 4.

Laing (1965) uses the term **mystification** to describe how some families deal with conflict and contradictory viewpoints within a family by befuddling, obscuring, or masking what is going on. Such a masking effect may not avoid the conflict, but it clouds over what the conflict is all about. In everyday family life, one person may mystify another by confirming the content of the experience the second person is having but disconfirming that person's interpretation of the experience. Suppose a young, ambitious husband, moonlighting on a second job in the evening after a day's work, comes home to find his wife sitting in front of the TV set, a six-pack of beer nearby, still wearing the dirty jeans he left her in early in the morning. The breakfast dishes are still unwashed in the kitchen sink. Frustrated, harassed by her three pre-school children all day, with the entire responsibility for raising them since her husband is rarely home before 10 P.M., she barely manages a smile when he arrives. He looks grim.

W: Are you angry?
H: No—just tired.
W: How come you look angry?
H: It's just your imagination.
W: Why don't you admit it? I know you well enough to know when you are pissed with me.
H: I don't know where you dream up these ideas.

In actuality, the husband is furious, but is afraid to have an angry confrontation with her. Instead, he tries to mystify her by telling her she has misperceived the situation. However, his avoidance behavior, intended to escape conflict, only causes greater conflict in her. If she believes him, their relationship is maintained but she thinks she must be "crazy" to imagine he is angry; if she believes her own senses, she retains a firm grip on reality but must face their deteriorating relationship.

The prime function of mystification is to maintain the status quo. It is brought into play when one or more family members threatens that status quo by what they are experiencing. A child who complains of being unhappy is told by his or her parents that such a thing is not possible: "You have no right to feel that way. Haven't we given you everything you want? How could you be so ungrateful?" Through mystification, the parents simply deny or negate what the child is feeling or experiencing, as though whatever he or she reports as taking place does not really exist. They know better what the child is experiencing; his or her perceptions are denuded of validity. After admitting to her parents that she had sexual thoughts and sometimes masturbated, one adolescent girl was flatly told by her parents that she did not. As this pattern was repeated, she began to doubt the validity of her own feelings and thoughts and slowly withdrew into schizophrenia (Laing & Esterson, 1970).

The following vignette is from a meeting of a family and two hospital staff members.

MOTHER: It's nice to have such lovely weather. (It is pouring outside the window.)
DAUGHTER: I am Nikita Khrushchev.
FATHER: (Shakes head mildly and lights a cigarette.)
THERAPIST: Daughter seems to be responding to mother's nonfactual statement.
MOTHER: It is raining, but how are you, doctor? You look well.
FATHER: We had a good visit.
DAUGHTER: Can I have a cigarette?
THERAPIST: A good visit?
FATHER: Yes, of course, we didn't go out but I had some good talks with daughter.

THERAPIST: Yes?
DAUGHTER: (Leaves room.) [Fleck, 1976, p. 670].[2]

With such confusion, you probably are hard pressed to guess who might be the patient! From a family system perspective, however, notice instead how all the family members engage in this strange exchange where no one validates anyone else's statements or behavior. The mother's comment about the lovely weather, while it appears to be a pleasant and agreeable opening gambit, actually is idiosyncratic and distancing. No agreement with her statement is possible from others because it contradicts the obvious fact that it is raining. In turn, it elicits a bizarre response from the daughter. The father, after nonverbally indicating he intends to ignore what is taking place, later offers his own conventional gambit ("we had a good visit"), which is also nonfactual. He had wished to take his daughter home from the hospital but his wish was not granted and his visit, in that sense, was a failure because his mission remained unaccomplished. With so many misstatements about plainly observable facts along with mutual nonvalidation of what each person is saying, is it any wonder that the daughter can tolerate no more and disengages by leaving the room?

Symmetrical and Complementary Relationships

Family therapists are interested in far more than the verbal content of any communication between two or more people, as we can see from the exchange just described. At least as important in most cases is how the participants define their relationship: who has the right to say what to, and about, the other? Patterns of communication and relationships between people may be symmetrical or complementary. In the former, the participants mirror each other's behavior; if A boasts, B tries to top him, which causes A to boast still further and so on in this "one-upmanship" game. In complementary relationships, one partner's behavior complements the other; that is, if A is assertive, B becomes submissive, which encourages A to further assertion, demanding still further submission from B, and so on (Bateson, 1958). As an example of a symmetrical relationship, notice the following exchange between a husband (H) and his wife (W), talking to an interviewer (I). They have sought help because they feared their constant bickering might hurt the children:

[2] From "A General Systems Approach to Severe Family Pathology," by S. Fleck, *American Journal of Psychiatry*, 1976, *133*, 670. Copyright 1976, the American Psychiatric Association. Reprinted by permission.

Transcript	*Comments*
I: How, of all the millions of people in the world, did the two of you get together?	
H: We . . . both worked in the same place. My wife ran a comptometer, and I repaired comptometers, and . . .	H speaks first, offering a unilateral summary of the whole story, thereby defining his right to do so.
W: We worked in the same building.	W restates the same information in her own words, not simply agreeing with him, but instead establishing symmetry in regard to their discussion of this topic.
H: She worked for a firm which had a large installation, and I worked there most of the time because it was a large installation. And so this is where we met.	H adds no new information, but simply rephrases the same tautological sentence with which he began. Thus, he symmetrically matches her behavior of insisting on his right to give information; on the relationship level they are sparring for the "last word." H attempts to achieve this by the finality of his second sentence.
W: We were introduced by some of the other girls up there. (Pause)	W does not let it drop; she modifies his statement, reasserting her right to participate equally in this discussion. Though this new twist is just as passive an interpretation as their "working in the same building" (in that neither is defined as having taken the initiative), she establishes herself as "a little more equal" by referring to "the other girls," a group in which she was obviously the insider, not H. This pause ends the first cycle of symmetrical exchange with no closure.
H: Actually, we met at a party, I mean we first started going together at a party that one of the employees had. But we'd seen each other before, at work.	Though somewhat softened and compromising, this is a restatement which does not let her definition stand.

Transcript	*Comments*
W: We never met till that night. (Slight laugh) (Pause)	This is a direct negation, not merely a rephrasing, of his statement, indicating perhaps that the dispute is beginning to escalate. (Notice however that "met" is quite an ambiguous term in this context—it could mean several things from "laid eyes on each other" to "were formally introduced"—so that her contradiction of him is disqualified; that is, she could not, if queried, be pinned down to it. Her laugh also enables her to "say something without really saying it.")
H: (Very softly) Mhm. (Long pause)	H puts himself one-down by agreeing with her—overtly: but "mhm" has a variety of possible meanings and is here uttered almost inaudibly, without any conviction or emphasis, so the result is quite vague. Even more, the previous statement is so vague that it is not clear what an agreement with it might mean. In any case, he does not go further, nor does he assert still another version of his own. So they reach the end of another round, again marked by a pause which seems to signal that they have reached the danger point (of open contradiction and conflict) and are prepared to end the discussion even without closure of the content aspect.
I: But still, I have an image of dozens of people, or maybe more floating around; so how was it that the two of you, of all these people, got together?	Interviewer intervenes to keep the discussion going.
H: She was one of the prettier ones up there. (Slight laugh) (Pause)	H makes a strong "one-up" move; this dubious compliment places her in comparison with the others, with him as the judge.

Transcript	*Comments*
W: (Faster): I don't know, the main reason I started going with him is because the girls— he had talked to some of the other girls before he talked to me, and told them he was interested in me, and they more or less planned this party, and that's where we met.	She matches his condescension with her own version: she was only interested in him because he was initially interested in her. (The subject around which their symmetry is defined has shifted from whose version of their meeting will be told and allowed to stand to who got the trophy, so to speak, in their courtship.)
H: Actually the party wasn't planned for that purpose—	A straightforward rejection of her definition.
W: (Interrupting): No, but it was planned for us to meet at the party. Meet formally, you might say. In person. (Slight laugh) We'd worked together, but I didn't make a habit of—	After agreeing with his correction, W repeats what she has just said. Her nonpersonal formulation has been weakened, but she now relies on a straight self-definition ("I am this kind of person . . . "), an unassailable way to establish equality.
H: (Overlapping) She was certainly backward-bashful type of worker as far as associating with uh, uh strange men on the place, yeah, but the women knew it. (Pause) And I was flirtin' with lots of 'em up there. (Slight laugh) Nothing meant by it I guess, but just . . . (sigh) just my nature I guess.	H gives a symmetrical answer based on his "nature," and another round ends.

[Watzlawick, Beavin, & Jackson, 1967, pp. 111-113][8]

Symmetrical relationships, as in the above exchange, may be characterized by equality and the minimization of difference between the participants, or they may be competitive. In the latter case, as each partner's actions influence the reactions in his or her partner, there is the danger of a spiraling effect, or what is called *symmetrical escalation*. Quarrels may get out of hand and become increasingly vicious, as a nasty jibe from one is met by a nastier response from the other, which

---

[8] This and other selections are reprinted from *Pragmatics of Human Communication,* by Paul Watzlawick, Ph.D., Janet Helmick Beavin, A.B., and Don D. Jackson, M.D., with permission of W. W. Norton & Company, Inc. Copyright © 1967 by W. W. Norton & Company, Inc.

prompts the first person to become even more nasty, and so on and on.

Complementary interaction is based on inequality and the maximization of differences. In such forms of reciprocal interaction, one partner (traditionally the male) takes the dominant "one-up" position while the spouse (traditionally the female) assumes the submissive "one-down" position. However, despite appearances, this need not be taken as an indication of their relative strength or weakness. Each partner behaves in a manner that presupposes, while also providing reasons for, the behavior of the other. Theirs is an interlocking relationship in which dissimilar but fitted behaviors evoke each other (Watzlawick, Beavin, & Jackson, 1967).

The following transcript is of a complementary relationship, with the husband in the "one-up" position and the wife "one-down." The spouses are emotionally distant from one another and the wife is depressed. After the interviewer has asked the standard opening question about their first meeting, the husband responds first:

H: And—see, when'd you start there?
W: W—I haven't any i—
H: (Interrupting)—seems to me it was about, I came in October, the year before . . . and you probably started about . . . February uh, January or February—probably February or March 'cause your birthday was in December, that same year.
W: Mm, I don't even remember . . .
H: (Interrupting): So I happened to send her some flowers, you see, when—our first date out. And that never—we'd never gone anywhere had we?
W: (With short laugh): No, I was very surprised.
H: And we just went from there. It was about a year later I guess we got married. Little over a year.
I: What did you . . .
H: (Interrupting): Although Jane left the company very shortly after that. Mm, I don't think you worked there over a couple of months, did you?
W: You know, I'm sorry, I don't remember a thing about (slight laugh) how long it was or when I went—
H: (Interrupting): Yeah, a couple of months, and then you went back into teaching. (W: Mhm, mhm) 'Cause we—she found I guess that this war work was not contributing as much to the war effort as she thought it—was, when she went out there.
I: So you—you went to a school?
W: Yes, I'd been working in it, before (Int: Mhm) I went to work there.
I: And you continued the contact without interruption. (H: Oh yeah) What, uh, beside the fact that your wife is obviously attractive, what else do you think you have in common?
H: Absolutely nothing. (Laughing) We never have—had 'r we—(sharp breath). (Pause)

[Watzlawick, Beavin, & Jackson, 1967, pp. 114-115]

Here we see a good illustration of the reciprocal roles each plays in the complementary interaction pattern. Her apparent amnesia and helplessness make it possible for him to appear to be the strong, realistic male, while at the same time being the very factors against which his strength and realism are quite powerless. From this perspective, outward appearances of who is weak and who is strong may be quite misleading.

Every communication reflects a struggle for control of a relationship (Haley, 1963). While each exchange between two persons may be defined by both as either symmetrical or complementary, their overall relationship may alternate from one to the other, depending on the situation. The way they define their relationship in a restaurant (symmetrically exchanging ideas about what sounds good on the menu) may differ drastically from how they define it in the bedroom (as a complementary relationship where one controls and the other submits). Neither pattern is necessarily better or worse. However, one or the other communication pattern may characterize most of a couple's transactions, determining the roles and power structure of their relationship.

ENMESHMENT AND DISENGAGEMENT

In optimally functioning families, clear boundaries exist between people, giving each family member a sense of "I-ness" along with an ingroup sense of "we" or "us." That is, each member retains his or her individuality but not at the expense of losing a feeling of family belongingness. The boundaries of subsystems also remain clear and well defined for proper family functioning. Most family systems fall somewhere along the continuum between enmeshment (where boundaries are blurred) and disengagement (where boundaries are rigid and communication across subsystems becomes difficult).

Enmeshment refers to an extreme form of proximity and intensity in family interactions in which members are overconcerned and over-involved in each other's lives. In extreme cases, the family's lack of differentiation makes any separation from the family an act of betrayal (Minuchin, 1974a). Belonging to the family dominates all experiences, at the expense of each member developing a separate sense of self. Whatever is happening to one family member reverberates throughout the system. A child sneezes, his sister runs for the tissue, his mother for a thermometer, and his father starts worrying.

Subsystem boundaries in enmeshed families are poorly differentiated, weak, and easily crossed (Minuchin, et al., 1978). Children may act like parents and parental control may be ineffective. Excessive togetherness and sharing may lead to a lack of privacy, as members intrude on each other's thoughts and feelings, ever alert to signs of distress in one another. Members of enmeshed families run the risk of overemphasizing family belongingness to the extent that they yield autonomy and a willingness to explore and master problems outside the family.

At the other extreme, members of *disengaged families* may function separately and autonomously, but with little family loyalty. They frequently lack the capacity for interdependence or for requesting support from others when needed. Communication is difficult, and the family's protective functions are handicapped. In times of stress to an individual family member, the enmeshed family responds with excessive speed and intensity, while the disengaged hardly seems to respond at all. Minuchin (1974a) offers this graphic illustration: The parents in an enmeshed family may become enormously upset if a child does not eat dessert. In a disengaged family, they may feel unconcerned about his or her hatred of school.

In disengaged families, the boundaries are inappropriately rigid, so that only a high level of individual stress can reverberate strongly enough to activate support from other family members. Disengaged families tend not to respond when a response is necessary, since individual members may feel isolated from the family system. Such members can rarely form relationships outside of the family, because they have not had the experience within the family.

Delinquent-Producing Families

In one landmark study (Minuchin, Montalvo, Guerney, Rosman, & Schumer, 1967) of poor, disadvantaged, unstable families that produce **delinquent** children, the extremes of enmeshment or disengagement (or alternation between the two) characterize family interaction. Because the homes are largely without fathers or stable father-figures, the rearing and education of the children is left completely to the mother. She tends to be available for their nurturant needs, but becomes anxious when called on to provide guidance or exercise control. Mothers at the enmeshment extreme feel absolutely responsible for their children's behavior. If a child steals,[4] the mother reacts as if she were a failure; this evokes a complementary response in her child: "If I steal, I hurt my mother," rather than, "If I steal, I am a thief." The child does not learn responsibility for his actions because there is no clear demarcation between his own and his mother's behavior. Disengaged mothers, at the other extreme, rarely inquire about what is happening in the day-to-day life of the child, thus abdicating their super-

---

[4] Families for this study were drawn from the Wiltwyck School for Boys, a residential treatment center servicing the most disadvantaged ghetto areas in New York City. All resident children have been in trouble with the law.

visory role. Neither extreme prepares the child for dealing with stress and conflict or for focusing attention on solutions to problems in the outside world. The alternation between enmeshment and disengagement in some families is depicted in Figure 3-2. Generally speaking, the stresses depicted during the enmeshment period (lower portion of figure) usually occur before the family reaches the attention of social service agencies. The disengagement period (upper portion) usually occurs with the relinquishment of parental authority.

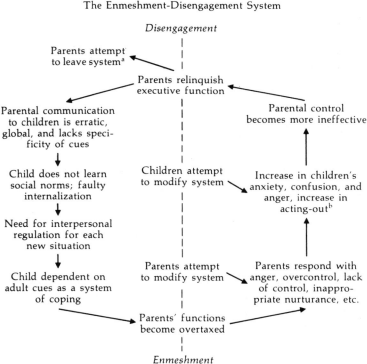

The Enmeshment-Disengagement System

Disengagement

Parents attempt to leave system[a]

Parents relinquish executive function

Parental communication to children is erratic, global, and lacks specificity of cues

Parental control becomes more ineffective

Child does not learn social norms; faulty internalization

Children attempt to modify system

Increase in children's anxiety, confusion, and anger, increase in acting-out[b]

Need for interpersonal regulation for each new situation

Child dependent on adult cues as a system of coping

Parents attempt to modify system

Parents respond with anger, overcontrol, lack of control, inappropriate nurturance, etc.

Parents' functions become overtaxed

Enmeshment

[a]When parental control becomes ineffective and parents relinquish executive functions, they may abandon the family altogether, but most of the time they segment the family by institutionalizing a child or children, acting-out (in illness, promiscuity, alcoholism, etc.), or allowing a sibling substructure to take over parental functions.

[b]At the point of increase in the children's anxiety and acting-out as an attempt to modify the system, children may turn to the siblings for control, guidance, or identification (delinquent or not); they may abandon the family, e.g., run away; or they may join a delinquent gang.

FIGURE 3-2. Alternations between enmeshment and disengagement found in some disorganized and disadvantaged families. (From Figure 1 of *Families of the Slums: An Exploration of Their Structure and Treatment*, by Salvador Minuchin et al. © 1967 by Basic Books, Inc., Publishers, New York. Reprinted by permission.)

Psychosomatic Families

In families where asthma, diabetes, or **anorexia nervosa** (self-starving) threaten a child's life, the locus of pathology may be in the family itself, rather than in the medical problem of the affected individual. Although the **etiology** of the disease may be physical and not psychological, the **psychosomatic** element of the disease lies in the exacerbation of the underlying symptoms triggered by emotional stress. For example, an allergy-prone child may react to an emotional arousal within the family (such as marital problems between the parents) by having an asthmatic attack.

Minuchin and associates (1978) indicate that families of children who manifest these psychosomatic problems are characterized by certain transactional patterns (see related discussion on page 122) that encourage somatization. Enmeshment is common, subsystems function poorly, individual boundaries are too weak to allow for individual autonomy. Psychosomatic families tend to be overprotective, again retarding the child's chance to develop a sense of independence, competence, or interest in activities outside the safety of the family. The child, in turn, feels great responsibility for protecting the family. Sometimes the physiologically vulnerable child protects them by manifesting symptoms over which they then may all become concerned. Any outside stress on the family (for example, father changes jobs, mother goes to work outside the home), especially in rigid families committed to maintaining the status quo, overloads their dysfunctional coping mechanisms, precipitating illness in the child. Such families typically have a very low threshold for conflict, which they feel they must avoid or diffuse for the sake of harmony and consensus. Unable to permit disagreement among themselves, they refuse to confront differences or negotiate their resolution.

The child's psychosomatic symptoms have a regulating effect on the family system. Parents who cannot deal with each other directly unite in protective concern over their sick child, avoiding dealing with their underlying marital conflict through this detouring maneuver. The sick child is thus defined as the family problem, and the other children join the parents in worrying or being exasperated over the burden. In such cases, as concern for the child's health absorbs the family, marital strife is ignored. The sick child in enmeshed psychosomatic families is thus often cast in the role of family conflict defuser. By returning the family to its previous homeostatic condition, he or she receives reinforcement for manifesting the symptoms, increasing the probability of their reappearance whenever a similar threat to the family occurs.

SCAPEGOATING

People learn, adopt, and are assigned roles within any social system, the family being no exception. As we pointed out in the first chapter, children in particular are often selected and inducted into playing specific family roles. Commonly, some chance characteristic that distinguishes the child from other family members—it need not even be an obnoxious trait, as long as it differentiates the person—is singled out and focused on by the others, increasing the contrast between the child and them. Bell (1975) contends that such roles are externally imposed because the family has discovered that this structuring is the best way to handle the complex interrelationships that exist within their group. Once such roles become established, especially if they are labeled or **typecast** as **pathological,** the basis for chronic behavioral disturbance is established. Bell argues, as do most family therapists, that when a family has a disturbed child, it is generally true that the family is motivated to preserve that disturbance by seeking to perpetuate the child's pathology. It follows that individual therapy with that child—the traditional route to alleviating his or her disturbance—is doomed to failure, since the family will very likely reinstitute the disturbance. Intervention at the family level offers the best chance to change the interactions out of which the disturbance in the one person emerged. The following is a case in point.

Larry P, by the time he was 14 years old, was failing at school and had been apprehended by the school authorities for vandalism on more than one occasion. A bright youngster, according to the school counselor who had given him an intelligence test, Larry nevertheless was receiving Ds and Fs in all his classes. He was habitually late arriving at school and almost invariably turned in all assignments at least a week late. On numerous occasions, he simply overslept and missed school, complained of being ill, or left in the morning but skipped class by going to a movie or pinball parlor for the day. Invariably, these actions resulted in shouting matches with his mother.

Life at home for Larry was a series of struggles with his parents (especially his mother) and his two younger brothers, Bill, aged 12, and John, aged 7. He felt blamed by his parents for everything that went wrong or anything that was missing in the house. By contrast, his brothers were held up to him by his parents as good children. Bill was a straight-A student (although probably no more intelligent than Larry), helped out at home after school, and never caused his parents any trouble. John was the family "pet," cute and playful; any deviation in his behavior from what his parents expected was quickly dismissed as insignificant, something he would grow out of soon enough.

Scapegoated as the family deviant, Larry proceeded to show them how deviant he could be. He stole money from his mother's purse, became a drug user and dealer, sometimes sold family possessions to raise more money. He destroyed some kitchen chairs in a rage one day, even wrote obscene words on the living-room wall using a spray can of paint. He refused to bathe or clean his room, much to his mother's distress. More and more, he stayed in his room listening to his portable radio. However, when he discovered the battery was dead one day, his ability to tolerate frustration was so low that he hurled the radio through the closed bedroom window.

Distraught by his behavior, Larry's parents finally sought professional help for him. Reluctantly, Larry consented, although his behavior with the psychologist repeated his pattern at home: he frequently missed sessions without notifying the therapist, or if he attended, sometimes damaged things in the office, as when he dropped a lighted cigarette on the sofa. After several months, Larry seemed to feel more trusting of the psychologist, but little progress was being made. Finally, the psychologist suggested family therapy.

From the start, the following consistent family portrait began to emerge: Mr. P was a passive, dependent man, overwhelmed by pressures from his business and family. Chronically frustrated and angry at his wife for presenting him with problems (usually involving Larry) when he arrived home in the evening, he nevertheless suppressed his anger because he worried that she might leave him. However, he secretly got some satisfaction from Larry fighting with Mrs. P, since Larry was acting out something Mr. P was feeling but was afraid to express. Mrs. P, on the other hand, was an insecure woman filled with a multitude of self-doubts. Unsure of her own judgment in almost all situations, she looked to her husband for family leadership or counsel, neither of which he seemed willing to give. Her anger at Larry was at least in part a displacement of her rage at her husband, with whom she appeared to get along beautifully on the surface. Both parents thus had a stake in perpetuating Larry's deviant behavior, since it allowed them to gain some satisfactions without risking open hostility toward each other.

What of the children? Bill was suffering under the strain of being a model child, and ultimately complained that he was merely trying to keep his parents together, but was building up resentment over losing out on being a child. He no longer wished to be compared with Larry. John found being a "pet" harder to give up, but finally saw that he was losing out on the privileges of being considered more grown up. Larry sensed the underlying strain between his parents; his acting-out behavior seemed a smokescreen or distraction from the family dealing with their problems over leadership, cohesiveness, and respect for each other's individuality. The parents were the most resistant to change. After six months of therapy with the entire family, all of the children felt ready to terminate, including Larry, whose deviant behavior had almost entirely ceased. Mr. and Mrs. P together joined a couples group (made up of five couples) and continued treatment for several months longer.

The scapegoat who develops symptoms is usually the identified patient who is carrying the pathology for the entire family. Note, however, that scapegoating is a mutual causal process, not simply one in which one member is victimized. All members, including the scapegoat, participate in the process. As we have just seen, by displacing their conflicts onto a child, parents frequently maintain harmonious relationships at the expense of the child's emotional development. The child, in turn, may be struggling to keep the family intact, even if it means sacrificing himself or herself. Scapegoating may take a variety of forms, depending on how the family typecasts its deviant members. Common guises are: "the mascot, the clown, the sad sack, the erratic genius, the black sheep, the wise guy, the saint, the idiot, the fool, the imposter, the malingerer, the boaster, the villain, and so forth" (Hoffman, 1971, p. 296). Different family members may switch roles during the family life cycle as needs change, crises come and go, and different persons offer themselves for scapegoating purposes.

PERSISTENT FAMILY MYTHS

Individuals as well as entire families have their myths—ill-founded, self-deceptive, well-systematized beliefs held uncritically about themselves. Within families, these myths, shared by all members, help shape interactions between members, assign complementary roles and partly determine the nature of intrafamilial relationships. Glick and Kessler (1974) have outlined some common myths regarding marriage held by many people coming for family therapy (Table 3-1).

Mutual make-believe as well as elements of distortion and denial of reality are often a part of the myths that are subscribed to by a family and convincingly presented to the outside world (Ferreira, 1966). Sometimes these myths infer general family characteristics: "Our fam-

TABLE 3-1. Some Common Myths Concerning Ways to Achieve Marital Happiness

Common Marital Myths	Family Systems Perspective
1. Marriage and families should be totally happy; each member should expect all or certainly most gratifications to come from the family unit.	A romantic myth; overlooks fact that many of life's satisfactions are commonly found outside family setting.
2. "Togetherness" through close physical proximity or joint activities leads to satisfactory family life and individual gratification.	Varies greatly from one family to another; cannot be considered ideal pattern for all families under all conditions.
3. Marital partners should be totally honest with one another at all times.	While openness and frankness are usually desirable, especially in the service of a constructive, problem-solving approach, they may also be damaging if used in the service of hostile, destructive feelings.
4. In happy marriages there are no disagreements; when family members fight it means they hate each other.	Differences between family members are inevitable and often lead to arguments; if these clarify feelings and are not personal attacks, they may be constructive and preferable to covering up differences by always appearing to agree.
5. Marital partners should see eye to eye on every issue and work toward identical outlook.	Differences in background, experiences, personality make this impossible to achieve; actually different outlooks, if used constructively, may provide family with more options in carrying out developmental tasks.
6. Marital partners should be unselfish and not think of their individual needs.	Extremes of self-absorption or selflessness undesirable; satisfactions needed as an individual, not merely appendage to others (for example, mother lives only to serve family).
7. Whenever something goes wrong in the family, it is important to determine who is at fault.	Rather than blaming a single individual, dysfunction in the family interactions should be examined so that all members accept responsibilities.
8. Rehashing the past is helpful when things are not going well at present.	Endless recriminations about past errors usually escalate present problems, not reduce them, since they usually invite retaliation from the partner.
9. In a marital argument, one partner is right and the other wrong, with the goal of seeing who can score the most "points."	Marriages generally suffer when competition rather than co-operation characterizes marital interactions.
10. A good sexual relationship inevitably leads to a good marriage.	Good sexual relationship is important component of a satisfactory marriage, but it does not preclude presence of interpersonal difficulties in other areas.

TABLE 3-1. (continued)

Common Marital Myths	Family Systems Perspective
11. In a satisfactory marriage, the sexual aspect will more or less take care of itself.	Not necessarily; sexual difficulties may be brought into marriage or related to stresses outside of the marriage.
12. Marital partners understand each other's nonverbal communications and therefore do not need to check things out with one another verbally.	Less likely to be true in dysfunctional families, where misperceptions and misinterpretations of each other's meanings and intent are common.
13. Positive feedback is not as necessary in marriage as negative feedback.	Positive feedback (attention, compliments) increases the likelihood that desirable behavior will reoccur, rather than taking for granted that it will and focusing on what's wrong with the other's behavior.
14. Good marriages simply happen spontaneously, and require no effort.	Another romantic myth; good marriages require daily input by both partners, with constant negotiation, communication, and mutual problem solving.
15. Any spouse can (and often should) be reformed and remodeled into the shape desired by the partner.	A poor premise in marriage, and one likely to lead to frustration, anger, and disillusionment. Working on improving the relationship should make partners more compatible and sensitive to each other's needs.
16. In a stable marriage, things do not change and there are no problems.	All living systems change, grow, and develop over time. Fixed systems sooner or later are out of phase with current needs and developments.
17. Everyone knows what a husband should be like and what a wife should be like.	Untrue, especially in modern society, where new roles are being explored.
18. If a marriage is not working properly, having children will rescue it.	On the contrary, children usually become the victims of marital disharmony.
19. No matter how bad a marriage, it should be kept together for the sake of the children.	Not necessarily true that children thrive better in an unhappy marriage than with a relatively satisfied divorced parent. In marriages where partners stay together as "martyrs" for the children's sake, children usually bear the brunt of resentment partners feel for one another.
20. If marriage does not work out, an extramarital affair, or divorce and marriage to another spouse will cure the situation.	Occasionally true, but without gaining insight similar choices will be made and the same nongratifying patterns repeated.

Based on information in Glick and Kessler, 1974, pp. 30–36.

ily is easy-going and happy-go-lucky. Our neighbors are stuffy and uptight." "We are good, responsible parents; our friends are too casual and indifferent about the welfare of their children." Sometimes, these myths differentiate family members: "My side of the family has humor and is fun-loving, yours are a bunch of sourpusses." "The males in this family are intellectually superior to the females, who are too emotional." While to an outsider these may appear to be blatant misstatements of the facts in the family, they nevertheless tend to be shared and supported by all family members as if their truth were beyond challenge.

What is important about these myths, as Ferreira (1966) points out, is that they are organized beliefs in the name of which the family initiates, maintains, and justifies many interactional patterns. He offers the following examples to illustrate how important interactional patterns within a family operate under rules not openly stated:

> In Family A, the husband has to drive the wife wherever she may need to go, oftentimes to the detriment of his business activities, since she does not know how to drive a car, nor does she care to learn. Although this pattern has been in operation since they were married some sixteen years ago, she explains it in terms of not being "mechanically inclined," a statement which the husband immediately endorses and corroborates.
>
> In Family B, no friend is ever invited to the house since no one quite knows when father is going to be drunk. The mother, who pointedly "does not drink," not only provides most of the family income (part of which goes, of course, for the father's liquor), but also stands vigil over who comes in the house lest someone will think that "he is almost an alcoholic."
>
> In Family C, the delinquency of a teen-age son is becoming the increasing concern of the local Juvenile Authorities. The parents profess total bewilderment on how to direct their son on a less troublesome path. They consider themselves a "very happy" family, with a "happiness" marred only by their son's encounters with the law. In this regard, the parents claim that they are constantly out-argued by their son, who happens to be, in the mother's proud and public statement, "the legal mind in the family" [Ferreira, 1966, p. 86].[5]

Note how certain family patterns and rules are translated into family myths, beliefs, and expectations about each other that lead automatically to action without further thought. In Family A, for example, the myth about the wife who is not "mechanically inclined"

---

[5] From "Family Myths," by A. J. Ferreira, *Psychiatric Research Reports No. 20*, 1966, 86–87. Copyright 1966 by the American Psychiatric Association. Reprinted by permission.

influences the behavior of the husband. The reason is that if both husband and wife agree that she is nonmechanical, there is the implied statement that he is mechanical. Therefore, he is prepared to carry out a complementary role vis-à-vis the wife. The myth helps define the nature of the relationship.

Similarly, in Family B, defining the husband as an alcoholic or near-alcoholic clearly establishes that the wife, a teetotaler, plays a counter-role: stable, responsible, dependable, protective. That playing of complementary roles very likely influences most, if not all, of their interactions. The "legal mind" delinquent in Family C undoubtedly is part of a family with members who do not have legal minds (but take some satisfaction from the fact that he does). Despite their protests, they may have a vested interest in keeping the situation intact.

All of this is significant because a family, by labeling one of its members as "sick," "crazy," or a "patient," is making a statement that the other family members are all well! This myth, once it becomes operational, may stay on (sometimes passed on from generation to generation) as an integral part of the family's transactions, a buffer against sudden change, the basis for explaining all interactions involving that labeled person. Because of its usefulness as a homeostatic mechanism, the myth is resistant to change. Despite efforts by the family to seek help for that "sick" person, they are likely to resist change and fight to maintain the status quo. To abandon the myth is to open up the issue of their own disturbances or dysfunction as a family.

Pseudomutuality

Dysfunctional families are often conspicuous for numerous myths. Wynne, an early researcher studying the family organization of schizophrenics, has suggested that such families, overburdened by their own mythology, often relate to one another by **pseudomutuality** (Wynne, Ryckoff, Day, & Hirsch, 1958). By this he means they make a strong attempt to maintain the appearance of a relationship, the illusion that they have an open, mutually understanding way of interacting, when in reality they maintain great distance between one another. What they do have in common is a shared maneuver designed to defend against pervasive feelings of meaninglessness and emptiness among all the family members. Pseudomutuality is thought to be characteristic of family settings in which schizophrenia develops. Anxious about separating from an established and familiar relationship, family members together develop the illusion of a perfect fit between their behavior and expectations and those of each other member. Divergence in viewpoint is intolerable; the illusion of family unity must be maintained. Any potential for growth or autonomy is squashed, sacrificed for the purpose of holding the group together.

Instead of developing relationships in which each member forms a separate and unique identity while respecting and appreciating the individuality in each of the other members (what Wynne calls *mutuality*), or having casual contact with others for specific purposes without

FIGURE 3-3. Lyman C. Wynne, M.D. (Photo courtesy of Lyman C. Wynne.)

developing any close or personal relationship, as between a customer and sales clerk *(nonmutuality)*, in pseudomutuality there is a determination to fit together into formal roles at the expense of participants losing their individual identities. Since divergence in viewpoint, interest, or attitude may lead to a disruption of the family relationships, it is forbidden. As a consequence, members fail to separate from one another or to fulfill their own potentialities. A strong sense of personal identity, which requires testing out through honest and meaningful feedback information from others in order to develop, cannot be formed under such circumstances. Moreover, efforts to assert such individuality are likely to be perceived as a threat to the facade of mutuality.

Particularly in families with a schizophrenic member (although not necessarily limited to those families), people become locked into fixed roles from which it becomes extremely difficult to escape. In a normal family, each person sees himself or herself as a member of the family group and also of the community and society as a whole. Growing up in a pseudomutual setting, by contrast, is to feel part of a self-sufficient social unit with its own continuous but unstable and flexible family boundaries with the outside world. Wynne describes such a family boundary as a **rubber fence**—it stretches its boundaries to include whatever can be interpreted as complementary to its structure and contracts to extrude that which it considers alien. The individual family member is prevented from recognizing or taking part in any activity that differentiates that person either within or without the family role structure. The surrounding walls expand and contract; one's own perceptions cannot be trusted; escape is impossible.

Through various myths, each person learns to forsake individuality and behave with uniformity and primary allegiance toward the family. Because of family pressure to remain within the rigid self-contained unit, the preschizophrenic learns a prescribed role but fails to develop a personal identity or to be equipped to deal with life outside the family circle. A common family myth in such a situation is that open divergence from the family and its assigned role will lead to a catastrophe or personal disaster. According to Wynne, an acute schizophrenic episode is most likely to occur when the individual must leave the family boundaries, struggle to become an individual, and learn to relate to others in unfamiliar surroundings and unrehearsed ways. The schizophrenic behavior is a reaction to an identity crisis caused by the threat of separation from the familiar pseudomutuality of the family.

SUMMARY

One way to study a family's functioning is to consider how it copes with various crises that occur during different phases of its life cycle. While some families learn more effective coping strategies, others continue in familiar dysfunctional transactional patterns. Four common expressions of dysfunctional behavior within a family are considered: pathological communication, enmeshment and disengagement, scapegoating, and the persistence of family myths.

To function effectively, families must establish and maintain clear communications channels. In dysfunctional families, pathological communication may take the form of double-bind messages or the use of mystification. In the former, the receiver of such a contradictory message is doomed to failure whatever response is made. In the latter, the recipient is confused and befuddled by a message whose intent is to cloud over any real conflict taking place. Beyond verbal content, communication between two or more people defines a relationship. Symmetrical relationships are characterized by equality and the minimization of differences between participants; in complementary relationships, the reverse is true.

In enmeshed families, boundaries between subsystems are blurred and members are overinvolved in each other's lives; in extreme cases, to separate from the family is to betray them. Because family membership is all-important, individuals often fail to develop a separate sense of self. In disengaged families, boundaries are rigid and members feel separate and isolated from one another. Without the experience of closeness within the family, they often cannot form relationships to people in the outside world either. Poor, disadvantaged, unstable families that produce delinquent children commonly interact at one extreme (enmeshment) or the other (disengagement). Psychosomatic families typically are enmeshed.

By scapegoating one member, a family distinguishes that person from the other members, usually labeling him or her as pathological and the cause of family disharmony. By displacing family conflicts onto this person, underlying sources of conflict within the family can be covered over. Another self-deceptive mechanism may involve the persistence of family myths, subscribed to by all family members and convincingly presented to the outside world. Through these myths, families may initiate, maintain, and justify many of their dysfunctional interactional patterns. Pseudomutuality—the myth that the family has an open, mutually understanding way of interacting, when in reality they do not—is thought to be characteristic of family settings in which schizophrenia develops.

Part Two

HISTORICAL AND THEORETICAL FOUNDATIONS

4

THE EVOLUTION OF THE
FAMILY THERAPY MOVEMENT

We have looked at various levels of family competence in the preceding chapters, ranging from those described as optimally functioning to those we have labeled as severely disturbed or dysfunctional. Before we attempt to develop some theoretical formulations for conceptualizing why certain families establish—or fail to establish—successful adaptational skills and competencies (Chaper 5), we first need to examine some historical developments in a number of areas that blended into the family therapy movement, or "family movement," in the 1950s. Presenting a brief history in this way should offer a broad context for understanding contemporary developments in the field of family therapy.

HISTORICAL ROOTS OF THE FAMILY
THERAPY MOVEMENT

The family movement, now approximately 30 years old, might be said to have gotten underway in the aftermath of World War II. With the sudden reuniting of families came a number of problems—social, interpersonal, cultural, situational—for which the public sought solutions by turning to mental health specialists. These professionals, accustomed to working with individuals, found themselves called on to help with problems involving marital discord, divorce, emotional breakdowns in family members, delinquency in children, problems with in-laws, and so on—all calling for help at the family level. While many of these clinicians continued to offer help to the individual with the dysfunctional behavior (someone we now refer to as the **identified patient** but not necessarily the only or even necessarily the most disturbed family member), others began to look at family relationships, transactions between family members that needed amelioration if individual well-being was to be achieved.

At least 15 behavioral sciences and professional disciplines have directed their attention to examining and better understanding family functioning (see Table 4-1). For our purposes, it seems best to focus on five seemingly independent scientific and clinical developments that coalesced in the late 1940s and early 1950s into what we now call the family movement. These include: (1) the extension of psychoanalytic treatment to a full range of emotional problems, eventually including work with whole families; (2) the introduction of general systems theory, with its emphasis on exploring relationships between parts that make up an interrelated whole; (3) the investigation of the family's role in the development of schizophrenia in one of its members; (4) the evolvement of the fields of child guidance and marital counseling; and (5) the increased interest in new clinical techniques such as **group therapy** and milieu therapy.

Psychoanalysis

Psychoanalysis, the theory and set of therapeutic techniques advanced by Sigmund Freud, had become the dominant ideology in American psychiatry after World War II. Shortly before the war, a large migration of European psychologists and psychiatrists, psychoanalytic in their orientation, had come to this country to escape the Nazi regime. The American public had been receptive to Freud's ideas since early in this century. With the arrival of these clinicians, psychoanalysis began to gain greater acceptance among medical specialists, academicians, and clinicians in the psychology community, as well as sociologists and psychiatric social workers.

Freud had been aware of the impact of family relationships on the individual's character formation, particularly in the development of neurotic behavior. For example, in his famous case of Little Hans, a child who refused to go out into the street for fear that a horse might bite him, Freud hypothesized that Hans was displacing anxiety that had been associated with his Oedipus complex. That is, Freud believed Hans unconsciously desired his mother sexually but felt competitive with, and hostile toward, his father, as well as fearful of his father's reaction to his hostility. Hans had witnessed a horse falling down in the

TABLE 4-1. Behavioral Sciences and Disciplines Involved in the Study of the Family

Disciplines	Illustrative Studies	Representative Researchers*

Anthropology
  Cultural anthropology
  Social anthropology
  Ethnology
	Cultural and subcultural family forms and functions
	Cross-cultural comparative family patterns
	Ethnic, racial, and social status family differences
	Families in primitive, developing, and industrial societies
		Ruth Benedict
		Allison Davis
		Clyde Kluckhohn
		Oscar Lewis
		Ralph Linton
		Helen and Robert Lynd
		Margaret Mead
		George Murdock
		W. Lloyd Warner

Counseling
  Counseling theory
  Clinical practice
  Evaluation
	Dynamics of interpersonal relationships in marriage and family
	Methods and results of individual, marriage, and family counseling
		Rollo May
		Emily Hartshorne Mudd
		James A. Peterson
		Carl Rogers

Demography	Census and vital statistics on many facets of family life Cross-sectional, longitudinal, and record-linkage surveys Differential birth rates Family planning and population control	Donald Bogue Hugh Carter Harold Christensen Ronald Freedman Paul Glick Philip Hauser P. K. Whelpton
Economics	Consumer behavior, marketing, and motivation research Insurance, pensions, and welfare needs of families Standards of living, wage scales, socioeconomic status	Robert C. Angell Howard Bigelow Milton Friedman John Kenneth Galbraith John Morgan Margaret Reid

Education
  Early childhood
  Early elementary
  Secondary
	Child-rearing methods
	Developmental patterns
	Educational methods and evaluation
	Family life education
		Orville Brim
		Catherine Chilman
		Cyril Houle
		Harold Lief

TABLE 4-1 (continued)

Disciplines	Illustrative Studies	Representative Researchers*
College Parent Professional	Motivation and learning Preparation for marriage Sex education	Nevitt Sanford Ralph Tyler James Walters
History	Historical roots of modern family Origins of family patterns Predictions of the future of families Social influences on the family Social trends and adaptations	Arthur Calhoun Franklin Frazier Bernard Stern Edward Westermarck Carle Zimmerman
Home economics Family relationships Home economics education Home management Nutrition	Evaluation of practices and measurement of educational results Family food habits and nutrition Home management practices Relationships between family members	Muriel Brown Irma Gross Paulena Nickell Evelyn Spindler Alice Thorpe
Human development Child development Adolescent development Middle age and aging	Character development Child growth and development Developmental norms and differences Nature of cognitive learning Cross-cultural variations Personality development Social roles of aging	Nancy Bayley Urie Bronfenbrenner Erik Erikson Dale Harris Robert Havighurst Lois Barclay Murphy Bernice Neugarten Jean Piaget
Law	Adoption and child protection Child care and welfare Divorce and marital dissolution Marriage and family law Parental rights and responsibilities Sexual controls and behavior	Paul Alexander John Bradway Marie Kargman Harriet Daggett Max Rheinstein Harriet Pilpel
Psychoanalysis	Abnormal and normal behavior Clinical diagnosis and therapy Foundations of personality Stages of development Treatment of mental illness	Nathan Ackerman Erik Erikson John Flugel Irene Josselyn Harry Stack Sullivan

TABLE 4-1 (continued)

Disciplines	Illustrative Studies	Representative Researchers*

Psychology
  Clinical
  Developmental
  Social
	Aspirations and self-concepts
	Drives, needs, and hungers
	Dynamics of interpersonal interaction
	Learning theory
	Mental health
	Therapeutic intervention
		Rosalind Dymond
		Gerald Gurin
		Robert Hess
		Eleanore Luckey
		Frederick Stodtbeck
		John Whiting

Public health	Epidemiology and immunization Family health and preventive medicine Maternal and infant health Noxious materials research Pediatric health education Venereal disease	Cecelia Deschin Nicholson Eastman Earl L. Koos Niles Newton Clark Vincent
Religion	Church policies on marriage and family Families of various religions Interfaith marriage Love, sex, marriage, divorce, and family in religious contexts	Stanley Brav Roy Fairchild Seward Hiltner John L. Thomas John C. Wynn

Social work
  Family casework
  Group work
  Social welfare
	Appraising family need
	Devising constructive programs for family assistance
	Measuring family functioning
		Dorothy F. Beck
		L. L. Geismar
		James Hardy
		Charlotte Towle

Sociology	Courtship and mate selection Family formation and functioning Effects of social change on families Family crises and dissolution Prediction of family success Social class influence on families	Ernest W. Burgess Ruth S. Cavan Harold Christensen Reuben Hill Judson Landis Marvin Sussman

*Illustrative of those research workers whose published findings may be available to students of the family in various disciplines; not an all-inclusive listing.

Table 6-1 (pp. 127–129) from *Marriage and Family Development*, 5th Edition, by Evelyn Millis Duvall. Copyright © 1957, 1962, 1967, 1971, 1977 by J. B. Lippincott Company. By permission of Harper & Row, Publishers, Inc.

street, and Freud speculated that he unconsciously associated the scene with his father, since he wanted his father hurt too. According to Freud, Hans unconsciously changed his intense fear of castration by his father into a **phobia** about being bitten by the horse, whom Hans had previously seen as innocuous. Having substituted the horse for his father, Hans was able to turn an internal danger into an external one. The fear was displaced onto a substitute object, a prototype of what takes place in the development of a phobia. In this celebrated 1909 case (Freud, 1955), the boy was actually treated by the father, under Freud's guidance.

The case of Little Hans, a 5-year-old boy, is actually of significant historical importance conceptually as well as technically. Conceptually, Freud was able to elaborate on his earlier formulations regarding psychosexual development in children and the use of **defense mechanisms,** such as displacement, as unconscious **ego** devices a person calls on as protection against being overwhelmed by anxiety. Moreover, he was able to establish his developing viewpoint that inadequate resolution of a particular phase of psychosexual development may lead to neurotic behavior such as phobias. Technically, as Bloch and LaPerriere (1973) point out, the case of Little Hans represents the first case both of child analysis and family therapy.

From the case of Little Hans and similar examples from among Freud's published papers, we can appreciate how family relationships came to provide a rich diagnostic aid in his psychoanalytic thinking. For the most part, however, Freud and his followers preferred to work therapeutically with an individual and his or her intrapsychic conflicts. In fact, as Bowen (1975) notes, one psychoanalytic principle that may have retarded the earlier growth of the family movement involves efforts to safeguard the personal privacy of the therapist/patient relationship as well as to prevent "contamination" of the therapist by contact with a patient's relatives. Bowen reports that some hospitals went so far as to have one therapist deal with the patient's carefully protected intrapsychic processes and another help handle reality matters and administrative procedures, while a third team member, the social worker, talked to relatives. According to Bowen's early experiences, failure to observe these principles was considered "inept psychotherapy." It is only recently that this principle began to be violated—more often than not for research rather than clinical purposes—and that families began to be seen therapeutically as a group.[1]

---

[1]Just how much change in attitude has taken place in the last 25 years may be gleaned from the fact that family therapists are especially willing to demonstrate their work with families quite openly, as often as not before a large professional audience

Nathan Ackerman, a psychoanalyst and child psychiatrist, is generally credited with adapting psychoanalytic formulations to the study of the family. In an early work (Ackerman, 1958), he characterized the family as "a kind of carrier of elements predisposing to both mental illness and mental health" (p. 104). Ackerman (1970a) credits psychoanalysis with giving pointed emphasis to the role of family conflict in mental disorders, although he acknowledges that psychoanalysts are divided between those who favor family diagnosis and treatment and those who are critical and antipathetic toward such a technique. Ackerman himself became a leader of the former group, seeing the family approach as offering a "new level of entry, a new quality of participant observation in the struggles of human adaptation" (1970a, p. 6).

Ackerman (1970a) saw the family as a system of interacting personalities. Treating the family involved intervention at several levels—the internal organization of personality of each member, the dynamics of family role adaptation, and the behavior of the family as a social system. What at the individual level may be seen as an intrapsychic conflict, a defense (for example, displacement) and a symptom (for example, phobia) take on a broader definition at the family level as part of a recurring, predictable, interactional pattern, intended to assure stasis for the individual, but actually impairing family homeostasis. Such phenomena produce distortions in the balance of family role relationships. An individual's symptom, in family terms, is a unit of interpersonal behavior reflected in a constellation of shared family conflict, anxiety, and defense.

Homeostasis, to Ackerman, signifies the capacity for the family system to adapt to change; it means much more than restoring the system to a previous balance or accustomed level of functioning. A disturbed person's symptoms and behavior unbalances the family homeostasis and at the same time reflects emotional distortions within the entire family. There is a *failure of complementarity* between roles played by various family members vis-à-vis each other, to use Ackerman's terms. Change and growth within the system become constricted. Roles either become rigid, narrow, or stereotyped or else shift rapidly, causing confusion and a breakdown of role **complementarity**. According to Ackerman, the family in which this occurs must be helped to "accommodate to new experiences, to cultivate new levels of complementarity in family role relationships, to find avenues for the solution of conflict, to build a favorable self-image, to buttress critical forms of

---

without benefit of one-way mirrors or other devices to separate participants from viewers. Families typically report that any initial self-consciousness is usually quickly overcome.

defense against anxiety, and to provide support for further creative development" (Ackerman, 1966, pp. 90–91).

General Systems Theory

First proposed by Ludwig von Bertalanffy, a biologist, in the 1940s, **general systems theory** represents an effort to provide a comprehensive theoretical model embracing all living systems and applicable to all the behavioral sciences. Bertalanffy's major contribution is in providing a framework for looking at seemingly unrelated phenomena and understanding how together they represent interrelated components of a larger system.

A system is a complex of component parts that are in mutual interaction. Rather than viewing each part as isolated and simply adding the parts to make up an entity, this viewpoint stresses the relationships between the parts; the various components can be understood best as functions of the total system. (The application to a family, made up of members, each of whom influences and, in turn, is influenced by all other members, has been discussed in Chapter 2.) To understand how something works, we must study the transactional process taking place between the components of a system, says Bertalanffy, not merely add up what each part contributes.

Systems differ in their degree of openness (Bertalanffy, 1968). A closed system admits no matter from outside itself and therefore is subject to entropy (the tendency toward disorder or disorganization). Such a system operates within its own impermeable boundaries through which no energy or information can be transmitted. (A chemical reaction taking place within a sealed, insulated container has no transactions with the outside environment and will ultimately stop.) Open systems exchange materials, energies, or information with the environment, because their boundaries are at least partially permeable. All living systems are open. For example, plants exchange energy with their surroundings, receiving input (carbon dioxide) and discharging output (oxygen) into these environments. On a larger scale, ecosystems operate within an open system. Open systems tend to maintain a steady state of negentropy (a high degree of orderliness or low entropy) although some entropic changes may occur in them.

Living systems, according to Miller (1978), a behavioral scientist who has attempted to conceptualize them for over a quarter of a century, are a special subset of open systems. He contends that all biological and social systems are organized and operate at each of seven hierarchical levels (see Figure 4-1): cells, organs (composed of cells), organisms (independent life forms), groups (families, committees), or-

Supranational System
(Common Market, United
Nations, satellite communications
network)

Societal System
(one nation, a large part
of a nation)

Organizational System
(industrial concern, social
agency, professional
association)

Group System
(family, work team,
recreational group,
animal group)

Organismic System
(individual person,
animal, or plant)

Organ System
(nervous system,
alimentary system)

Cell System
(individual cells
within a body)

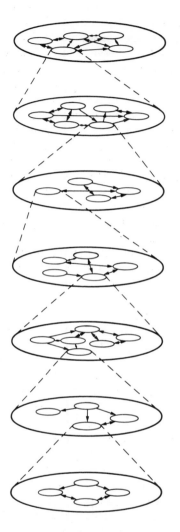

FIGURE 4-1. Living systems exist in a hierarchy of levels. Each level is made up of subsystems that have a relationship with other parts of their own system and to systems at other levels. Behavior at an individual (organismic) level is different than that individual's behavior at a group or family level, because of characteristics of that higher level (family rules, roles, power structure, ways of communicating). Family members relate to each other with greater intensity than they do to others outside the family boundary, but they also relate to others in society, a higher system. (From Sundberg/Tyler/Taplin, *Clinical Psychology: Expanding Horizons*, 2nd Ed., © 1973, p. 101. Reprinted by permission of Prentice-Hall, Inc., Englewood Cliffs, New Jersey. Based on the theory presented by Miller, 1971.)

ganizations (universities, multinational corporations, cities), societies or nations, and supranational systems. Each higher-level system encompasses all lower-level ones and provides the environment for the systems on the level directly below. Since cells evolved, about 3 billion years ago, the general direction of evolution has been toward ever-greater complexity, according to Miller's thesis.

Nothing and nobody exists in isolation; the world is made up of systems within systems. The emotionally disturbed person is just one part of a subsystem in the family system, but the entire family system is influenced by and influences the disturbed person. Dysfunctional families who seek treatment at a social agency are components in that agency's organizational system. They in turn affect disbursement of government funds, training grants for research on family life or educating family counselors, and so on. Consider, too, that a person is an organization of many subsystems, and that the organismic system is part of a larger scheme, as we have shown. Suppose, to use an example offered by Bloch and LaPerriere (1973), a woman becomes depressed. At what level would intervention be most effective? At the organ system level her depression might be related to hormonal changes during her menstrual cycle; at the organismic level, to her way of handling aggressive impulses; at the group level, to her way of dealing with her family; at the society level, to her learned female mode of damming up assertive impulses. How do we best help her and how do we best describe her? We take the position that intervention at the family level encompasses many of her problem areas and offers an effective method for expediting change.

Open, living systems exist by virtue of their interaction with the environment. They change constantly, as environmental and biological demands impinge and create stresses and strains (Beavers, 1977). We saw in Chapter 3 how the family, as a living system, goes through a series of changing situations during the life cycle, producing changing pressures and calling for new solutions. Systems also contain self-regulating processes or *homeostatic mechanisms* (see Chapter 2) in order to maintain a steady state when the system must deal with abrupt or drastic changes. Another aspect of keeping a system functioning is its *feedback mechanisms*. While feedback may be positive (exhilirating the system's activities) or negative (reversing the activities), the latter is more important in governing the process, since it tends to correct a system in trouble and reestablish its previous state. Foley (1974) points out that at the family level, the role of the "identified patient" clinically illustrates negative feedback. Thus, when the relationship between mother and father becomes overly intense—threatening the family system's stability—the "identified patient," often the family scapegoat, will develop symptoms requiring attention, enabling the parents to unite for their child's sake, keeping the family system from disintegration.

We will return to the application of general systems theory at the family level in Chapter 5. Here we must stop, however, and ask what is its significance in the historical development of the family movement. For one thing, in contrast to psychoanalysis, with its psychopathological orientation, general systems theory views man as a complex being operating within a system where concepts such as "sick" or "well" are irrelevant; a symptom developing in one person merely means that the system (that is, the family, or the community, or society in general) must be studied because it has become dysfunctional. In contrast to the psychoanalyst, who remains apart from the patient, many family therapists intervene directly and become participating components in the family system. The patient is not reduced, mechanistically, to **id/ego/superego** struggles of an intrapsychic nature but rather the emphasis is on multiple causality at various levels. Dealing with present styles of communication, feedback, and efforts to achieve homeostasis replaces searching for causality in the unresolved conflicts of the individual's past and undoing the earlier damage. Thinking in systems terms provides family counselors and therapists with a new paradigm or conceptual framework. It allows for a new set of assumptions about what should be studied, what data are relevant, and how such studies should be carried out. Minuchin (1974a) and Bowen (1978) are generally considered the leading exponents of this viewpoint, as we shall see in some detail later in this and the following chapter.

Schizophrenia and the Family

What role does a disturbed family environment play in the development of schizophrenia in a family member? Lidz and Lidz (1949), early investigators of the characteristics of mothers of their schizophrenic patients, found serious inadequacies and psychological disturbances in the mother/child relationship. Fromm-Reichmann (1948) introduced the term **schizophrenogenic mother** to denote a domineering, cold, rejecting, possessive, guilt-producing person—who, when combined with a passive, detached, and ineffectual father, causes her male offspring to feel confused and inadequate, and ultimately to become schizophrenic. These family pathology studies, extending into the 1950s, sought to establish a linear cause-and-effect relationship between a pathogenic mother, an inadequate father, and schizophrenia in the male child. Thus, the search was on for studying the family environment from which the schizophrenic emerges. Soon, this psychological view was joined by a broader and more systematic psychosocial view (the family as a group of individuals influencing each other) and by a sociological viewpoint that perceived the family as a dysfunctional system supporting the disturbed person (Waxler, 1975).

During the mid-1950s, the major impetus for family research in the area of schizophrenia came from three sources: Gregory Bateson at the Mental Research Institute in Palo Alto, California; Theodore Lidz at Yale University; Murray Bowen and later Lyman Wynne, both at the National Institute of Mental Health (NIMH) (Reiss, 1976).

Bateson, an anthropologist affiliated initially with the Veterans Administration Hospital in Palo Alto, received a grant in 1952 to study patterns and paradoxes of communication in animals as well as humans. Soon he was joined by Jay Haley, a communications specialist, John Weakland, a research associate with training in cultural anthropology, and Don Jackson, a psychiatrist. As a result of their investigations over several years, they began to study the relationship between patterns of communication and behavior. More specifically, their work led them into the realm of "pathological" communication and its relation to behavior within groups such as families. In 1956 this interdisciplinary team published a landmark paper (Bateson, Jackson, Haley, & Weakland, 1956) in which they introduced the "double-bind" theory to account for the development of schizophrenia in a family member.

According to this theory, a double-bind situation is one in which a person receives contradictory messages from the same individual; he or she is called upon to make some response, but is doomed to failure whatever response he or she chooses. This study gives the following poignant example:

> A young man who had fairly well recovered from an acute schizophrenic episode was visited in the hospital by his mother. He was glad to see her and impulsively put his arm around her shoulders, whereupon she stiffened. He withdrew his arm and she asked, "Don't you love me any more?" He then blushed, and she said, "Dear, you must not be so easily embarrassed and afraid of your feelings" [p. 259].

The authors go on to report that the distressed patient promptly became violent and assaultive when he returned to his ward.

Bateson and his associates believed that double-bind situations occur with great regularity in some families. They frequently involve real but not always readily apparent contradictions between what is said aloud and what is simultaneously communicated by gesture or tone. For example, a father may verbally inquire with simulated interest and enthusiasm what his daughter did at school today but at the same time reveal his disinterest through his nonverbal behavior by not looking up from the newspaper he is reading while she is attempting to respond to his question. When children are confronted by love and hate, approach and avoidance, both emanating from the same person, and when they are unable to form any satisfactory response to the contradictory messages, they become confused—responding leads to rejection, and failing to respond leads to the loss of possible love. Thus, they are damned if they do and damned if they don't. If the parent then denies simultaneously sending contradictory messages, this adds to the confusion. Bateson and his colleagues suggested that repeated and prolonged exposure to this kind of impossible situation typically results in the child's learning to escape hurt and punishment by responding with equally incongruent messages. As a means of self-protection, he or she learns to deal with all relationships in this distorted manner and finally loses the ability to understand the true meaning of his or her own or others' communications. At this point the child begins to manifest schizophrenic behavior. The interdisciplinary group at the Mental Research Institute in Palo Alto, led by Bateson, thus focused on schizophrenia as a prototype of the consequences of failure in a family's communication system.

The double-bind hypothesis has grown into one of the most scientifically respectable theories of schizophrenia-producing family interaction (Sluzki & Ransom, 1976). However, recent research (Hirsch & Leff, 1975) points out that double-bind messages do not occur in such families alone—they sometimes occur in "normal" families too—and thus are not specific to the parents of schizophrenics. Rather, as Shean (1978) concludes, such communication patterns are only one aspect of a more complex family interaction pattern frequently associated with the development of schizophrenic disorders.

At about the same time that Bateson and his colleagues were doing family research with schizophrenia on the West Coast, Theodore Lidz on the East Coast (Baltimore, and later New Haven, Connecticut) began publishing his research on the family's role in schizophrenic development of one or more of its children. These studies (Lidz, Fleck, & Cornelison, 1965) represented an extension of psychoanalytic concepts to the family, although these concepts are broadened somewhat in the transition. For example, Lidz and his coworkers saw oral fixation, which orthodox psychoanalytic formulations consider the primary factor in the development of schizophrenia, as only one aspect of the disease. To this team, schizophrenia is a "deficiency disease" resulting from the family's failure to provide the essentials for integrated personality development. More specifically, they suggested that a parent's (usually the mother's) own arrested personality development leads to an inability to meet the child's nurturance needs, so that the latter is likely to grow up with profound insecurity and be unable to achieve autonomy. They also postulated that an unstable marriage, in which there is considerable conflict between husband and wife long before the patient is born, provides poor role models for the children. The consequence, at least for some of the children, is the inability to acquire the adequate or appropriate age- and sex-related social roles that are necessary for interactions with others outside the family. You can see from this brief description that, to Lidz, it was the **psychodynamics** of the parents, rather than the family as a social system, that was primarily responsible for the development of schizophrenic behavior in their child. Such parents typically fail to transmit the basic adaptive techniques that are necessary for the children to function effectively in the culture. Failing to teach children how to fill their ultimate social roles adequately, the parents fail to help them develop adequate coping skills for adapting successfully to independent adult living.

Lidz and associates (1965) described two patterns of chronic marital discord that are particularly characteristic of families of schizophrenics (although each may exist in "normal" families to a lesser extent). **Marital schism** refers to a disharmonious situation in which each parent, preoccupied with his or her own problems, fails to create a satisfactory role in the family that is compatible with and reciprocal to the spouse's role. Each parent tends to undermine the worth of the other, especially to the children, and they tend to compete for the loyalty, affection, sympathy, and support of the children. Because they do not value or respect each other, each may voice fears that the child will grow up behaving like the other parent. Threats of separation or divorce are common; it is usual in such families for the father to become ostracized and a nonentity if he remains in the home. In the pattern of **marital skew**, which these researchers have also observed in families with a schizophrenic offspring, the continuity of the marriage is not threatened, but mutually destructive patterns nevertheless exist. The serious psychological disturbance of one parent (such as psychosis) usually dominates this type of a home. The other parent, who is often dependent and weak, accepts the situation and goes so far as to imply to the children that the home situation is normal. Such a denial of what they are living through may lead to further denials and distortions of reality by the children. This study concludes that male schizophrenics usually come from skewed families in which there is a dominant, emotionally disturbed mother, impervious to the needs of other family members but nevertheless intrusive in her child's life. At the same time, skewed families usually contain fathers who can neither counter the mother's child-rearing practices nor provide an adequate male role model.

If marital skew is often an antecedent of schizophrenia in a son, marital schism often precedes schizophrenia in a daughter. Here there is open marital discord and each parent particularly wants the daughter's support. However, the father's disparagement of the mother (or perhaps all women), plus his seductive efforts to gain the daughter's love and support, leads to the daughter's confusion about her identity as a woman, as well as to doubt about her later ability to carry out her female role in society successfully. Pleasing one parent means rejection by the other. In some cases, as Shean (1978) notes, such a child may become a family scapegoat, causing problems that mask and divert attention from parental incompatibility. Unfortunately, the diversion is at the expense of the child's own developmental needs.

First at the Menninger Foundation in Topeka, Kansas, in the early 1950s, and later at the National Institute of Mental Health near Washington, D.C., Murray Bowen began having families move in with schizophrenic patients in order to study the family as a unit, especially possible symbiotic mother/child interactions. As he later reported (Bowen, 1960) in a book edited by Don Jackson, which for the first time brought together various family theories related to the etiology of schizophrenia, families of schizophrenics often demonstrate interaction patterns resembling Lidz's findings about marital schism. Bowen termed the striking emotional distance between parents in such a situation **emotional divorce**. He described relationships of this kind as vacillating between periods of overcloseness and overdistance. Eventually the relationship becomes fixed at an emotional distance between the parents to avoid anxiety; they settle for "peace at any price." One area of joint activity—and, commonly, conflicting views—is the rearing of their children, particularly of children who show signs of psychological disturbance. It is as if the parents maintain contact with each other and therefore a semblance of emotional equilibrium by keeping the disturbed child helpless and needy. Thus, adolescence, a period in which the child usually strives for a measure of autonomy, becomes especially stormy and stressful. This is typically the time when schizophrenic behavior is first manifested. Bowen proposed the intriguing notion that schizophrenia is a process that spans at least three generations before it is manifested in the behavior of a family member. He suggested that one or both parents of a schizophrenic are troubled, immature individuals who have themselves experienced serious emotional conflict with parents, and are now subjecting their offspring to similar conflict situations.

Succeeding Bowen at NIMH, Lyman Wynne focused his research on the blurred, ambiguous, and confused communication patterns in families with schizophrenic members. In a series of papers (Wynne, Ryckoff, Day, & Hirsch, 1958; Wynne & Singer, 1963), he and his colleagues have addressed themselves to the social organization of such families. If schizophrenics interpret the meaning of what is happening around them in unusual and idiosyncratic ways, these researchers believe that the family's recurrent and characteristic fragmented and irrational style of communication may have contributed to their vulnerability. As noted in Chapter 3, Wynne offered the term *pseudomutuality*—giving the appearance of a mutual, open, and understanding relationship without really having one—to describe how such families conceal an underlying distance between members. Pseudomutuality is a shared maneuver designed to defend all of the family members against pervasive feelings of meaninglessness and emptiness.

To grow up in a pseudomutual family setting is to fail to develop a strong sense of personal identity. This handicaps the person from interactions outside the family and makes involvement within one's own family system all-encompassing. According to Wynne, the preschizophrenic becomes afraid to trust his or her capacity to accurately derive meaning from a personal experience, preferring instead to return to the familiar, self-sufficient family system with its enclosed (but safe) boundaries.

By 1950, the Group for the Advancement of Psychiatry formed a committee to look into the subject of family behavior (Spiegel, 1971). Within a few years (in 1957) a number of schizophrenic-family researchers met together for the first time at a national convention of the American Orthopsychiatric Association, an interdisciplinary group, in order to exchange research ideas. While no separate organization was formed from this yet small group, considerable enthusiasm was aroused for the new field of "family therapy" with schizophrenics. During subsequent national meetings, Bowen (1976) reports presentations by dozens of new therapists (rather than researchers) eager to describe clinical intervention techniques now involving entire families. Boszormenyi-Nagy and Framo together edited *Intensive Family Therapy* in 1965, bringing together for the first time reports by 15 authorities on their work with schizophrenics and their families. The researchers of a decade earlier, studying the relationship between family processes and the development of schizophrenia (Goldstein & Rodnick, 1975) had laid the groundwork for what was to become the major impetus to the growth of the emerging field of family therapy.

Marital Counseling and Child Guidance

Two techniques of clinical intervention, both involving at least two individuals and the relationship between them, helped broaden our outlook on how best to help emotionally troubled persons. As precursors of family therapy, both marital counseling and child guidance helped establish the view among therapists that psychological disturbances arise from conflicts *between* persons as well as *within* one or the other individual. To be effective, then, any therapeutic endeavor required working simultaneously with marital partners or parent(s)/child pairs between whom conflict existed.

Informal marriage counseling has certainly existed for as long as has the institution of marriage, if we assume that people have always been ready to advise or seek advice from others. Formal counseling from a professional marriage counselor, on the other hand, probably came into being about 50 years ago in the United States, beginning with the opening of two marriage clinics in February of 1929 (Mudd, 1961). Paul Popenoe founded the American Institute of Family Relations in 1930, offering premarital guidance as well as aid in promoting marital adjustment. Emily Mudd opened the Marriage Council of Philadelphia in 1930. By 1942, the American Association of Marriage Counselors (now the American Association of Marriage and Family Therapists) was formed, bringing together various professionals—educators, social workers, clinical psychologists, sociologists, clergymen, physicians, and lawyers—concerned with the new interdisciplinary field of marriage counseling (Reevey, 1967). When Gurin, Veroff, and Feld (1960) conducted a nationwide survey of 2460 persons on the nature of personal problems for which people seek professional help, as part of the groundbreaking work of the Joint Commission on Mental Illness and Health, they found that only one person in seven had ever sought such help. However, as indicated in Table 4-2, marriage and family problems together were by far the most common reasons given

TABLE 4-2. Nature of Personal Problems for Which People Sought Professional Help (*N* = 345)

Problem Area	Percent*
Spouse; marriage	42
Child; relationship with child	12
Other family relationships—parents, in-laws	5
Other relationship problems; type of relationship problem unspecified	4
Job or school problems; vocational choice	6
Nonjob adjustment problems in the self (general adjustment, specific symptoms)	18
Situational problems involving other people (that is, death or illness of a loved one) causing extreme psychological reaction	6
Nonpsychological situational problems	8
Nothing specific; a lot of little things; can't remember	2
Not ascertained	1

*Total is more than 100% because some respondents gave more than one response.

From Table 10.1 in *Americans View Their Mental Health*, by Gerald Gurin, Joseph Veroff, and Sheila Feld, © 1960 by Basic Books, Inc., Publishers, New York. Reprinted by permission.

for seeking professional help. Today, a variety of clinical services are available at marriage counseling clinics, sex therapy centers, and family service associations, as well as from private practitioners specializing in psychiatry, clinical psychology, psychiatric social work, or more specifically in professions dealing with marriage and family counseling. There are indications that such services are being used today more than ever before.

According to Silverman (1972), marriage counseling differs from individual treatment in that it centers primarily on the marriage pair and the problems arising from this relationship. It is concerned not only with the growth of two individuals as separate persons, but with their growth as they relate to each other in an intimate emotional and sexual relationship. Unlike the deeper probing of most forms of psychotherapy, such counseling tends to concern itself with reality problems and to facilitate the couple's conscious decision-making process.

Most people who seek marriage counseling are attempting to cope with a crisis (marital discord, infidelity, threat of divorce, disagreements regarding child-rearing, money problems, in-laws, sexual incompatibilities, and so on) that has caused an imbalance in the family equilibrium. Each partner enters counseling with different experiences, different expectations and goals, and different degrees of commitment to the marriage. Both partners probably have some stake in staying married or they would not seek professional marriage counseling, although the strength of the determination to stay together may vary greatly between them. Most marriage counseling is brief, problem-focused, and pragmatic. The marriage counselor, in treating the relationship, is likely to assess each individual's personality, role perceptions, and expectations as husband or wife (and how each perceives the partner's counter-role), patterns of communication (including sexual patterns), disruptive and inconsistent patterns of verbal communication, and the couple's ability to function together as a working unit in dealing with problems and reaching decisions (Cromwell, Olson, & Fournier, 1976).

A forerunner of family therapy, marriage counseling helped change the focus from individual psychotherapy to a **conjoint** therapeutic relationship. Previously it had been assumed that through individual treatment the patient would overcome his or her personal difficulties and the marriage would benefit. Actually in many cases the marriage got worse! A change in one partner often was so disruptive that the marital balance was more precarious than ever. Far more common today is a "couple therapy" approach, sometimes with several couples and a counselor or therapist, in which marital patterns are explored, with the goal of better understanding the intermeshing nature of their problems. A variety of handbooks are currently available on marriage counseling and therapy (Ard & Ard, 1977; Martin, 1976).

Turning to historical developments in the child guidance movement, Kanner (1962) points out that the systematic study of early childhood simply did not exist until early in this century. Rubenstein (1948), in a careful survey of the child psychiatry literature before 1900, could find no reference to the psychological and developmental aspect of the normal child. Thus, with the possible exception of studying the "mentally defective" child who had subnormal intelligence, little if anything that is known today in the fields of child psychology and psychiatry was published before 1900.

Early in this century, however, social reforms and changes in the legal status of children occurred, leading to restrictions on child labor, universal compulsory education, and a greater recognition of children's rights. Inevitably, a movement began to set up groups of experts who might work as a team to help emotionally disturbed children—the start of the child guidance movement (Rosenblatt, 1971). By 1909, William Healy, a psychiatrist, founded the Juvenile Psychopathic Institute (now known as the Institute for Juvenile Research) in Chicago, a forerunner of later child guidance clinics. Healy was specifically concerned with treating (and if possible, discovering ways of preventing) juvenile delinquency. By 1917, Healy had moved to Boston and established the Judge Baker Guidance Center devoted to diagnostic evaluations and treatment of delinquent children (Goldenberg, 1973a). The American Orthopsychiatric Association, largely devoted to preventing emotional disorders in children, was organized in 1924. Although few in number until after World War II, child guidance clinics now exist in almost every city in the United States.

One important innovation Healy introduced was to have a team of professionals from different disciplines assess both the child and his or her family. (The practice of utilizing a team made up of a psychiatrist, a clinical psychologist, and a psychiatric social worker to examine the child through interviews, psychological tests, and history taking, respectively, became a tradition in child guidance clinics. The same may be said for involving one or both parents in the treatment. The psychiatrist was generally responsible for most clinical decisions as well as psychotherapy, the psychologist for educational and remedial therapies, and the social worker for casework with the parents and liaison with other agencies in order to help improve the family's social environment.) If therapy is undertaken with the child, it is common for the parent(s) to visit the clinic regularly for therapy also, although usually with a different therapist from the one seen by the child. This collaborative approach, with the two therapists presumably consulting one another frequently, is traditional by now in child guidance clinics. As Cooper (1974) notes, direct work with the parents of emotionally disturbed children has three basic aims: (1) to establish an alliance with the parent that will support the child's growth in therapy, (2) to secure pertinent information about the child's experiences and the family situation, and (3) to help change the environment, thus aiding the child's growth and development. What is most germane to our purposes is the establishment of the principle that the child's disturbance may very likely arise from interaction with one or both parents, and also that therapeutic change is best brought about by changing the nature of that problem-causing interactive pattern. Child guidance clinics have functioned on the basis of early intervention into a child's (family's?) emotional problems in order to avert more serious disabilities later.

Group Therapy

Group therapy has been practiced in one form or another since the beginning of the 20th century, but the impetus for its major expansion came from the need for clinical services during and immediately after World War II. The earliest use of the group process in psychotherapy can be credited to Jacob Moreno, an Austrian psychiatrist who, around 1910, combined dramatic and therapeutic techniques to create **psychodrama** (Back, 1974). Moreno, whose psychodramatic techniques are still used today (Greenberg, 1974), believed that it is necessary to recreate in the therapeutic process the various interpersonal situations the patient was enmeshed in that may have led to his or her psychological difficulties. Since this cannot be easily accomplished in the one-to-one therapist/patient situation, Moreno, as therapist/director, utilized a stage in which the patient could act out his or her significant life events in front of an audience. In these psychodramas, various people (frequently, but not necessarily, other patients) represented key persons ("auxiliary egos") in the patient's life. At certain junctions, the director might instruct the patient to reverse roles with one of the players, so that he or she could gain a greater awareness of how another person saw him or her. Moreno introduced psychodrama into the United States in 1925; in 1931 he coined the term *group therapy* (Gazda, 1975).

Independently, at the Tavistock Institute in London, influenced largely by the theories developed by British psychoanalyst Melanie Klein, considerable interest developed during the 1930s in group processes. Several therapists began experimenting with group intervention techniques (Bion, 1961). In particular they emphasized dealing with current problems ("here and now") rather than searching for past causes or reconstructing early traumatic experiences in their patients. At about the same time, in the United States, Samuel Slavson, an engineer by training, began to do group work at the Jewish Board of

Guardians in New York City, from which emerged his activity-group therapy techniques (using play groups) with children and disturbed adolescents (Slavson, 1964). Slavson's approach was based on concepts derived from psychoanalysis, group work, and progressive education. In 1943, the American Group Psychotherapy Association was formed, largely through Slavson's efforts.

The sudden influx of psychiatric casualties during World War II, along with a shortage of trained therapists to work with these individuals, led to an increased interest in briefer and more efficient therapeutic techniques, such as group therapy. Shortly after the war, *human-relations-training groups* (T-groups)—sometimes referred to as "therapy for normals"—came into being at the National Training Laboratory (NTL) at Bethel, Maine. Here the focus was on group discussion and role-playing techniques; these were part of an educational effort to provide feedback information about interpersonal perceptions to the participants, so that they could gain a better understanding of the group process, examine their attitudes and values, and become more sensitive to others. (T-groups are sometimes referred to as **sensitivity-training groups** on the West Coast.) In the 1960s, stimulated by the emergence of various growth centers around the United States, particularly the Esalen Institute in Big Sur, California, the *encounter* (or **human-potential**) **movement** exploded onto the scene and seemed to gain the immediate approval of large numbers of people, who were mostly from the upper-middle social classes. Today, that enthusiasm has waned considerably, although traditional group therapies, NTL groups, and encounter groups continue to exist side by side (Goldenberg, 1977).

Fundamental to the practice of group therapy is the principle that a small group can act as a carrier of change and strongly influence those who choose to be considered its members. Thus, a therapy group is a meaningful and real unit in and of itself, more than a collection of individuals, more than the sum of its parts. Another way of putting it is that the group is a collection of positions and roles, and not of individuals (Back, 1974). In the Tavistock version of group therapy this last point is seen most clearly: the group is treated as if it were a disturbed patient, hurting because certain functions are not being carried out successfully. In a Tavistock group, the leader attempts to help the group function in a more balanced, coordinated, mutually reinforcing way, so that the group may accomplish productive work more efficiently. The implications for family therapy with a dysfunctional family should be obvious.

As group therapy is practiced today, most groups meet at least once a week, consist of between five and ten members plus a leader, meet in one-and-a-half to two-hour sessions, and sit in a circular arrangement so that each member can see and readily talk to every other member, including the therapist. The groups are usually heterogeneous, although under special circumstances homogeneous groups (for example, women's consciousness raising groups, groups composed of rape victims, groups of parents who are real or potential child abusers) are formed. NTL groups, which are more likely to meet over a two-week period away from participants' homes, tend to focus on training community, business, and government leaders in organizational development; these laboratories have expanded from their beginnings in Bethel in 1946 to various parts of the world today. Encounter groups, which are no longer restricted to growth centers (of which there are fewer today than there were in the 1960s), are now readily available in most medium-sized or larger cities, college campuses, and churches, and in some unions and large industrial organizations. Goldenberg (1977) has summarized some of the unique advantages of group therapy (Table 4-3).

DEVELOPMENTS IN FAMILY THERAPY

The 1950s: Schizophrenia in the Family

By 1957 the family movement surfaced nationally (Guerin, 1976) as family researchers and clinicians in various parts of the country began to learn of each other's work. At these early national meetings, families containing a hospitalized schizophrenic member were the main focus of interest, and as indicated earlier in this chapter, Jackson's (1960) edited volume on the etiology of schizophrenia brought together in one place a number of family-related studies on this important topic. At this point, schizophrenia as well as a number of other severely incapacitating disorders were seen as resulting from a destructive family environment, the so-called "pathogenic" family (Zuk & Rubinstein, 1965). Bowen (1960), studying such families first hand, for example, offered a **three-generation hypothesis,** that is, that schizophrenia as a process requires three or more generations to develop. He illustrates this idea with the following case.

This brief history from one of the families will be used to illustrate the points that I currently consider to be most important in the three-generation process: The paternal grandparents (first generation) were relatively mature and highly respected members of the farming community in which they lived. Their eight children were also relatively mature except for a son (second generation), who was the father of the patient and who was

TABLE 4-3. Some Special Advantages of Group Therapy over Individual Therapy

Principle	Elaboration
Resembles everyday reality more closely	Therapist sees patient interacting with others, rather than hearing about it from the patient and possibly getting a biased or distorted picture; adds another informational dimension regarding his or her customary way of dealing with people.
Reduces social isolation	Patient learns that he or she is not unique by listening to others; thus he or she may be encouraged to give up feelings of isolation and self-consciousness.
Greater feelings of support and caring from others	Group cohesiveness ("we-ness") leads to increased trust; self-acceptance is likely to increase when patient is bolstered by acceptance by strangers.
Imitation of successful coping styles	New group members have the opportunity to observe older members and their more successful adaptational skills.
Greater exchange of feelings through feedback	Group situation demands expression of feelings, both positive and negative, directed at other members who evoke love, frustration, tears, or rage; patient thus gains relief while also learning from responses of others that intense affect does not destroy anyone, as he or she may have feared or fantasized.
Increases self-esteem through helping others	Patient has the opportunity to reciprocate help, to offer others empathy, warmth, acceptance, support, and genuineness, thereby increasing his or her own feelings of self-worth.
Greater insight	Patients become more attuned to understanding human motives and behavior, not only in themselves but also in others.

From *Abnormal Psychology: A Social/Community Approach*, by H. Goldenberg. Copyright © 1977 by Wadsworth, Inc. Reprinted by permission of the publisher, Brooks/Cole Publishing Company, Monterey, California.

much less mature than his siblings. As a child he was very dependent on his mother. The other siblings regarded him as mother's favorite, but she either denied this and affirmed that she loved all her children equally, or she implicitly agreed and said that she would have done as much for any of the other children if they had needed as much attention as this son. With the need to begin functioning in the outside world that came with adolescence, he suddenly became distant and aloof from his mother and began to function much more adequately outside the home. He applied himself to school and later to his business. He became more successful in business than his siblings and colleagues, but he was aloof, shy, and uncomfortable in close personal relationships. He never rebelled against his parents, but he maintained a distant, compliant relationship with them.

There was a similar pattern on the mother's side of the family. The maternal grandfather (first generation) was a respected professional man in a small town. It was the oldest daughter (second generation) who became the mother of the patient. She was the one in her sibling group who had the most intense attachment to her mother. At adolescence, she reacted to the parental attachment in a different way from that in which the father reacted in his family. He attained his area of adequacy outside the home, while she gained her area of adequacy in the home. She suddenly changed from a shy, dependent girl who could do nothing without her mother to a socially poised and resourceful young woman who could run the home without help. Here were two people with high levels of immaturity, but both had managed to deny their immaturity and to function adequately in certain areas. Both were lonely people and somewhat aloof in their relationships with others. They met while he was working in the town where she lived. Neither had been serious about marriage before they met. On one level there was a "made only for each other" quality about the relationship, but on the surface they appeared casual or even indifferent to each other. The casual relationship continued for a year. They married suddenly, a few days before the husband was transferred to a job in another state. Their relationship became conflictual as soon as they began to live together.

According to the speculative three-generation idea, these two people will have at least one child with a very high level of immaturity, and this child may develop clinical schizophrenia in an attempt to adapt to the demands of growing up. It is stressed that this is not a specific proposition about the origin of schizophrenia but that such a pattern has been present in several of the families. We have speculated about the implications of this pattern. It suggests that one child in each sibling group acquires a higher level of immaturity than the other siblings, that the immaturity is in the one who had the most intense *early* attachment to the mother, and that the immaturity is roughly equivalent to the combined levels of immaturity in the parents. It is a consistent clinical experience, among those who work with husbands and wives, that people choose spouses who have identical levels of immaturity but who have opposite defense mechanisms. To sum-

FIGURE 4-2. Murray Bowen, M.D. (Photo courtesy of Murray Bowen.)

marize this three-generation idea, the grandparents were relatively mature but their combined immaturities were acquired by
one child who was most attached to the mother. When this child
married a spouse with an equal degree of immaturity, and when
the same process repeated itself in the third generation, it resulted in one child (the patient) with a high degree of immaturity,
while the other siblings are much more mature. We have not
worked with families with complicated family histories involving the death of a parent, divorces, remarriages, or multiple neuroses and psychoses in the same sibling group.

There are some characteristics of the early married life of the
parents that are important in our theoretical thinking. A constant
finding in all eleven father-mother-patient families has been a
marked emotional distance between the parents. We have called
this the "emotional divorce" [Bowen, 1960, pp. 352–354].[2]

[2] From "A Family Concept of Schizophrenia," by Murray Bowen, pp. 352–354 in
The Etiology of Schizophrenia, edited by Don D. Jackson, M.D. Copyright 1960 by Basic
Books, Inc., Publishers, New York. This and all other quotations from this source are re-
printed by permission.

By "emotional divorce," Bowen referred to the married life of parents of schizophrenics, both of whom are immature. However, one denies the immaturity, functioning with a facade of being overadequate, while the other accentuates the immaturity and is overtly inadequate in behavior. Neither is capable of any behavior midway between overadequate or inadequate; the former must always appear stronger and surer than is realistic, the latter more helpless than is truly the case. As Bowen explains:

> There are some constantly recurring situations that accompany the overadequate-inadequate reciprocity. One is the "domination-submission issue." On personal issues, especially decisions that affect both parents, the one who makes the decision becomes the overadequate one and the other becomes the inadequate one. The overadequate one sees self as being forced to take responsibility and the other as a shirker. The inadequate one sees self as being "forced to submit" and the other as "dominating." The "domination-submission" term was introduced by the inadequate one who complains the most. This brings in the problem of "decisions." One of the outstanding clinical characteristics of the families is the inability of the parents to make decisions. They avoid responsibility, and the anxiety of "submission," by avoiding decisions. All levels of decisions are left undecided, to be decided by time, by circumstance, or by advice from experts. Decisions that are routine "problems to be solved" by other families become "burdens to be endured" by these families. The inability to make decisions creates the impression of weak families. One father illustrated the decision problem clearly. He said, "We can never decide together on anything. I suggest we go shopping Saturday afternoon. She objects. We argue. We end up doing nothing." When decision paralysis becomes intense, the mothers more often assume the decision-making function against the passive resistance of the fathers [p. 355].

Bowen found parental conflict beginning within weeks of being married, as overadequate/inadequate reciprocal functioning caused anxiety in both as soon as they needed to engage in any cooperative activity. Unable to handle their problems together, they distance themselves from each other, although they may maintain the facade of a happy marriage. With the birth of a baby later destined to become schizophrenic, Bowen believes it is common for the mother to project her own sense of inadequacy onto the child, which the child accepts. Any moves, as in adolescence, to become independent, become a threat to the mother, who forces her child back into an inadequate role. The child is thus locked into the family's "emotional relationship system" (Bowen, 1978).

Bowen, Jackson, Lidz, and Wynne and their associates were the early workers in studying families of schizophrenics. Carl Whitaker was another psychiatrist who in the early 1950s was interested in exploring the possibility of working therapeutically with schizophrenics and their families, but his later work involved normal families and particularly the role of the extended family members in the family therapy process.

The 1960s: Widening the Focus—New Families, New Settings, New Techniques

The early 1960s saw greatly increased curiosity regarding family therapy on the part of many therapists. Family therapy began to be viewed as a new way of conceptualizing the origins of mental disorders and their amelioration rather than simply one more method of treatment. As a number of therapists began working with whole families, many continued to be individual-oriented, recognizing that the "identified patient" was the victim of family strife but working with each family member separately in a family group setting. Others, more family-oriented, did more than treat individuals in a family context; they began to realize that the disordered family must be changed (Goldenberg, 1973a). For this latter group, as Haley (1971b) points out, the focus of treatment was on changing the family structure and interaction patterns, not changing an individual's perception, affect, or behavior per se. The goal of therapy shifted from changing the person to changing the sequences of behavior between intimates. At the same time, new families (for example, poor White and non-White minority families) and new outpatient settings (for example, community mental health centers) became involved in family therapy programs, which now were no longer directed solely at hospitalized schizophrenics and their families (Zuk, 1971a).

One important example of extending family therapy to a broader spectrum of families came from the work of Minuchin and associates (1967). Twelve impoverished, unstable, disorganized minority families containing delinquent children were compared to a matched group of disadvantaged but non-delinquency producing families. More than three-fourths of the experimental group had no fathers or stable father-figures, forcing the mother to head the single-parent family. Typically, communication was sparse. In those families with the father present, he was considered a peripheral member and rarely spoke with his wife. Similarly, the children communicated little with each other, although each child might talk to the mother. Minuchin and associates distinguished two types of family interaction (see previous discussion in Chapter 3): enmeshed (intertwined) and disengaged (in which parents abdicated authority). Thirty weekly family therapy sessions with the delinquency-producing families resulted in seven of the twelve families judged improved. In general, they tended to be better able to explore alternate ways of coping with family stress and to interact without going to either extreme of enmeshment or disengagement. A greater range of emotional expression developed—parents accepted their roles more readily, and they showed improved guidance and control over their children.

By 1962, Nathan Ackerman in New York and Don Jackson in California joined forces to publish the field's first interdisciplinary journal, *Family Process,* with Jay Haley as editor. Ackerman, who had published a paper with a family orientation as early as 1937, had been busy during the 1940s and early 1950s sending his staff on home visits to families. Working with a wide range of nonschizophrenic families, Ackerman founded the Family Institute in New York City in 1965 to teach his emerging views.[3] Other psychoanalysts, such as Grotjahn (1960), began to modify their strict patient/doctor dyadic relationship in order to deal with neurotic interactions taking place within families.

A number of the leading family therapists (for example, Satir, Jackson, Whitaker) presented verbatim transcripts of their family therapy interviews in 1967 and then answered questions about their theoretical positions and intervention techniques in a volume edited by Haley and Hoffman (1967). Quite clearly this was in response to a growing interest among therapists as to how family therapy sessions were conducted and why the process in each case occurred as it did. At the same time, their more research-oriented colleagues were becoming interested in the development of experimental techniques for studying the patterns of interaction and communication within families in which one member had been labeled schizophrenic, in hope of determining whether such families follow certain distinctive patterns, and, further, what influences these patterns may have on the development of schizophrenia (Mishler & Waxler, 1968).

The 1970s: Consolidation and Innovation

By the end of the 1960s, enough interest and enthusiasm had been generated for family therapy that numerous well-attended regional meetings and workshops were taking place in various parts of the United States and Canada. A number of cities had established family therapy centers (sometimes also known as family centers or family

---

[3]Following Ackerman's death in 1971, the institute was renamed The Nathan W. Ackerman Family Institute to honor his pioneering work in the field. It remains today an outstanding facility for offering both training and clinical services to families at all socioeconomic levels.

learning centers) or had their child guidance clinics change their major thrust in the direction of working with entire families (for example, The Philadelphia Child Guidance Clinic under Minuchin's direction). In some cases, community mental health centers established "family units" (Framo, 1976), although the change in philosophy and orientation to the human condition underlying the family therapy approach sometimes met with considerable legal problems (by law, centers are mandated to treat "psychiatric illness") as well as resistance from administrators and clinicians with an individual orientation.

Two efforts at conceptualizing what was transpiring in the still relatively new field of family therapy deserve mention. The so-called GAP report (Group for the Advancement of Psychiatry, 1970) acknowledged the increasing awareness among clinicians of the family's role in symptom and conflict formation as well as the limitations of the traditional psychoanalytic emphasis on intrapsychic processes. Their survey of a sample of family therapists found them largely to be made up of members of three disciplines (psychologists, social workers, and psychiatrists), although practioners also included marriage counselors, clergymen, nonpsychiatric physicians, child psychiatrists, nurses, sociologists, and others. Most were young, reported having been dissatisfied with the results of individual treatment, and were looking for a more efficient method of therapeutic intervention. When asked to indicate their primary and secondary goals from among eight classes of possible goals, over 90% of the 290 respondents listed "improved communication" within the family as their primary goal; not a single respondent said it was rarely or never a goal. Over half of the respondents had as a primary goal, either with all or certain families, all eight of the possible goals stated in the questionnaire (see Table 4-4). However, improvement in individual task performance or individual symptomatic improvement was more likely to be a secondary goal (see Table 4-5). This indicates that these goals had by no means been abandoned, but that change in only part of a family was given less emphasis than such family-wide change as improved communication.

Practicing family therapists in the 1970 GAP Report survey rank-ordered the following as most influential in the field at that time:

> Satir
> Ackerman
> Jackson
> Haley
> Bowen
> Wynne
> Bateson
> Bell
> Boszormenyi-Nagy

TABLE 4-4. Primary Goals Stated by Therapists with Families Actually in Treatment (N = 290)

Primary Goals	Percent of All Families	Percent of Certain Families	Total Percent
1. Improved communication	85	5	90
2. Improved autonomy and individu-ation	56	31	87
3. Improved empathy	56	15	71
4. More flexible leadership	34	32	66
5. Improved role agreement	32	32	64
6. Reduced conflict	23	37	60
7. Individual symptomatic improvement	23	33	56
8. Improved individual task perform-ance	12	38	50

From *The Field of Family Therapy*, GAP report No. 78. Copyright 1970 by the Group for the Advancement of Psychiatry, Inc. Reprinted by permission of the Committee on the Family, Group for the Advancement of Psychiatry.

TABLE 4-5. Secondary Goals Stated by Therapists with Families Actually in Treatment (N = 290)

Secondary Goals	Percent of All Families	Percent of Certain Families	Total Percent
1. Improved individual task performance	16	29	45
2. Improved symptomatic improvement	23	15	38
3. Reduced conflict	17	18	35
4. Improved role agreement	17	15	32
5. More flexible leadership	11	19	30
6. Improved empathy	17	8	25
7. Improved autonomy and individuation	7	5	12
8. Improved communication	8	1	9

From *The Field of Family Therapy*, GAP report No. 78. Copyright 1970 by the Group for the Advancement of Psychiatry, Inc. Reprinted by permission of the Committee on the Family, Group for the Advancement of Psychiatry.

In another effort at classifying and bringing order to the developing field, Beels and Ferber (1969) observed a number of leading therapists conducting family sessions and studied videotapes and films of them working with families. As a result, they distinguished two types of family therapists: **conductors** and **reactors.** As therapists, conductors are active, aggressive, and colorful family-group leaders who place themselves in the center of a family's star-shaped verbal communication and are very willing to state their value systems to families. Here they include Ackerman, Satir, Bowen, and Minuchin. Reactors are less public personalities, more subtle and indirect, observing and clarifying the family-group process, responding to what the family presents to them, negotiating differences between family members. Whitaker, Framo, Zuk, Boszormenyi-Nagy, Haley, Jackson, and Wynne are included here. Each group is effective in directing and controlling the family sessions and in providing the family with possible new ways of relating to one another; the conductors are more obvious but not necessarily more successful in helping provide a new family experience as the basis for changing their interactive behavior patterns. (A more detailed discussion of actual family therapy techniques will be found in Chapters 7 and 8.)

In the 1970s, the systems-based ideology began gaining many followers among family therapists, as the view of the family moved more and more toward seeing them as interacting individuals whose behaviors influence each other and not simply as providing "crazy-making" environments in which to grow up. As we shall see in the following chapter, no single theory dominates the field yet, although we can begin to discern certain positions. However, most family therapists agree that the family must be considered as a social system, that therapeutic intervention must aim beyond the treatment of individuals to the treatment of families, and beyond separately treating individuals who comprise the family to treating the family as a unitary group. As Bell (1976), a family pioneer, notes, the locus of the problems or the center of pathology is placed within the family in this perspective; any outcome of treatment must be evaluated in terms of family well-being.

A variety of innovative techniques have been proposed and are currently being pursued; these will form the basis of much of the second half of this book. These include: working with several families simultaneously as in **multiple family therapy** (Laqueur, 1976); visiting families occasionally or regularly for therapy sessions at home (Speck, 1964); bringing families together for an intensive, crisis-focused two days of continuing interaction with a team of mental health professionals, as in **multiple impact therapy** (MacGregor, Ritchie, Serrano, & Schuster, 1964); working in the home with a family group, including the extended family members, friends, neighbors, employers, and so on, as in **network therapy** (Speck & Attneave, 1973); utilizing behavior modification principles for changing family interactive patterns (LeBow, 1972); brief therapy focusing on specific problem resolution (Weakland, Fisch, Watzlawick, & Bodin, 1974); outpatient family crisis intervention in place of hospitalizing a disturbed, scapegoated member (Langsley, Pittman, Machotka, & Flomenhaft, 1968); and many more. Videotaping family therapy sessions for immediate playback to family members (Alger, 1976a) and using a family sculpturing and choreography technique (showing physically and visually through poses how each person sees each other rather than using words to do so) (Papp, 1976) seem to be especially promising new ideas for diagnosing and changing dysfunctional family patterns.

Experimentation with new techniques, a more systematic evaluation of results, and an effort to provide some more cogent body of theory for family therapy seem to provide the areas of challenge as we enter the 1980s.

SUMMARY

Five roots of present-day family therapy are considered. *Psychoanalysis*, as proposed by Freud, considered the impact of family relationships on the individual's personality development, although its techniques of treatment were individual-oriented. Ackerman, a psychoanalyst, is considered a founding father of family therapy. *General systems theory*, as proposed by Bertalanffy, a biologist, attempts to relate seemingly unrelated phenomena as components of a self-regulating total system with feedback mechanisms for governing the process; Minuchin is the family therapist most identified with this viewpoint. Research on *schizophrenia* by Bateson and his colleagues on double-bind situations, Lidz on marital schism and marital skew, Bowen on symbiotic mother/child interactions, and Wynne on pseudomutuality helped focus on the family as a source of disturbance in the etiology of schizophrenia and set the stage for studying interaction patterns in all families. The fields of *marital counseling* and *child guidance* brought into treatment pairs of family members (husband/wife, parent/child), thus modifying the traditional emphasis on single parents. Finally, *group therapy* encouraged the use of small group processes for therapeutic gain, a forerunner of therapy with entire families.

As the family therapy movement gained momentum and national visibility in the 1950s, its initial thrust was in the study of families with schizophrenic members. By the 1960s, the pioneering family therapists of the previous decade were joined by more individual-oriented therapists who were attracted to this new way both of conceptualizing dysfunctional behavior and treating such behavior. Poor, disadvantaged families, rarely seen in psychotherapy before, began to be treated in outpatient settings by family therapists with favorable results. During the 1970s, efforts were underway to conceptualize what was taking place in this new field and attempt to classify practitioners and their therapeutic activities. Innovative techniques were introduced and the search continued for a conceptual central core of theory for what brings about changes through family therapy.

5

THEORETICAL MODELS
OF FAMILY INTERACTION

While all family therapists are apt to regard the family as a social system, there nevertheless are significant differences in theoretical assumptions about the nature and origin of psychological dysfunction, views of family interactions, and plans for therapeutic intervention between different models of family therapy. Aside from the common factor of differentiating themselves from the approach of individual therapy, family therapists can be further distinguished from one another on the basis of key theoretical suppositions and therapeutic techniques. Although positions have not yet hardened into "schools," we will attempt to differentiate special features of each of the following: (1) family psychodynamic theory, (2) family communications theory, (3) structural family theory, and (4) family behavior theory.

FOUR PARADIGMS OF FAMILY INTERACTION

Family Psychodynamic Theory

The psychodynamic view of individual behavior, based largely on a psychoanalytic model, focuses on the interplay of opposing forces within a person as the basis for understanding that person's motivation and sources of discomfort and anxiety. The neurotic individual, for example, may be seen as someone torn by inner conflict between his or her sexual wishes or urges and a punitive, guilt-producing conscience. Extrapolated to the family level, advocates of this view seek to discover how the inner lives and conflicts of family members interlock and the effect of the binding together on disturbances in family members.

In an early paper, Ackerman (1956) presented a conceptual model of **interlocking pathology**[1] in family relationships, arguing for family sessions where such entanglements might be demonstrated to the family members as they occur, in order for them to begin working toward eliminating them. Concerned with the impact of the family environment on the development of childhood disorders, Ackerman was one of the first to point out the constant interchange of unconscious processes occurring between family members as they are bound together in a particular interpersonal pattern. Under such circumstances, any single member's behavior represents a symptomatic reflection of possible confusion and distortion occurring in the entire family. With notions such as that of "interlocking pathology," Ackerman, a Freudian by training but attuned to social interactions by personal inclination, was able to wed many of the psychoanalytic concepts of intrapsychic dynamics to the psychosocial dynamics of family life. Framo (1970) summarized this position well when he stated: "Departing from the conventional, simplistic view of symptoms as intrapsychic entities and as stemming from a central illness, it is the author's view that symptoms are formed, selected, faked, exchanged, maintained and reduced as a function of the relationship context in which they are naturally embedded" (Framo, 1970, p. 127).

In addition to Ackerman, many of the family therapy pioneers (Don Jackson, Theodore Lidz, John Bell, Murray Bowen) tended to develop techniques based on psychoanalytic theory. According to Bowen (1976), probably the leading theorist in family therapy today, psychoanalysis provided two basic concepts still followed by mental health professionals: (1) that an emotional disturbance in an individual is developed in relationship with others, and (2) that the therapeutic relationship is the most effective and universal way to treat that disturbance.

---

[1] The pattern of *interlocking pathology* had long been known to therapists, many of whom had made the disquieting observation that sometimes, when their patient improved, his or her marriage broke up (Walrond-Skinner, 1976). This seemed to many to suggest that the patient had been locked into a neurotic interaction before, and following treatment was no longer willing to be so; therefore, he or she sought to leave the marriage. If, during the psychoanalytic treatment, the spouse became upset at changes in the patient, individual help with another therapist usually was recommended. It is not surprising that as a patient "improved" under this approach, the change was greeted as a threat and reacted to with anxiety and suspicion by family members, who sometimes would subtly undermine the effects of the analysis. It was not until family therapy began to be practiced that all of the persons involved—the entire family—were treated together.

More concerned with theory-building than was Ackerman, Bowen began to study the degree to which people are able to distinguish between the feeling process and the intellectual process within themselves. He observed differences between people in the ways feelings and intellect are either fused or differentiated from each other. Those with the greatest **fusion** between the two, he concluded, functioned the poorest. Those who could best distinguish between feeling and thinking had the most flexibility and adaptability in coping with life stresses. Turning to family relationships, Bowen (1966) introduced the concept of **undifferentiated family ego mass,** derived from psychoanalysis, to convey the idea of a family emotionally "stuck together," one where "a conglomerate emotional oneness . . . exists in all levels of intensity" (p. 171). For example, the symbiotic relationship of interdependency between mother and child may represent the most intense version, while the father's detachment may be the least intense. The degree to which any one member is involved from moment to moment depends on that person's basic level of involvement in the family ego mass. Sometimes the emotional closeness can be so intense that family members know each other's feelings, thoughts, fantasies, and dreams. This may shift to uncomfortable "overcloseness," according to Bowen, ultimately leading to a phase of mutual rejection between two members. In other words, within a family system, emotional tensions shift over time (sometimes slowly, sometimes rapidly) in a series of alliances and rejections.

Bowen (1966) developed a scale (Figure 5-1) for evaluating a per-

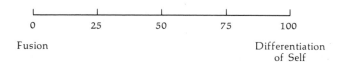

FIGURE 5-1. The theoretical Differentiation of Self scale, according to Bowen's conception, distinguishing people according to the degree of fusion or differentiation between their emotional and intellectual functioning. Those at the lowest level of differentiation (0–25) are emotionally fused to the family and others and lead lives in which their thinking is submerged and their feelings dominate. The lives of those in the 25–50 range are still guided by their emotional system and the reactions of others; goal-directed behavior is present but carried out in order to seek the approval of others. In the 50–75 range, thinking is sufficiently developed so as not to be dominated by feeling when stress occurs, and there is a reasonably developed sense of self. Those rare people functioning between 75–100 routinely separate their thinking from their feelings; they base decisions on the former but are free to lose themselves in the intimacy of a close relationship. Bowen (1978) considers someone at 75 to have a very high level of differentiation and all those over 60 to constitute a small percentage of society.

son's "differentiation of self" from the family ego mass. The greater the degree of undifferentiation (no sense of self or a weak or unstable personal identity), the greater the emotional fusion into a common self with others (the undifferentiated family ego mass). A person with a strong sense of self ("these are my opinions . . . this is who I am . . . this is what I will do, but not this . . .") does not negotiate it away for the sake of marital bliss or to please parents or achieve family harmony, although some fusion of selves occurs between husband and wife as well as between all family members.

People at the low extreme are those whose emotions and intellect are so fused that their lives are dominated by the feelings of those around them. As a consequence, they are easily stressed into dysfunction. Those far fewer individuals at the high end are emotionally mature; their intellectual functioning can retain relative (although not complete) autonomy during stressful periods, so that their actions can remain highly independent of the emotionality around them. In between are persons with relative degrees of fusion or differentiation. Note that the scale eliminates the need for the concept of normality. It is entirely possible for lower-scale people to keep their lives in emotional equilibrium and be symptom-free, thus appearing to satisfy the popular criteria of being "normal." However, they are more vulnerable to stress than those higher on the scale and under stress are apt to develop symptoms from which they recover far more slowly than do those others. A more differentiated person can participate freely in the emotional sphere without fear of becoming too fused with others.

In addition to his emphasis on the degree of integration of self, Bowen's theory also emphasizes anxiety or emotional tension within the person or in his or her relationships. The basic building block in a family's emotional system is the **triangle,** according to Bowen. During calm periods, when anxiety is low and external conditions are ideal, two persons may engage in a comfortable back and forth flow of feelings. Even under the best of circumstances, however, this condition becomes unstable, as one or both people become upset or anxious, either because of internal stresses or those from outside the twosome. When a certain intensity level is reached, the two persons will involve a vulnerable third person. According to Bowen (1978), the twosome may "reach out" and pull in the other person, the emotions may "overflow" to the third person, or that person may be emotionally "programmed" to initiate involvement. This triangle dilutes the anxiety; it is more stable and flexible than the twosome, and has a higher tolerance for dealing with stress. When anxiety in the triangle subsides, the emotional configuration returns to the calm twosome plus the lone outsider. However, should anxiety in the triangle increase, one person in the triangle may involve another outsider, and so forth.

Sometimes such **triangulation** can reach beyond the family, involving social agencies or the courts.

By definition, a two-person system is unstable (Bowen, 1975) and forms itself into a three-person system under stress. As more people become involved, the system becomes a series of *interlocking triangles.* As an example, conflict between siblings quickly involves a parent. He or she feels positively toward both children, who at the moment are in conflict with each other. If the parent can control his or her emotional responsiveness and manage not to take sides, while staying in contact with both children, the emotional intensity between the original two-some, the siblings, will diminish.[2] (As we shall see in describing Bowen's therapeutic technique in Chapter 7, the same situation exists when a couple comes to a marriage counselor or family therapist. If the counselor, as the triangled person, can remain involved with both without siding with one or the other, they may be able to each see themselves as individual selves as well as persons involved together in a marriage. But unless the triangled person remains in emotional contact with them, the twosome will triangle in someone else.)

We have noted previously (Chapter 4) Bowen's early (1960) three-generation hypothesis to account for the development of schizophrenia in a family member requiring at least three generations to develop. In a more recent formulation (1976), Bowen has proposed the broader concept of a *multigenerational transmission process,* in which one offspring, most fused into the family system,[3] emerges with a lower level of differentiation than the parents and functions more poorly than they in life. Other siblings, less involved with these parents, will fare better. If the impaired child with the poorest sense of self is followed over several generations, Bowen anticipates that the line of descent will produce persons with lower and lower levels of differentiation. Bowen now believes that the process may slow down or remain static over a generation or two so that perhaps eight or ten generations may be required until the level of impairment is reached that is consistent with schizophrenia. If the family encounters severe stress, however, schizophrenia may develop in an earlier generation. In some less stressful cases, he now believes, poorly differentiated people may keep

[2]A parallel situation exists when parents quarrel and a child is drawn into the triangle in an attempt to dilute and thus reduce the strain between the combatants.

[3]Bowen (1976) believes the child so selected by the parents, who themselves are immature, will be the one who is most infantile of all the children, regardless of his or her birth order in the family. Bowen stresses the sibling position of the parents in their families of origin as clues as to who is chosen in what he calls the "family projection process." Most emotionally attached to the parents of all the children within a family, that child will end up with the lowest level of differentiation of self and will have the most difficult time in separating from the family. Alfred Adler, an early associate of Freud's, also gave considerable credence to the influence of sibling position on later personality development.

their relationship system in relatively symptom-free equilibrium for several generations longer. This process may be reversed, of course, should someone in this lineage marry a person considerably higher on the differentiation-of-self scale. However, Bowen observes that most persons choose mates at more or less their own level of differentiation.

Although he was initially decidedly psychoanalytic (notice the use of such terms as **symbiosis** and *ego mass*), Bowen began early to move toward a systems view. However, he insists his more recent outlook has emerged from previous psychoanalytic thinking, not Bertalanffy's general systems theory. He is concerned, as are most family therapists, in the "facts of functioning in human relationships systems" (Bowen, 1978, p. 416)—*what* is happening, and *how, when,* and *where* it is happening—as far as the trained observer can determine those facts. Avoided are efforts to search out and uncover *why* things are happening—a cornerstone of traditional psychoanalytic treatment.

Ackerman, considered by at least one authority (Guerin, 1976) as the family movement's most creative and zealous psychoanalytic proponent, had also begun moving away from classical psychoanalytic thinking during the late 1960s. By 1970, Ackerman urged the consideration of a broadened "biopsychosocial" model to conceptualize personality dynamics. He had begun shortly before his death to view individual symptoms not as walled-off intrapsychic phenomena, but rather as recurring, predictable, interactional patterns, intending (unsuccessfully) to achieve homeostasis for the person, but actually producing progressive distortions in the balance of family role relationships. Today, as the center of the field has moved toward viewing families as systems, Boszormenyi-Nagy (Boszormenyi-Nagy & Spark,

FIGURE 5-2. Ivan Boszormenyi-Nagy, M.D. (Photo courtesy of Ivan Boszormenyi-Nagy.)

1973), Framo (1965), and Whitaker (Napier & Whitaker, 1978) remain the leading theoreticians attempting to bridge psychoanalysis and family theory.

Family Communications Theory

The traditional psychoanalytic or psychodynamic view of, say, conflict between mother and adolescent daughter, may be viewed as the mother overidentifying with her child and perhaps projecting her own unresolved problems from her own adolescence onto her. The daughter, in turn, rebellious and with a still incompletely formed sense of personal identity, may be introjecting many of her mother's characteristics, but undergoing an "identity crisis" at the same time. It is possible, however, that this same pattern may be viewed not as two persons, each with "problems," but as a *dysfunctional relationship,* which manifests itself, among other ways in faulty communication. If we adopt the latter view, notice how the emphasis has shifted—from the past to here and now, from analyzing the inner dynamics of each to studying their pattern of interaction and communication, from seeing pathology in one or both to understanding how each has defined her role and adapted to the other. Their recurring struggle may be circular: "I nag because you defy me." "No, mom, it's the other way around; I defy you because you nag."[4] To Haley (1963), every relationship contains within it an implicit power struggle over who defines the nature of that relationship, and the pattern just described is no exception. The mother is not the cause of her daughter's behavior, nor is the daughter causing her mother's behavior. Both are caught up in a circular system and have evolved "rules" for behaving toward each other.

To communication theorists (Don Jackson, Jay Haley, Virginia Satir), all behavior is communication; just as it is impossible not to behave, so communication cannot be avoided. The wife who complains in utter frustration that her husband "refuses to communicate" with her but instead stares at the television set all evening is responding too literally to his failure to "talk" to her. On a nonverbal level, she is receiving a loud and clear message that he is rejecting her, withdrawing from her, may be angry or bored with her, wants distance from her, and so on. Communication occurs at many levels—gesture, body language, tone of voice, posture, intensity—in addition to the content

---

[4]This circular interaction continues because each participant imposes her own "punctuation" on the ongoing system. Many clinical problems seen by family therapists involve punctuations parallel to those seen in children quarreling: "You started it!" ("I'm only reacting to what you did.") "No, you started it first!" and so on. Actually, it is pointless to search for the starting point because we are dealing with a complex repetitive interaction and not a simple linear cause and effect situation (Weakland, 1976).

of what is said. Sometimes, as indicated earlier in the previous chapter, a message is sent in the form of a double-bind, contradicting itself, as in the following:

> IGNORE THESE INSTRUCTIONS

To follow instructions, one must not follow instructions, which becomes very confusing.

It is clear that there is no such thing as a simple message. Rather, people are forever sending and receiving a multiplicity of messages by both verbal and nonverbal channels, and every message is qualified and modified by another message on another level of abstraction (Weakland, 1976). People can say one thing and mean another, modifying, reinforcing, or contradicting what they have just said. In other words, they are both communicating ("How are you?") and communicating *about* their communication ("I do not really expect you to answer, nor do I especially want to know the answer—unless you say you are fine."). To summarize, people cannot help but communicate, and all communication takes place at two levels—the surface level, one of content, and a second level that qualifies what is said on the first level. This second level is called **metacommunication** (Watzlawick, Beavin, & Jackson, 1967). Problems may arise when a message at the first level ("Nice to see you.") is contradicted by a facial expression or voice tone ("How can I make a quick getaway from this boring person?"), which communicates at the second level. As we have seen, communications theorists, following the work of Bateson and his coworkers, propose that such contradictions occur in families that produce schizophrenic children—we love you (hate you), we want you close by (go away), and so on. It is as though the parent is saying "I order you to disobey me" to a confused child who cannot escape, to whom the relationship is important, and who must develop a response to the incongruent messages occurring at two different levels. In that situation he or she may develop an incongruent way of communicating back, sometimes in a schizophrenic manner.

While the early work of communications theorists was carried out at the Mental Research Institute in Palo Alto and dealt mainly with families with schizophrenic members, it has since expanded rapidly to other family therapy centers around the country and to other aspects of family functioning. In the meantime, the Mental Research Institute has continued as a research, training, and family therapy center, emphasizing the interactional view of behavior (Watzlawick & Weakland, 1977) and developing new therapeutic techniques—such as brief family therapy, a direct, time-limited, pragmatic approach intended to help families better deal with changes in their relationships as new developmental stages in family living are experienced (Watzlawick, Weakland, & Fisch, 1974).

Jackson, Haley, and Satir, all originally associated with the institute during the 1950s, began conceptualizing human problems in terms of interaction and in particular tried to develop ways of improving family communication. Jackson, psychoanalytic by training but influenced by Bertalanffy's general systems theory, stressed the family's feedback system, its homeostasis, the emergence of its rules, and the ways the family deals with conflict. Cognitive in his approach, seeking to reduce problem-maintaining behavior, he saw marriage, for example, as a voluntary, long-term, collaborative relationship where rules arise out of the partners' interaction experiences (rather than from individual actions), and where something akin to bargaining takes place through what he called the "marital quid pro quo" (literally "something for something") (Jackson, 1965a). Quid pro quo refers to a relationship based on a recognition and acceptance of differences between the partners and a clear division of labor defining the contribution made by each. For example: he handles intellectual matters more capably but is less practical; she is a more realistic person and also more sensitive to others and more social. Or as a second example: he actually prefers marketing and cooking but is too casual about finances; she prefers working to being home, hates cooking, enjoys arranging and sticking to a budget. The point is that an exchange is made, a kind of contract, not based on stereotyped sex roles but on abilities and interests.

In the first example, she can avoid becoming frustrated waiting for him to invite friends over and he can avoid frustration waiting for her to introduce intellectual issues into their conversation. In the second example, handling money would not be entrusted to him nor would remembering to pick up groceries on the way home from work be expected of her. While this is simple (perhaps too simple), Jackson was beginning to develop a theory of marriage based on these relationships and not individuals, with a language to aid observing the interaction pattern and a way of teaching a couple "rules" for governing their relationship. Jackson was developing these further at the time of his death in 1968.

The notion of the family attempting to maintain a homeostatic balance is central to Jackson's thinking. You will recall from Chapter 2 that Jackson (1965b) likened the family's operations to those of a home heating system, where a sudden change in temperature initiates a number of events designed to establish the equilibrium. Analogously, when a teenager announces she is pregnant, or a grandmother moves in with her children and grandchildren, or there is a divorce between parents, or chronic illness in a child, or a family member becomes schizophrenic—these and similar events are equivalent to flinging open a window when you've warmed the house to the temperature you desire. The family goes to work to reestablish its balance. Ironically, a family that is disintegrating and disunited can strive to become functional once again to cope with such a crisis. In some cases, the family's very stability may be maintained by their child's periodic illnesses (Napier & Whitaker, 1978).

A family's communication pattern reveals the sender/receiver's relationship. If it is a relationship based on equality, it is symmetrical; if not, then it is complementary. (These concepts, along with detailed transcripts of a husband and wife talking to a therapist, are presented in Chapter 3.) The former may be a simple open exchange of views or perhaps highly competitive, but it is between peers, while the latter inevitably involves one person assuming a superior position and the other an inferior one. Here Jackson is joined by Haley (1963), who underlines the struggle for power and control in every relationship through the messages that sender and receiver exchange with each other. Who will define the relationship? Will that person turn it into a symmetrical or complementary one? Who decides who decides? Observe a couple deciding on how to allocate expenditures, or what television program to watch, or whether to make love late in the evening (when one prefers mornings), or who will answer the telephone, balance the checkbook, go out to buy some ice cream, or pick up the dirty socks and underwear from the floor, and see if you do not learn a great deal about how they define their relationship!

Haley believes that all symptoms are strategies for controlling a relationship when other strategies have failed, and then to deny doing so by claiming the symptom is involuntary. As an example, he cites the case of a woman who insisted her husband be home every night because she suffered anxiety attacks if left alone. However, she refused to acknowledge thus controlling his behavior, but rather blamed it on the anxiety attacks, over which she presumably had no control. The husband faces a dilemma: he cannot acknowledge that she is controlling his behavior (it is, after all, her anxiety that is doing that), but he also cannot refuse to let her control his behavior, for the same reason. He is in a double-bind situation. The family therapist would seek changes in the nature of their relationship and ways of communicating with each other.

Haley, then, focuses on the power struggles within a family and how each family member constantly seeks to define or redefine the relationship. ("You can't boss me around anymore; I'm not a baby." is a familiar taunt in the teenager's effort to change old family "rules.") Jockeying for control, according to Haley, occurs in all families and in every relationship between two or more people. Most couples work out a suitable means of dealing with struggles for control. People who develop symptoms (as the woman with the anxiety attack described above) deny efforts to control but develop subtle, indirect methods (and pathological relationships) instead. Haley's (1976) therapeutic approach is to treat individual problems as symptoms of an improperly functioning family organization. He seeks to directly cause a change in the patient's behavior that will alleviate the symptom.

Virginia Satir, a psychiatric social worker, was among the first to report in book form on the work she and her colleagues in Palo Alto were carrying on in teaching families more honest and effective communications patterns (Satir, 1967). More concerned with practice than theory (as is also true of many family therapists), Satir offered numerous illustrations of her family-oriented techniques, including verbatim transcripts of family sessions, based on the communication viewpoint. She emerges as a direct, caring person who herself is a model of clear, open, simple communication patterns. Among the early workers in family therapy, Satir, along with Ackerman, is usually credited as being one of the two initial charismatic leaders of the field (Beels & Ferber, 1969).

Under stress, people in any relationship with one another handle their communications in one of five ways, according to Satir's classification (Satir, Stachowiak, & Taschman, 1975). The *placater* always agrees, apologizes, tries to please; the *blamer* dominates, finds fault, and accuses; the *super-reasonable* person remains detached, calm, supercool, and not emotionally involved; the *irrelevant* person distracts and seems unrelated to anything going on; only in the *congruent* way of communicating does the person appear real, expressive of genuine feelings, and sending out straight (not double-binding or other confusing) messages. Various combinations exist in families; for example, take the case of a blaming wife, a blaming husband and a placating child triad ("it's the school, they don't teach anything anymore . . . it's the child down the street, that's where she's learned those bad words . . . it's the way you've raised her, she's just like you . . . I'll try to do better, daddy, you're absolutely right. I'll stop watching TV tomorrow, go to the library, and so on . . . leave the dishes and I'll do them tomorrow after school . . ."). In the blamer/super-reasonable dyad, the wife might complain with great intensity that "we hardly ever make love anymore, don't you have any feelings for me?" The husband might respond coldly, "of course I do or I wouldn't be married to you. Perhaps we define the word 'love' differently." Satir tends to work with families at the level of their day-to-day functioning. She deals with their emotional experiences with one another and attempts to teach them congruent ways of communicating by helping them restore the use of their senses and get in touch with and accept what

TABLE 5-1. Four Communication Stances Adopted under Stress (Satir)

Category	Caricature	Typical Verbal Expression	Body posture	Inner Feeling
Placater	Service	"Whatever you want is okay. I'm just here to make you happy."	Grateful, bootlicking, begging, self-flagellating	"I am like a nothing. Without you I am dead. I am worthless."
Blamer	Power	"You never do anything right. What is the matter with you?"	Finger pointing, loud, tyrannical, enraged	"I am lonely and unsuccessful."
Super-Reasonable	Intellect	"If one were to observe carefully, one might notice the workworn hands of someone present here."	Monotone voice, stiff, machine-like, computer-like	"I feel vulnerable."
Irrelevant	Spontaneity	Words unrelated to what others are saying. For example, in midst of family dispute: "What are we having for dinner?"	In constant movement, constant chatter, distracting	"Nobody cares. There is no place for me."

Adapted from R. Bandler, J. Grinder, and V. Satir, *Changing with Families*, Palo Alto, Calif.: Science and Behavior Books, 1976.

they are feeling. Thus, she helps families build their sense of self-worth, and opens up the possibilities of making choices and bringing about changes in their relationships.

Structural Family Theory

Strongly committed to the systems outlook, the structuralist position, primarily developed and advanced by Minuchin (1974a), emphasizes the active, organized wholeness of the family unit. He describes his viewpoint as follows:

> In essence, the structural approach to families is based on the concept that a family is more than the individual biopsychodynamics of its members. Family members relate according to certain arrangements, which govern their transactions. These arrangements, though usually not explicitly stated or even recognized form a whole—the structure of the family. The reality of the structure is of a different order from the reality of the individual members [p. 89].

Like the communications theorists, the structuralists are interested in how the components of a system interact, how balance or homeostatis is achieved, how the family feedback mechanisms operate, how dysfunctional communication patterns may develop, and other systems factors. However, there are also important differences between the two theories. Rather than observe the basic elements in a family transaction—what messages members send back and forth—the structuralists adopt a more holistic view, observing the activities and functions of the family as a clue to how the family is organized or structured (Ritterman, 1977). Put another way, the focus here is on using the content of a transaction in the service of understanding how the family organizes itself; the structuralists in general are more concerned with *how* family members communicate than *what* they communicate.

Minuchin rejects what he calls the "linear" framework for understanding human behavior and instead insists on using a systems frame of reference. A linear approach zeros in on the individual and his or her intrapsychic problems (the psychodynamic view) or learned maladaptive behavior (the behavioral view) in attempting to conceptualize and then treat that particular individual's symptom. A systems approach, on the other hand, builds on the work of the linear approaches but goes beyond them to look at that person in context (Minuchin, et al. 1978). That is, the systems model analyzes the individual's psychological and behavioral makeup by focusing upon the influences family members have on one another from that individual's earliest life to the present. Although they recognize that the person's past life experiences do transcend the family system, the structuralists believe that experiences within the family govern the range of each family member's behavior. The systems approach thus operates with a wider lens than does the linear.

Members define themselves and their place in the family organization by their interactions. We begin to catch on to how a family functions by watching these interactions. The members' actions and transactions with one another tell us how they accommodate to one another, the degree to which they are assimilated into the family, whether the family operates as an open or closed system, what boundaries and subsystems exist, and lots more. For example, the structuralist may ask himself or herself: Who is the family spokesman? Are roles established by age, sex, power, or some other factors? Is what is being said during a family therapy session supported or contradicted by the family's behavior? What transactional patterns and boundaries exist and how are they set up? Are these patterns functional or dysfunctional? Minuchin (1974a) describes this process of forming a structural diagnosis as deriving a family "map," an organizational scheme of family interactions. This map forms the basis for determining therapeutic goals. As needed, **structural family therapy** is directed toward changing the family organization, the social context in which an individual member's "symptoms" may develop. Minuchin argues that, when the structure of the family group is transformed, the positions of its members will be altered accordingly and, as a result, each person will experience change.

The family is a social unit that advances through distinct stages of development, during each of which new developmental tasks or challenges must be met (see Chapter 1). Each stage calls for reorganization of the family system usually accompanied by changes in functions among members. A recently married couple must learn to mutually accommodate to numerous small routines (when to go to bed, when to rise, how to share the bathroom, sexual pattern preferences, meal times, and so on). In the process, they develop a set of patterned transactions for triggering as well as monitoring each other's behavior. The birth of a first child changes the organization. A child imposes new demands on their time and differentiates their parenting functions (who is responsible for feeding and dressing the baby, changing diapers, buying clothes, going to the doctor, baby's bed time, baby's play time, and so on), thereby changing the spouse's previous transactional patterns. New subsystems are introduced, grandparents may enter the picture, new alliances are created, boundaries changed. With each new stage of development, restructuring is called for, new accommodations and changes in the relative strengths and productivities of family members.

Thus, a family is always subject to inner pressures brought about by changes in its members and subsystems as well as outer pressures to accommodate to significant social institutions (as, for example, when an immigrant family must adopt to a new culture) (Minuchin, 1974a). Some families, under stress to change, become increasingly rigid in their transactional patterns and boundaries, resisting any exploration of alternative ways of interacting. As we saw in Chapter 3, families Minuchin has labeled as "enmeshed" become too involved, intertwined with one another, and overintrusive on personal boundaries; disengaged families are too rigidly separated. Minuchin stresses that boundaries or delineations between a family's subsystems need to be clear for proper family functioning. Members of one subsystem (for example, parents) must be allowed to carry out their functions without too much interference (say, from a grandmother), but contact between members of the subsystem and others must be maintained. A parental subsystem may even include a grandparent so long as the lines of authority and responsibility are clearly drawn in the family. It is when boundaries are too blurred and the family communicates only within itself that it is said to be enmeshed. At the other extreme, if boundaries become overly rigid and communication across subsystems becomes difficult, then the family becomes disengaged. Members of disengaged families are apt to lack a feeling of family loyalty and belonging; they find it difficult to depend on other members or to request help or support from them when needed. Members of enmeshed families achieve their heightened sense of belonging by yielding their autonomy or ability to act independently. Minuchin's early work at the Wiltwyck School (see footnote 4, Chapter 3), where he dealt with many disorganized, low socioeconomic, multiproblem families with delinquent children, led him into developing his theories on the importance of understanding the family structure and process as well as developing more concrete, here and now therapeutic techniques for reaching the entire family that did not require a high level of verbal sophistication (Minuchin, Montalvo, Guerney, Rosman, & Schumer, 1967).

Minuchin has recently extended his work to the area of psychosomatic illnesses such as anorexia nervosa in children (Minuchin, et al., 1978). Instead of the customary psychiatric (that is, linear) view that the child is the passive recipient of noxious environmental influences, Minuchin and his coworkers have begun to look at the individual in his or her social context and at the feedback processes between individual and context. From a systems viewpoint, certain types of family organizations, such as those that encourage somatization, are related to the development and maintenance of psychosomatic symptoms in physiologically vulnerable children. In turn, the child's psychosomatic symptoms play an important role in maintaining the family homeostasis. Each family member's behavior is simultaneously caused and causative of behavior in other members (see Figure 5-3). The system can be activated at various points, with feedback mecha-

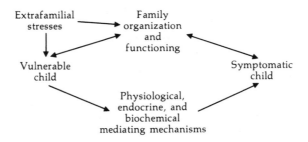

FIGURE 5-3. An open systems model of psychosomatic disease. (Reprinted by permission of the publishers from *Psychosomatic Families: Anorexia Nervosa in Context,* by Salvador Minuchin, Bernice Rosman, and Lester Baker. Cambridge, Mass.: Harvard University Press. Copyright © 1978 by the President and Fellows of Harvard College.)

nisms causing reverberations throughout the system. Increased stress, coming from within the family system or brought about by outside forces, can trigger physical symptoms such as anorexia nervosa in a vulnerable child, causing the family to modify its temporary dysfunctional interactional patterns. Thus, family members, including the anoretic child, through feedback processes, constrain and regulate each other's behavior.

Various psychosomatic illnesses, such as bronchial asthma and certain forms of diabetes in children, in addition to anorexia nervosa, have been found (Minuchin, Baker, Rosman, Liebman, Milman, & Todd, 1975) to occur with particular frequency in families with the following transactional patterns: (1) *enmeshment* (poorly differentiated, weak, and easily crossed subsystem boundaries); (2) *overprotectiveness* of each other, not limited to the identified patient (nurturing constantly elicited and supplied, each member hypersensitive to signs of distress in others); (3) *rigidity* (retaining accustomed ways of interacting when no longer appropriate, stunting growth and autonomy in a child); and (4) *lack of conflict resolution* (leaving problems unresolved, problems that later reactivate the system's avoidance circuits and lead to the reappearance of symptoms). While no one of these family characteristics alone may be sufficient to spark the appearance of psychosomatic symptoms, the cluster of all four transactional patterns is believed by Minuchin and his colleagues to be characteristic of a family process that encourages somatization. In such families, "illness" becomes a mode of communication as the symptomatic child helps the family avoid its real conflicts. In Chapter 7, we will offer a brief example of an anoretic adolescent girl and Minuchin's therapeutic technique for dealing with the transactional issues within the family that the appearance of her symptoms has accentuated.

Family Behavior Theory

Learning-oriented clinicians have extended the principles underlying behavior modification or **behavior therapy** with individuals to the realm of marital and family intervention. Assuming that deviant behavior within a family is subject to the same laws governing all human behavior, they argue that the relearning procedures useful in changing any behavior can be applied to changing deviant behavior within a family. Before intervention can take place, however, one must have an assessment process for defining, observing, and recording behavioral and stimulus events occurring within a family. Behaviorists insist on recording actual events and scrupulously avoid inferences about the motives and feelings of the people involved. Thus, instead of inferring from a verbal exchange between husband and wife that one or both are feeling angry (that is, instead of explaining why they spoke or behaved as they did) behaviorists find it more exact and scientific to record the behavior of each spouse (what each said, and what each did) and the temporal relationships existing between antecedent and consequent events related to each behavior. They are more interested in changing the behavior than in ferreting out its exact causes. If one partner offers a self-report of an internal state ("I'm feeling very angry at you now") that is acceptable data, but unconfirmed inferences about another person's private thoughts or feelings is not (LeBow, 1972).

The behaviorally oriented therapist sees the family therapy situation as an opportunity to induce significant behavioral changes in the family members by restructuring their interpersonal environments (Liberman, 1970). After creating a positive therapeutic alliance between himself or herself and the family members, the therapist makes a behavioral analysis of the problems within the family. What behavior is maladaptive (that is, should be increased or decreased) in the identified patient? What specific changes would each person like to see in other family members? Answers to questions such as these force the therapist to specify the behavioral goals of the treatment, something behaviorists argue is glaringly absent in other therapeutic approaches. In addition, the behavior therapist wants to know what environmental and interpersonal contingencies currently support the problematic behavior. Such a behavioral analysis continues throughout the family therapy sessions; as problem behavior changes during treatment, so must the analysis of what maintains these behaviors (Liberman, 1970).

FIGURE 5-4. Robert P. Liberman, M.D. (Photo courtesy of Robert Liberman.)

The process of family behavior therapy consists of guiding family members toward altering reinforcement contingencies. For example, instead of being caught up in, and rewarding, maladaptive behavior with attention responses that socially reinforce the undesirable behavior (by nagging, showing sympathy or anger, or babying), family members learn to recognize, approve, and thereby positively reinforce only each other's desirable behavior. The point here is that the deviant member will continue his or her undesirable, manipulative behavior or set of symptoms only so long as other family members express interest or concern or otherwise respond, positively or negatively, with attention (saying, in effect, "you'll continue to receive our special attention as long as you misbehave"). The behavior therapist helps the family set up conditions by which social reinforcement such as attention-giving is made contingent on the desired behavior.

A number of learning-theory principles are involved in family behavior therapy. The most frequently employed is undoubtedly **positive reinforcement,** a reward (smile, kiss, gift, attention) for a desirable behavioral pattern which strengthens that pattern and increases the probability of its recurrence as a response. **Shaping,** another frequently employed technique, involves an **operant conditioning** process in which successive approximations of desired behavior are reinforced until the desired behavior is achieved. Liberman (1970) utilized shaping principles to help a married couple deal with specific problems, as illustrated in the following case.

Mr. and Mrs. F have a long history of marital strife. There was a year-long separation early in their marriage and several attempts at marriage counseling lasting three years. Mr. F has paranoid trends which are reflected in his extreme sensitivity to any lack of affection or commitment toward him by his wife. He is very jealous of her close-knit relationship with her parents. Mrs. F is a disheveled and unorganized woman who has been unable to meet her husband's expectations for an orderly and accomplished homemaker or competent manager of their five children. Their marriage has been marked by frequent mutual accusations and depreciation, angry withdrawal and sullenness.

My strategy with this couple, whom I saw for 15 sessions, was to teach them to stop reinforcing each other with attention and emotionality for undesired behavior and to begin eliciting desired behavior in each other using the principle of *shaping*. Tactically, I structured the therapy sessions with an important "ground-rule": No criticism or harping were allowed and they were to spend the time telling each other what the other had done during the past week that approached the desired behaviors. As they gave positive feedback to each other for approximations to the behavior each valued in the other, I served as an auxiliary source of positive acknowledgment, reinforcing the reinforcer.

We began by clearly delineating what specific behaviors were desired by each of them in the other and by my giving them homework assignments in making gradual efforts to approximate the behavioral goals. For instance, Mr. F incessantly complained about his wife's lack of care in handling the evening meal—the disarray of the table setting, lack of tablecloth, disorderly clearing of the dishes. Mrs. F grudgingly agreed that there was room for improvement and I instructed her to make a start by using a tablecloth nightly. Mr. F in turn was told the importance of his giving her positive and consistent attention for her effort, since this was important to him. After one week they reported that they had been able to fulfill the assignment and that the evening meal was more enjoyable. Mrs. F had increased her performance to the complete satisfaction of her husband, who meanwhile had continued to give her positive support for her progress.

A similar process occurred in another problem area. Mr. F felt that his wife should do more sewing (mending clothes, putting on missing buttons) and should iron his shirts (which he had always done himself). Mrs. F was fed up with the home they lived in, which was much too small for their expanded family. Mr. F resolutely refused to consider moving to larger quarters because he felt it would not affect the quality of his wife's homemaking performance. I instructed Mrs. F to begin to do more sewing and ironing and Mr. F to reinforce this by starting to consider moving to a new home. He was to concretize this by spending part of each Sunday reviewing the real estate section of the newspaper with his wife and to make visits to homes that were advertised for sale. He was to make clear to her that his interest in a new home was *contingent* upon her improvements as a homemaker.

Between the third and sixth sessions, Mrs. F's father—who was ill with terminal lung cancer—was admitted to the hospital and died. During this period, we emphasized the importance of Mr. F giving his wife solace and support. I positively reinforced Mr. F's efforts in this direction. He was able to help his wife over her period of sadness and mourning despite his long-standing antagonism toward her father. Mrs. F, in turn, with my encouragement, responded to her husband's sympathetic behavior with affection and appreciation. Although far from having an idyllic marriage, Mr. and Mrs. F have made tangible gains in moving closer toward each other [pp. 114-115].[5]

Stuart (1969) utilizes operant conditioning theory and what he calls **operant-interpersonal therapy** to treat marital discord. He assumes, to begin with, that the exact pattern of interaction taking place between spouses at any point in time is the most rewarding of all available alternatives—that's why they chose it. (A wife who complains that her husband spends too much time with his friends and not enough with her should not simply be angry at him but should face up to the fact that his friends offer greater relative rewards for him than she does.) Stuart assumes further that successful marriages involve a quid pro quo ("something for something") arrangement; here he is in agreement with communications theorist Don Jackson (see page 115). In behavioral terms, successful marriages can be differentiated from unsuccessful ones by the frequency and range of reciprocal positive reinforcements the partners exchange. ("I'll be glad to entertain your parents this weekend if you accompany me on that fishing trip [or ballet performance] within the following month.") In unsuccessful marriages, coercion, withdrawal, and retaliatory behavior are more common. Presumably, the rejected wife in the example above

[5] From "Behavioral Approaches to Family and Couple Therapy," by R. P. Liberman, *American Journal of Orthopsychiatry*, 1970, 40 (1), 106–118. Copyright © 1970 by the American Orthopsychiatric Association, Inc. Reproduced by permission.

must take the "positive risk" of changing her behavior (that is, making a positive move toward her mate before expecting one from him). In behavioral terms, she must be willing to give reinforcement before receiving it. The consequences of her behavioral change increase the likelihood of a "positive risk" from her spouse. The new social exchange reshapes and redefines their relationship.

In a troubled relationship, according to Stuart, the couple is "locked into" a problematic pattern of interaction, each requiring a change in the other before changing his or her own behavior. Stuart proposes that the couple make explicit reinforcement contracts with each other, negotiating exchanges of desired behavior. Restating negative statements and complaints in terms of specifically desired positive behavior (wife: "I would like you to spend at least 30 minutes with the children before their bedtime"; husband: "I would like you to have dinner on the table within 15 minutes after I arrive home"), each person records the frequency with which the other completes the desired behavior. Stuart even suggests a token system, somewhat in the style of hospital **token economy** programs, to facilitate behavioral change. The husband may earn tokens for conversing with his wife, let us say, for at least 30 minutes of each hour (these criteria can be negotiated depending on circumstances). Conversation tokens accumulated by the husband could later be redeemable for increased physical affection and sexual activity. Hickok and Komechak (1974) have reported the use of a token system to monitor and then begin to change the undesirable, mutually provocative behavior in a couple contemplating divorce. Each partner was taught how he or she previously had been inadvertently reinforcing precisely that behavior in the other that he or she had so strongly criticized.

Considerable behavioral work, following a social learning model, has been directed at child-management problems within a family. Rather than dealing therapeutically with the family as a dysfunctional social system, this approach attempts to reprogram the social environment (Patterson, McNeal, Hawkins, & Phelps, 1967) in an effort to socialize the disturbed behavior of a child within the family. Such an effort typically teaches social learning principles such as **modeling** and the use of social reinforcers directly to parents to apply at home, utilizing their daily contact with the child to act as change agents (or, in a sense, as behavior therapists) in bringing about a modification of the child's undesirable behavior (Berkowitz & Graziano, 1972).

Social learning theory, when applied to families, emphasizes that parents control many of the contingencies influential in the child acquiring and maintaining certain behavior patterns, and therefore are logically in a position to change that behavior, if properly taught to do so. In *Families*, Patterson (1971) outlines some procedures for parents to acquire "behavior management skills" in order to carry out good child management. Presumably, in many well-run homes managed by adults, these skills occur "naturally," that is, without deliberately following a prescribed program. For those less fortunate, Patterson spells out a plan for parents—observing behavior to establish a baseline, pinpointing the specific behavior they wish to change, observing and graphing one's own behavior, negotiating a contract with the child, and so on. Figure 5-5 represents a checklist constructed for a boy who

Dave's Program						
	M	T	W	T	F	S
Gets to school on time (2)	2					
Does not roam around room (1)	0					
Does what the teacher tells him (5)	3					
Gets along well with other kids (5)	1					
Completes his homework (5)	2					
Work is accurate (5)	3					
Behavior on the schoolbus is OK (2)	2					
Gets along well with brother and sisters in evening (3)	0					
TOTAL 13						

1. If Dave gets 25 points, he doesn't have to do any chores that night and he gets to pick all the TV shows for the family to watch.
2. If Dave gets only 15 points, he does not get to watch TV that night.
3. If Dave gets only 10 points, he gets no TV and he also has to do the dishes.
4. If Dave gets only 5 points or less, then he gets no TV, washes the dishes, and is grounded for the next two days (home from school at 4:00 and stays in yard).

FIGURE 5-5. A parent/child negotiated contract checklist indicating specific duties to be performed and a point system based on the degree of goal achievement. (From *Families: Application of Social Learning to Family Life*, by G. R. Patterson. Copyright 1971 by Research Press Company. Reprinted by permission.)

displayed a wide range of out-of-control behavior. The parent/child contract, developed together, stipulated the former would check with the teacher daily to get the necessary information and would provide the consequences for the child's behavior (no dishwashing chores, allowed to watch TV, and so on). These consequences included mild but fair punishment for continued problem behaviors in addition to providing the aforementioned "payoffs" for adaptive behavior. In establishing the contract, the child helps set the "price" in points for each item, sees the results daily (the program is posted in a conspicuous place at home, such as the refrigerator door), and negotiates the backup reinforcers (for example, TV programs) for the accumulated points.

Recent research (Arnold, Levine, & Patterson, 1975) suggests that the behavior of siblings as well as that of an identified problem child need to be altered by parent-training programs, because a family may contain more than one "deviant" child, although only one child may be so labeled by the parents. If only one child is treated, siblings may continue to "trigger" the problem child's deviant behavior, thus counteracting the possible positive effects of the parents' management program. These researchers were able to plot positive changes in the siblings of socially aggressive boys, as well as these boys themselves, when parents were trained in social learning techniques of child management. As most family therapists of whatever theoretical persuasion ultimately conclude, effective treatment requires changes in the family system.

SUMMARY

Four theoretical models of family interaction are differentiated in this chapter. *Family psychodynamic theory*, based largely on a psychoanalytic model, stresses an interlocking pathology in family relationships. Many early family therapists, such as Ackerman and Bowen, began with this theoretical framework, developing concepts couched in psychoanalytic terms while attempting to view the family as an ongoing system. *Family communications theory* emphasizes the central role of faulty, contradictory, or double-bind messages in a dysfunctional family relationship. Its leading advocates are Jackson (communication and family homeostatic balance), Haley (struggle for power and control in every communication message), and Satir (family communication roles). *Structural family theory*, as proposed by Minuchin, takes a holistic view of the family's organization as the determining factor in its transaction patterns. Here the focus is on the relationship between various subsystems within a family, the flexibility of boundaries, and the family's ability to reorganize and accommodate to changing stages of development. *Family behavior theory* utilizes learning theory principles such as positive reinforcement and shaping to explain how certain maladaptive behavior patterns developed between family members. Liberman, Stuart, and Patterson are leading behavior therapists who use these same principles to guide families to alter their reinforcement behavior.

Part Three

TECHNIQUES OF
FAMILY THERAPY

6

THE PROCESS OF
FAMILY THERAPY

In Part One of this book, we considered a variety of family transactional patterns, some less functional than others. We described a family as a natural social system with its own rules of behavior, its own degree of closeness among members, its own power structure. Each family develops and perpetuates its own myths, has its own way of coping with crises, and its unique communication patterns. In Part Two, we looked at how the family therapy movement evolved and what theoretical models exist today for the practice of family therapy.

We are now ready to look at various controversial issues and forms of clinical practice in the family therapy field. In this chapter, some definitions and basic features of family therapy will be considered. The following two chapters will be devoted to a discussion of some contemporary therapeutic techniques.

BASIC CHARACTERISTICS OF FAMILY THERAPY

Family Therapy versus Individual Therapy

Family therapy is a psychotherapeutic technique for exploring and attempting to alleviate the current interlocking emotional problems within a family system by helping its members change the family's dysfunctional transactional patterns together. Unlike individual psychotherapy, which focuses on the person's intrapsychic difficulties while sometimes recognizing that the patient's disturbed interpersonal relationships may have contributed to those difficulties, family therapy zeros in on the relationships (for example, alliances, rules, covert loyalty pressures) as they transpire during therapeutic sessions. The family therapist is interested in the family *of* the psychiatric patient, and, as much or sometimes more to the point, in the family *as* the psychiatric patient (Bloch, 1974). More and more, according to Spiegel (1974), family therapy is becoming the center of service delivery systems in the United States, as nationwide efforts continue to develop a comprehensive system of community mental health care.

Family therapy may be further differentiated from individual therapy along three dimensions: (1) views of the nature and location of forces active in personality development, (2) views of symptom formation, and (3) the approach to therapeutic change (Robinson, 1975). In family therapy, it is assumed that external forces dominate personality formation in the organized behavioral characteristics of the family by which the family manages and regulates the interpersonal lives of its members. In individual therapy, internal events (thoughts, fears, conflicts) are believed to be dominant. From the former perspective, it is the family, as a rule-governed, change-resistant transactional system evolved over several generations, that sustains itself by evoking conformity among its members. Robinson cites the example of a mother/infant relationship being influenced as much by the quality of the mother's relationship with her husband and the satisfactions derived from her marriage as by the specific characteristics of the infant. If the infant ultimately fails to develop into a mature adult, independent of the mother, it is less a reflection of his or her unresolved internal conflicts than of a family conspiracy of needs. Parental marital tensions may have exaggerated the mutually dependent mother/child relationship in order to satisfy the void in the marital relationship.

Similarly, where individual therapies emphasize symptom formation as a result of conflict (for example, id/ego/superego conflict in psychoanalysis) between component parts of the self, family therapy locates conflict in the transactional interface between the emerging person and the dysfunctional family system. A disturbed person becomes trapped in a role designated for him or her by the family system, which results in impaired or arrested development. Efforts to become independent may lead to high levels of anxiety and guilt.

In regard to treatment, the individual therapist structures the sessions to assist the patient in achieving **insight** or having new experiences in order to understand previous failures and gain relief from disabling symptoms. Family therapists, on the other hand, see the family as committed to the status quo, behaving in a repetitive manner, protecting itself and maintaining homeostasis by opposing change in

one of its members. Robinson (1975) sees the job of the family therapist as helping them as a unit to isolate and change family behavior
patterns that support the appearance of symptoms in family members,
allowing individuals in each generation to separate from the family
and become independent as they mature and establish emotional
bonds with their peers. Zuk (1971b) puts the goal of family treatment
somewhat differently, but also feels that it involves a change in the
family's homeostatic balance. He attempts to "shift the balance of
pathogenic relating among family members so that new forms of relating become possible" (p. 213).

Indications and Contraindications for Family Therapy

A systems orientation dictates that the family therapist never lose
sight of the family system as he or she works; it does not necessarily
demand that even family members be present at all sessions. In practice, the family therapist may choose to work with entire families, subsystems within the family (for example, husband and wife, both parents plus all children over the age of nine, father and adolescent son,
mother and school-phobic daughter), or individual family members in
order to bring about change in the functioning of the overall family
social system. In some cases, the therapist may combine all three or
parts thereof during different stages of treatment. A common sequence, according to Glick and Kessler (1974), is for the entire family
to begin treatment together, and then for various dyads or triads to be
separated out for special attention. Most probably it is the marital pair
that remains for further therapeutic help; it is even common nowadays
for family therapy to eventually become marital therapy (Framo,
1975).

Generally speaking, family therapy is indicated when the family's ability to perform its basic functions becomes inadequate. In some
cases, a teenage family member may begin individual treatment, but
the therapist and adolescent may reach a therapeutic impasse as the
enmeshed, pathology-producing family resists therapeutic efforts to
bring about changes in the patient and upset the longstanding homeostatic balance in the family. In this event, the entire family may then
be seen for a period of time, or the adolescent and his or her parents,
minus siblings, may come together for family therapy aimed at disen-
tangling the overinvolvement, creating clearer boundaries, and breaking the impasse. In another case, again with a youngster, improvement
as a result of individual psychotherapy may lead to considerable distress and the appearance of symptoms in one or more of the other family members, again suggesting family sessions. In both these situa-

tions, a clinician with a family therapy orientation is likely to assume that the identified patient is the symptom bearer for a disturbed or dysfunctional family system.

There are situations in which family therapy is clearly mandatory, where the presenting problem appears in obvious systems terms. Marital conflict, severe **sibling rivalry,** and intergenerational conflicts are the clearest examples of such situations (Bloch & LaPerriere, 1973). The individual-oriented therapist who simply chooses to treat the most obviously disruptive or most obviously suffering family member may miss the point of the disturbed transaction. The therapist may waste a lot of time hearing from the patient how the other, absent person(s) is to blame and must change if the patient is to gain relief. In marital therapy, for example, Martin (1976) believes extensive changes in a relationship between a husband and wife can come about primarily if both partners are participants together in the treatment. Similarly, sexual problems are difficult to ameliorate on an individual basis, but are more likely to be helped if partners together deal with this jointly experienced marital problem. (We will return to some of the issues and techniques of sex therapy in Chapter 8.)

In some cases, intergenerational conflicts may involve three generations simultaneously, as in the following example.

The index patient was an eighteen-year old girl with an out-of-wedlock pregnancy. There was open and continued conflict between the parents and the girl over her behavior in general and in regard to plans for this pregnancy specifically. The parents wanted her to terminate the pregnancy with an abortion; her stated wish was to carry the child to term and place the baby for adoption. Much of the parental concern was centered around the issues of the reaction of the community to the pregnancy. While the generational conflict was the initial basis for the consultation, the first family interview revealed severe concealed disagreements between the parents, which were long-standing and antedate the present complaint, and seemed to be related to it, at least in the sense that the pregnancy restored and healed over a split between the girl's parents. Further study also demonstrated that the grandparental generation had opposed the parents' marriage and had been consistently involved in intense maneuvering designed to split the parental pair. The extended families of the girl's parents had never reconciled themselves to the marriage, nor had they been willing to free *their* children from bonds of dependency.

In the foregoing instance, it was necessary ultimately to involve elements of all three generations and of both extended families in order to explore and resolve the conflicts most efficiently. As the parents were able to clarify the nature of their own involvement with their own extended families and with *their* parents in particular, it was possible to reduce the intensity of their competitive struggle for their daughter's allegiance. This in turn permitted the girl to make an adequate decision about her pregnancy [Bloch & LaPerriere, 1973, p. 7].[1]

Family therapy is not a panacea for all psychological disturbances but rather a valuable addition to a therapist's repertoire. As we have just pointed out, it is especially useful—the treatment of choice—for certain systems problems within the family. Even if the therapist sees one family member at a time (the others may simply refuse to come in!), a family orientation in which an individual's problems are seen in a family context is still possible (Wynne, 1971).

Most clinicians who accept the premises of family therapy would undoubtedly agree with Wynne's (1965) general observation that this approach is applicable particularly for clarifying and resolving relationship difficulties within a family. Here Wynne is referring to those reciprocal interactional patterns in which all family members contribute, collusively or openly, consciously or unconsciously. While some members will continue to insist, months later, that the problem (for example, drug abuse in an adolescent or sexual dysfunction in a spouse) resides in some other family member (the identified patient), and that they are attending family sessions only to help that troubled member, they too may ultimately become active participants and benefit from the sessions, individually as well as for their family. What Wynne is getting at here is the idea that it is not necessary for all members to verbally acknowledge their motivation for treatment for family therapy to be effective.

Wynne (1965, 1971) cites a number of examples from his work at NIMH where family therapy was especially suited. Here he includes adolescent separation problems (for example, by rebellious, often delinquent teenagers trying to break away from a family or, in some cases, simply the separation necessary to go away to college), especially when the parents share in the adolescent's ambivalence and confusion about the pending separation. As indicated by his previously cited work on pseudomutuality (see Chapter 3), Wynne is also interested in families where a shared effort is made to avoid separation or the development of mutuality. In such families, boundaries to the outside

---

[1] From "Techniques of Family Therapy: A Conceptual Frame," by D. A. Bloch and K. LaPerriere. In D. A. Bloch (Ed.), *Techniques of Family Psychotherapy: A Primer.* Copyright 1973 by Grune & Stratton, Inc. This and all other quotations from this source are reprinted by permission of Grune & Stratton, Inc. and the author.

world are rather impermeable, so extrafamilial experiences are limited. Should the developing adolescent or young adult become exposed to totally unfamiliar feelings in the outside world (for example, hostile, angry feelings or even loving, tender feelings), he or she may suffer an abrupt breakdown and perhaps become schizophrenic. On the family level, according to Wynne, the breakdown is both dreaded and collusively supported. It is during the period of trying to cope with an acute schizophrenic episode in one of its members that Wynne has found family therapy exceedingly helpful in getting the family in touch with previously excluded and denied experiences that erupt during the episode.

Under what circumstances is family therapy contraindicated? Some family therapists take the extreme position that family therapy is the treatment of choice in all conditions where psychotherapy is indicated. The only practical exceptions to this rule might be the limited ability of the therapist to work with entire families or the unwillingness of the family system to cope with the changes necessary in all its members. That is, some families simply refuse to give up scapegoating the identified patient because all alternative behavior patterns cause intolerable discomfort, so that they are likely to discontinue treatment (Bloch & LaPerriere, 1973).

A more moderate view of contraindications is that not all disturbed families necessarily benefit from family therapy. For some families it may be too late to reverse the forces of fragmentation. In other families, it may be too difficult to establish or maintain a therapeutic working relationship with the family because key members are unavailable (for example, children away at school, parents hospitalized or dead, certain members refuse to attend family sessions). Sometimes one grossly disturbed member may so dominate the family with malignant, destructive motivation and behavior (openly violent and/or filled with paranoid ideation) that the family therapy approach is unworkable (Ackerman, 1970b). While family therapy may often be useful in treating schizophrenia in a family member, sometimes acute schizophrenics are so panicked that, without prior benefit of an established relationship with a therapist, they cannot tolerate the complexity and stress of family interviews (Wynne, 1965). In some cases, two fragile social isolates, married to each other, may have learned to stabilize their lives so long as few demands are made on them. Family therapy, in such a situation, may be catastrophic and may push them too far. Sometimes, as in the following example, this approach may even precipitate paranoid schizophrenic episodes.

> The wife was the index patient in this instance. She had adapted to a
> childless, lonely, restricted married life, spending most of her time

cleaning and caring for a tiny, immaculate apartment, while her highly successful executive husband occupied himself with 16-hour work days at his factory. This functioning adaptation was twice upset by efforts of the childless couple to become more intimate with each other, under the guidance of a family therapist. Each effort seemed brilliantly successful, with heightened sexual contact and enjoyment and an increase in shared activities, but each instance led to a psychotic decompensation for the wife, under the unmanageable pressures of this increased intimacy [Bloch & LaPerriere, 1973, p. 11].

Family therapy demands open communication and the courage to risk exposing the truth. Sometimes parents, unaccustomed to sharing personal or marital secrets with their children (or family secrets with their therapist) balk at family sessions.[2] Ackerman (1970a) has noted that some family members have such extremely rigid defenses that breaking through them may induce an acute depression, psychosis, or psychosomatic crisis. On the other hand, if the rigid defenses remain impenetrable, the individual remains walled off from his or her own feelings and inaccessible to the rest of the family, rendering intervention by family therapy ineffective.

None of these arguments necessarily rules out using family therapy. Instead, they indicate that certain family circumstances or characteristics may excessively handicap the potential benefits of therapeutic intervention on a family level.

FAMILY DIAGNOSIS

Is Diagnosis Necessary?

Is **diagnosis** an integral part of treatment planning and choosing of therapeutic goals in family therapy or merely an irrelevant counterproductive exercise in labeling left over from the **medical model**? Both views have their supporters and detractors among family therapists. Most closely identified with the proposition is Ackerman (Ackerman & Behrens, 1974), who stressed the interdependence of diagnostic and treatment procedures in family therapy. According to Ackerman,

---

[2] Handling secrets or other confidential items presents a special ethical problem in family therapy. In individual psychotherapy, the patient's privacy is protected; his trust in the therapist maximizes his openness. In family therapy, the situation is more complicated, with different family members feeling varying degrees of trust or openness in front of the rest of the family and the therapist. Many family therapists consider secrets to be part of the family's problems in communication. Consequently, they may announce at the start that, in an effort to facilitate more open communication, they will not keep secrets of one family member from the whole family.

there can be no scientific approach to treatment without a prior evaluative or diagnostic effort to conceptualize and categorize various family types.

Those who take the con position regarding diagnosis are equally
adamant in their views. Kempler (1973) considers history taking useless and analysis of others distracting. Haley (1971a) believes experienced family therapists need to intervene as soon as they have some
grasp of what is going on during a family session; they should not delay therapy for diagnosis. He contends that careful diagnosis, most
likely to be carried out by beginning family therapists, is done more to
allay the anxiety of the therapist than to benefit the family. Bell (1975)
also finds little of value in diagnosing individual family members in
advance of family meetings, preferring to observe directly how they
relate to each other once they are together. According to Bell, diagnosis and treatment go along simultaneously throughout the family sessions, up to termination.

Most family therapists would probably agree with Haley's (1976)
notion that to begin therapy by interviewing one family member is to
begin with a handicap. Such an approach, a carryover from individual
psychotherapy, assumes the therapist is dealing with a disturbed person whose symptoms indicate maladaptive or inappropriate behavior.
Thus, a wife experiencing anxiety attacks is assumed to be acting in a
way that is not adaptive to her surroundings and therefore she is in
need of treatment. From a family perspective, her "symptom" needs to
be seen in the context of her family life, where it may indeed be quite
adaptive to the husband/wife relationship she and her spouse have.
Family therapy attempts to deal with the interactional life of the family group, not merely the symptoms in its separate members.

Perhaps the staunchest advocate of formal family diagnosis in
planning therapeutic strategy is Howells (1975), a British psychiatrist.
Working preferably with as many family members as can be induced
to attend, he undertakes a broad investigation aimed at obtaining as
complete a picture as possible of the family's strengths and weaknesses, the areas where they function effectively and where dysfunction occurs. Essentially medical in orientation, Howells tries first to establish the nature of the "disorder" and then to seek its cause.
Beginning with the presenting complaint ("Our family is breaking
up." "We seem to quarrel all the time we're together."), he inquires
further into the family symptomatology ("My husband and I have not
had sexual relations for several years." "Both our children have a tendency toward depression.") and traces the history of these problems
with the family members. At the same time, he observes family interaction patterns for signs of psychopathology. Finally, he gives the
family a diagnosis—not simply a label (for example, "anxious family"

or "delinquent family"), but rather an indication of the degree of disturbance in each member and a brief description of family interaction patterns, as in the following:

(i) The individuals (symptomatology can be added in each case):
Marked degree of psychonosis[3] in father
Moderate degree of psychonosis in mother
Moderate degree of psychonosis in son
Severe degree of psychonosis in daughter
(ii) Internal interaction:
Father-Mother relationship—negative hostile relationship
Father-Children relationship—marked mutual antipathy to daughter and somewhat less to son
Mother-Children relationship—grossly overprotective to both with rejection of daughter, and hostility of children towards mother
(iii) General: Father isolated by rest of family members; fragmentation of family imminent
(iv) External interaction: Failure at employment with impending bankruptcy; school failure of daughter; delinquency of son; isolation of family
(v) Physical: Feeding difficulties in daughter; enuresis in son; gastric ulceration in father; frigidity in mother

The family diagnosis at this point may be:
(i) Unclear. Thus further investigations are required.
(ii) Provisional
(iii) Final

[Howells, 1975, pp. 207–208] [4]

Under Howells's system, therapeutic work may proceed with an individual, a pair, or the entire family, although most likely the entire family will be involved. Howells clearly distinguishes family diagnosis from family therapy. The former involves describing and understanding family events; family therapy, a separate procedure, focuses on changing dysfunctional family patterns.

Family diagnosis and family therapy are parallel, interdependent activities, according to Ackerman (Ackerman & Behrens, 1974). Just as family functioning is an ever-changing phenomenon, the diagnosis changes as the family changes. Thus family diagnosis, from this perspective, is a guide to action for the therapist, providing strategy and direction for therapeutic intervention. Although Ackerman would

[3]Howells's term for a form of psychopathology in which there is a disruption of psychological functioning as well as signs and symptoms indicative of dysfunction.
[4]From *Principles of Family Psychiatry*, by J. G. Howells. Copyright 1975 by Brunner/Mazel, Inc. Reprinted by permission.

agree with Howells on the need for family diagnosis, the two differ in their views of diagnostic procedures. While Howells is more structured and formal in his approach, being careful to keep the diagnostic and therapeutic phases of family interviews quite separate, Ackerman does not seem bound by such restrictions. He views family sessions as opportunities to participate in face to face confrontations with a troubled family, continuously testing out clinical hunches derived from his observations of the family and his knowledge of psychodynamic and psychosocial processes.

Ackerman believed therapists inevitably formulate judgments about the families they treat, even if some prefer to call this process one of evaluation rather than diagnosis. He understood that the concept of diagnosis was repugnant to many family therapists who were disenchanted with the medical model and critical of psychiatric labeling. Nevertheless, he believed a clinically oriented classification of families is necessary if we are truly to understand what distinguishes "well" from "sick" families. While acknowledging that diagnosis is often abused—pigeonholing people with scant information—he argued that the solution is better diagnosis, not ridding ourselves of the diagnostic responsibility altogether.

Ackerman was an active, engaging family diagnostician and therapist, someone who mobilized family interaction, cutting through denial, hypocrisy, and projection and forcing family members to be open with him (often more than they were with each other). In Beels and Ferber's (1969) classification of family therapists, he personified the "conductor" type—using his honesty and forthrightness to unfreeze a family afraid to deal with aggression or promoting a sexy interchange in a couple too frightened to deal with the subject of sex aloud. Diagnostically, Ackerman was apt to pay attention to appearance, mood, family roles, alliances and splits within the family, covered up family secrets, conspiracies of silence, rigid boundaries between family members, and so on. As a first step in diagnosis, Ackerman tried to focus on those destructive relationships that generate the most intense anxiety. By a technique he called "tickling the defenses," he would try to catch the family off guard, perhaps confronting them with their contradictions (for example, between their verbal utterances and their facial expressions or bodily postures), challenging their clichés and pat answers, inviting increasingly candid disclosures, encouraging deeper, more meaningful interaction, and in general seeing how family members cope and defend themselves in order to prevent change. What one member conceals, another reveals, as the therapist joins or jousts with one or another family member or family faction.

Diagnostically, Ackerman was interested for over 25 years in developing a classification system to cover family disturbances. Unfortunately, he failed to develop a unified theory before he died, offering instead a set of partial hypotheses regarding family functioning. The differential diagnosis of family types by potentials of health and growth still remains to be achieved.

Evaluating A Family's Functioning

Most family therapists find little, if any, use for formal psychiatric labels (neurotic, schizophrenic, psychopathic) originally intended for individual diagnosis. The reasons should be obvious: families are too complex, relationships do not remain static over time, current labels are inadequate to capture the full flavor of an ongoing family life. Even terms like "double-bind" or "scapegoating" are useless in characterizing families, according to Kempler (1973), since such patterns can be found at times in any family, refer to only one aspect of the family's overall functioning, and fail to offer guidance in planning specific treatment (as presumably a specific medical diagnosis would call for a specific treatment program).

Family therapists assume that psychopathology in a family member—the identified patient—is a response to that person's current situation. Consequently, observing the family together affords an excellent diagnostic opportunity (not available in individual therapy) to see how the members interact, how they communicate thoughts and feelings, and what alliances and coalitions are formed (parents versus children, males versus females, father and daughters versus mother and sons, and so on) that may be related to the symptomatic behavior in the identified patient. Haley (1971b) views the symptom as always having an adaptive function and therefore as appropriate behavior, rather than being irrational and maladaptive. Thus, rather than assume that a depressed family member has a predisposition to that behavior under stress, the family therapist tries to help the family become aware of how depression in one of its members is an appropriate response to what is happening to them here and now.

Those family therapists who prefer to evaluate a family before initiating treatment (or continually during the therapy process) are likely to pose the following questions to themselves as they observe the family together. What is the family mood today? How do they enter the consultation room and in what arrangement do they seat themselves? Who joins with whom, and against whom? Who speaks for the family? Who is silent? Who reaches out to the therapist or to other family members, who withdraws because of fear, distrust, or hostility? According to Ackerman and Behrens (1974), the family therapist examines the family's main patterns of conflict and coping, the pattern of

its complementarity, its secrets, its sources of anxiety, its various collu-
sions to prevent change, its image of itself, and finally, its capacity for
change and growth. Other therapists, such as Glick and Kessler (1974),
try to gauge the current phase of the family's life cycle during the initial interview, in an attempt to understand the family's organization
and ways of functioning, its probable stresses, tasks and phase-deter-
mined relationships. For example, a couple happily married for 25
years may begin to show their response to stress as the last child
leaves the home and the couple must deal with being alone together
for the first time in a quarter of a century.

Watzlawick (1966), a family therapist with a communications
viewpoint, has developed what he calls a "structured family interview" as an evaluative technique that reveals family patterns and re-
duces interview time in family therapy. Through a series of predeter-
mined questions to each member and the assignment of tasks for the
family to do together, the interviewer gathers data useful in evaluating the family's functioning. According to Watzlawick, it is even possible for the therapist to observe another interviewer and the family
through a one-way mirror and then to take over at the end of the interview to begin therapy with an understanding of the family's dynamics and patterns of interaction. More likely, the therapist will conduct the family interview as a prelude to initiating family therapy.

A structured interview might begin by asking each family member individually what he or she thinks are the family's main problems.
After each person is questioned separately, the family is brought together. The interviewer indicates there are discrepancies in their
viewpoints, although these are not disclosed because confidentiality is
protected. These discrepancies suggest the family may wish to discuss
their problems together now, and the interviewer leaves to go behind
the one-way mirror to observe and record their discussion. Their assignment is to reach a consensus on what are the family's main problems. In this way, the therapist is showing the family that each member has his or her own views, that all views are considered important,
that the problems belong to the family and not just the identified patient, and that the interviewer assumes the presence of a variety of
problems.

Later, the interviewer may ask the family to plan something they
can do together as a group, as he or she observes them through the
mirror. Here, of course, it is not so much the content of what they plan
(for example, a family picnic or trip by car) that interests the interviewer, but more the process (including possible conflicts and impasses) that is important. An interviewer may also question the parents alone, inquiring how they met.[5] Frequently such questioning

---

[5] The transcript of such an interview is reproduced in Chapter 3.

elicits highly significant patterns of marital interaction. The parents may also be asked to arrive at a mutually satisfactory interpretation of a proverb (for example, "A rolling stone gathers no moss") and then to teach its meaning to their children. Whether or not they agree on the meaning—the proverb may actually be interpreted in two ways[6]—and how they tolerate or otherwise deal with disagreement, involving the children in parent/child coalitions, is all of value in understanding family functioning.

Another evaluative approach, introduced by Moos (1974), attempts to assess the impact of the family environment on individual and family functioning. He assumes, to begin with, that all social climates have characteristics that can be portrayed accurately. For example, some are more supportive than others, some more rigid, controlling, and autocratic; in others, order, clarity, and structure are given high priority. Moos argues that the family environment greatly regulates and directs the behavior of the people within it. His Family Environment Scale, containing 90 true/false statements to be answered by family members ("Family members really help and support one another." "Family members often keep their feelings to themselves." "We fight a lot in our family."), helps characterize their family climate and its directional influence on behavior. Understanding the climate provides a framework for better comprehending relationships among family members, the directions for personal growth (for example, intellectual, religious) emphasized in the family, and the family's basic organizational structure.

Ten subscales make up the Family Environment Scale. As indicated in Table 6-1, three (cohesiveness, expressiveness, and conflict) are conceptualized as relationship dimensions. They characterize the interpersonal transactions that are perceived by members as taking place within the family. Five subscales (independence, achievement, intellectual-cultural and active recreational orientations, and moral-religious emphasis) refer to personal development or growth dimensions. They represent the emphasis within the family on certain developmental processes encouraged by the family atmosphere. The final two subscales (organization, control) refer to system maintenance dimensions. They provide information about the family structure and its roles. A score is obtained for each subscale and average scores for the family are placed on a family profile. The family in Figure 6-1, made up of parents and two children in their early twenties, is strongly upwardly mobile, emphasizing personal development (especially achievement and moral-religious emphasis) above other aspects of family life. These same two factors are deemphasized by the young couple (no

---

[6]Either that moss is desirable (roots, stability, friends) or that rolling is desirable (because it keeps a person from stagnating).

TABLE 6-1. Description of Subscales of Moos's Family Environment Scale

Relationship Dimensions

1. Cohesion	The extent to which family members are concerned and committed to the family and the degree to which family members are helpful and supportive of each other.
2. Expressiveness	The extent to which family members are allowed and encouraged to act openly and to express their feelings directly.
3. Conflict	The extent to which the open expression of anger and aggression and generally conflictual interactions are characteristic of the family.

Personal Growth Dimensions

4. Independence	The extent to which family members are encouraged to be assertive, self-sufficient, to make their own decisions and to think things out for themselves.
5. Achievement orientation	The extent to which different types of activities (i.e., school and work) are cast into an achievement oriented or competitive framework.
6. Intellectual-cultural orientation	The extent to which the family is concerned about political, social, intellectual and cultural activities.
7. Active recreational orientation	The extent to which the family participates actively in various kinds of recreational and sporting activities.
8. Moral-religious emphasis	The extent to which the family actively discusses and emphasizes ethical and religious issues and values.

System Maintenance Dimensions

9. Organization	Measures how important order and organization is in the family in terms of structuring the family activities, financial planning, and explicitness and clarity in regard to family rules and responsibilities.
10. Control	Assesses the extent to which the family is organized in hierarchical manner, the rigidity of family rules and procedures and the extent to which family members order each other around.

From *Combined Preliminary Manual: Family, Work and Group Environment Scales*, by R. H. Moos. Copyright 1974 by Consulting Psychologists Press. Reprinted by permission.

children) depicted in Figure 6-2. They agreed that, for them, relationships are far more important, conflict is minimal, and control is low. This couple felt very positive about the social environment they had created. If desired, the differing perceptions of various family mem-

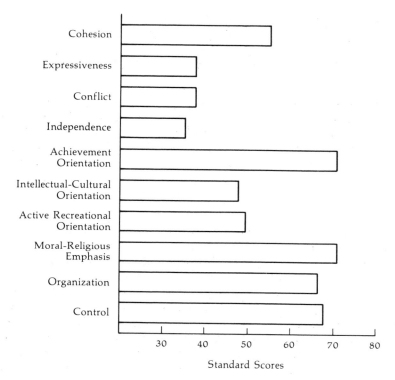

FIGURE 6-1. Family Environment Scale scores for an achievement-ori-
ented family. (Adapted from *Combined Preliminary Manual: Family,
Work and Group Environment Scales,* by R. H. Moos. Copyright 1974 by
Consulting Psychologists Press. Reprinted by permission.)

bers (for example, parents and children or husband and wife) can be
compared for possible widely divergent views of the family environment.

Dimensions for Family Assessment

In a survey (Fisher, 1976) of those parameters therapists use in
family assessment, it was found that family practitioners implicitly utilize a series of underlying dimensions to conceptualize a family's
functioning. These frameworks of assessment, in turn, provide the
conceptual format for how the therapist operates. Some therapists focus their evaluation on family conflict and how such families resolve
their differences. Others zero in on the distribution of power within
the family. For example, does power reside in one person exclusively

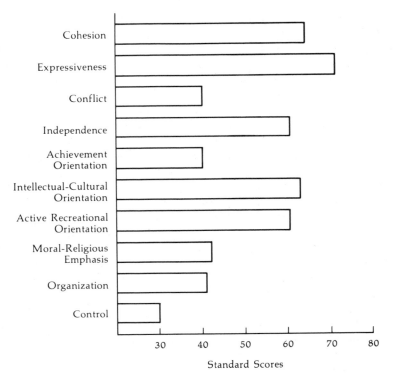

FIGURE 6-2. Family Environment Scale for a higher relationship, low control family. (Adapted from *Combined Preliminary Manual: Family, Work and Group Environment Scales,* by R. H. Moos. Copyright 1974 by Consulting Psychologists Press. Reprinted by permission.)

without input from others or is it shared more equitably? Is there one dominating power structure within the family regardless of what issues come up, or does the power shift with the content of the issue, such as money, sex, household decisions, outside jobs? Other therapists may look at family resources rather than conflict—how easily members communicate, how supportive they are of each other's efforts, how loyal they are to one another, how flexible in playing family roles, how close or remote as a family unit, or the extent to which they share common family goals.

Behaviorists like Liberman (1970) make a functional analysis of the problem, in collaboration with the family, mapping out specific behavioral goals based on how each person wishes others would change or how they themselves would like to be different. He also helps the family understand what environmental and interpersonal contingencies are operating to maintain the undesirable behavior. Instead of the family being caught up in and rewarding maladaptive behavior with attention (by nagging, babying, sympathizing, or becoming irritable) that socially reinforces that behavior, family members are taught to recognize and approve only each other's desired behavior. Manipulative behavior or a set of symptoms by any deviant member will cease once the family stops expressing an interest in (and thereby reinforcing) that behavior, according to Liberman.

Of the numerous conceptual schema available in the literature for family assessment, Fisher (1976) has derived five broad categories (see Table 6-2). Generally speaking, structural descriptors (roles, splits,

TABLE 6-2. An Overview of Dimensions Used by Practitioners in Making Family Assessments

I)   Structural Descriptors
    1) role: complementarity, acceptance, confusion, adequacy
    2) splits, alliances, scapegoating
    3) boundaries: internal and external
    4) patterns of interaction and communication: rules and norms of relating
    5) conflicts and patterns of resolution
    6) family views of life, people, and the external world
II) Controls and Sanctions
    1) power and leadership
    2) flexibility
    3) exercise of control
    4) dependency—independency
    5) differentiation—fusion
III) Emotions and Needs
    1) methods and rules for affective expression
    2) need satisfaction: giving and taking
    3) relative importance of needs vs. instrumental tasks
    4) dominant affective themes
IV) Cultural Aspects
    1) social position
    2) environmental stresses
    3) cultural heritage
    4) social and cultural views
V)   Developmental Aspects: appropriateness of structural, affective, and cultural aspects to developmental stage.

From "Dimensions of Family Assessment: A Critical Review," by L. Fisher, *Journal of Marriage and Family Counseling*, 1976, 2(4), 367–382. Reprinted by permission.

alliances, boundaries, patterns of interaction and communication, rules, conflict and its resolution, and the family views of life) offer the primary dimensions for family assessment. Note, however, how cultural aspects (social class, race, urban versus rural or suburban setting) and the phase of the family's life cycle (developmental aspects) help provide an essential background against which the family can be viewed and evaluated.

VALUES AND GOALS IN FAMILY THERAPY

Inherent in the family therapy approach are a set of moral values and sentiments that are largely middle class—belief in the institution of marriage, a stable and harmonious family life, the importance of exercising good child-rearing techniques adapted to the needs of each child, passing along the family's cultural values to the next generation, and so on. The very orientation of family therapy speaks for a value and belief system, according to Bloch and LaPerriere (1973), that holds that a family (of whatever type or composition) is necessary for maintaining good mental health, and that an individual who functions in isolation is underfunctioning or malfunctioning. Social critics such as British psychiatrist David Cooper (1970), a colleague of R. D. Laing, on the other hand, see the family structure in capitalist society as the ultimate form of imperialism, destroying individual initiative and spontaneity. Nevertheless, most family therapists, deliberately or unwittingly, consciously or unconsciously, proselytize for maintaining a family way of life.

The reader can easily glean from the theories discussed so far what are the dominant value-orientations of the leading family therapists: the avoidance of interlocking pathology within the family (Ackerman, Framo); the necessity of differentiating the self from the family ego mass (Bowen); developing relationships of mutuality within a family, rather than simply maintaining the appearance of a relationship, as in pseudomutuality (Wynne); the uncovering of self-deceptive family myths (Ferreira) and scapegoating; untangling family enmeshment so that clear boundaries can exist between family members (Minuchin); the belief in simple, straight communication of needs, feelings, and thoughts (Satir); and the importance of altering reinforcement contingencies so that family members learn to positively reinforce only desirable behavior in each other (Liberman).

Beyond these specific values (most of which are shared but given different emphasis by different therapists), there appears to be a common core of operational assumptions made by therapists working with families. Warkentin and Whitaker (1967) indicate the following as their "secret agenda" in working with couples and families: that marital partners have chosen each other with great wisdom (including the wisdom of their unconscious motives); that people are good for each other to the degree that they are intimate together; that the force or power of marriage is greater than the positive and negative sums of the two people; that a satisfying sexual relationship is the primary axis in the dynamics of a marriage; that the type and intensity of exchange of feeling in a marriage must be continuously balanced by the partners; that the usual rules of human social behavior (for example, fairness) do not apply to marriage or any other intimate relationship; that a normal marriage proceeds through a series of developmental crises or impasses as the years go by; that both partners bring their unconscious secret goals into marriage, and that these secret purposes determine the dynamic line of forces between them; that the course of marriage hinges on the conscious determination of two people to remain intimately related; and finally, that human character structure changes little once it is formed, so that someone who divorces and remarries may very likely choose as a second spouse someone who is a reasonable facsimile of the first and eventually get involved in similar marital struggles, so that the current marriage is probably the best he or she can achieve in his or her lifetime.

How do family therapists decide on treatment goals, on what they wish to change in a family? Ferber and Ranz (1972) caution that the therapist may, knowingly or unknowingly, attempt to impose on families his or her own version of what makes for a good family life (for example, less rigidity in family roles, better sex relations, more fun together). In such a case, the therapist's values, rather than the problems presented by the family, influence the direction of the treatment. Therapists and families from similar cultural and social-class backgrounds may share similar assumptions about what constitutes problems and how they should be solved. However, therapists and families from widely separate backgrounds may have different expectations about what the family problems are and how they can be resolved. Ferber and Ranz suggest as a general rule that the therapist try to deal with the problems the family labels as problems, or short of that, to explain to the family the basis on which he or she redefined their problems.

Generally speaking, the main purpose in therapeutic work with a family is to improve its functioning as a working, interdependent group. In addition, each member should derive personal benefit from the therapeutic experience. Haley (1976) attempts to obtain from the family in the first session some statement of what changes everyone wants; this helps the family focus on why they are in family therapy and helps set the goals of treatment. Satir (1967) suggests asking each family member to state his or her goals, what they hope to gain for the identified patient as well as for themselves, as a way of consolidating their commitment to the treatment. Behaviorists are apt to negotiate a contract with the family with clearly stated goals (for example, fewer quarrels, more frequent sexual relations, more help around the house from the children and more recognition of their contribution). Glick and Kessler (1974) suggest that, in general, family therapists have three broad therapeutic goals: to facilitate communication of thoughts and feelings between family members; to shift disturbed, inflexible roles and coalitions; and, to serve as role models, educators, and de-mythologizers, showing by example how best to deal with family quarreling and conflict.

A useful distinction is sometimes made between immediate, short-term goals and overall, long-term goals (Group for the Advancement of Psychiatry, 1970). The former vary, depending on the phase of therapy and the therapist's technique. Typically, the family therapist's initial goal is to discover if and how the identified patient's presenting problem is linked to the network of relationships within the family and in what ways family members might participate in the treatment. The therapist is likely to explore with the family the various ways family members are emotionally and behaviorally involved with each other. A second important goal may be to assess what combination of family members (if not all) should continue to undergo family therapy. As we have indicated, various combinations may be seen at different points over the course of therapy. A third short-term goal, once therapy is underway, is to sensitize the family members, through their participation, to the ways they currently communicate with each other, solve problems, resolve differences, or deal with family crises. One overall goal, undertaken from the start by most family therapists, is to involve all family members in the therapeutic process. This is especially important for those individuals who are resistant and deny they have problems but come for therapy reluctantly and allegedly only for the sake of the identified patient.

Longer-term goals depend upon the family therapist's theoretical orientation. For some this may mean helping strengthen a parental coalition, while for others reducing disengagement and facilitating greater family intimacy may be paramount. Some family therapists let long-term goals emerge from the treatment process, with no preconceived or preplanned goals of treatment, while others formulate quite definite long-term goals from the initial interview. A sampling of goals by therapists with families in treatment has been previously described in Tables 4-4 and 4-5.

STAGES OF FAMILY THERAPY

The Initial Interview

Family therapy gets underway with the first contact made by a family member concerning the presenting problem or symptom. Most often this contact is made by telephone by the identified patient or someone calling in his or her behalf (especially when the identified patient is a child). Family therapists assume that a symptomatic person is calling out for help for the entire family, regardless of whether the symptom is physical ("I have frequent headaches." "My child is hyperactive."), psychological ("I'm always frightened and apprehensive." "My husband has been depressed for two months now."), or interpersonal ("My teenage son and I have been at each other's throats all summer." "My wife and I stopped having a sexual relationship six months ago."). As Kempler (1974) puts it, the individual with the symptom is simply saying "Ouch! I have a pain in my family." Consequently, most family therapists prefer to ask everyone living in the household to come in together for the initial interview. Even if the therapist later chooses to work with only some members, excluding others (for example, young children), gathering information first hand about the family's style of operation and strategies for coping with the stress of the interview situation may later prove invaluable.

As we noted earlier, a family may refuse to involve one or more of its members (for example, the parent who states that it is not possible to leave work to attend, but who may also be avoiding the sessions out of fear of being blamed or exposed by the therapist or family). Most families, however, will include all members if the therapist indicates it is his or her way of working to see the entire family together. Therapists such as Bell (1975) point out over the telephone that in their experience such problems always involve the total family, so it is therapeutically best for all members to attend. Franklin and Prosky (1973) go so far as to regard the willingness of the entire family to participate as a favorable prognostic sign. They point out the risk of seeing one member (for example, an anguished spouse) alone, since the other members who later join her may see her as the person with the problem, or she may mistakenly look to "her" therapist for protection later on against the others. Family therapists report that, despite the protests of a telephone caller that his or her spouse would never agree to family sessions, most are willing to come in if troubled enough about the state of their marriage or other family relationships.[7]

What about children? Is there an age below which the child's short attention span is counter-therapeutic? If a child is the identified patient (for example, a 12-year-old bedwetter) should he or she and the parents come together for family sessions, or should all the other children in the family also attend? When should children be included,

---

[7]There are situations where only one person is available, of course, so that the initial session by necessity involves a one-to-one relationship only. A college student away from home, a member of the armed forces stationed far from his family, a person in jail or in a mental hospital may all need to be seen individually, although the therapist may retain a family-oriented outlook regarding the causes of the presenting difficulties and their alleviation.

for how long, and when excluded? Satir (1964) usually insists on seeing the husband and wife first for at least two sessions without the children, in order to emphasize to them that they are individuals and mates, not strictly parents. However, in the event that the family is so dysfunctional that the spouses cannot bear to look at their own relationship but must have the child present to focus on, Satir may make an exception and include the children from the start. Children under four years of age may attend some early sessions, according to Satir, but she prefers working with the marital pair and possibly including the young children later in the therapy. Children over four are usually included for most if not all the family therapy sessions. All the children in the family above four, and not merely the symptomatic child, are included in Satir's approach.

Bell (1975) also insists on seeing the parents first, then the entire family. He will not see one parent from an intact family (mother and father living together in one household) without the other—a practice followed by most family therapists. Bell's rule of thumb is to exclude children younger than nine because of their difficulty verbalizing and inability to think in abstract terms about the family's problems beyond their own self-centered feelings. Otherwise, all family members living together are included in the family sessions once the parents are oriented to the family therapy approach.

Some therapists compile a family life history (for example, Satir, 1967; Franklin & Prosky, 1973) during the initial interview, perhaps comparing each member's perspective on what to that person were significant past events. Other therapists (for example, Zuk, 1976) are interested in family history also but focus primarily on current family functioning and activities. Still others, such as Wynne (1971), determine the feasibility of family therapy through a series of exploratory conjoint family sessions, search for difficulties in current family interactions, and believe discussions of the past to be merely intellectual exercises unless an understanding of current experiences is achieved.

A number of family therapists, such as Haley (1976), proceed in a preplanned systematic way, viewing the initial interview as being composed of a series of stages during which the therapist negotiates with the family on what problem(s) need attention. The therapist then formulates a plan of intervention to change the dysfunctional behavior patterns in order to eliminate the problem(s). After a *social stage*, during which Haley observes family interaction and tries to get all family members to participate, he shifts to a *problem stage*, getting down to the business of why the family is there. Here he tries to get all family members to specify what changes in the family they want. Why is the family here and why now? In some cases it is best to start with the least involved child, the one seemingly most distant and detached, thus making it clear that all members are expected to participate, not merely the adults. In what Haley calls "problem-solving therapy," the focus is clearly on establishing the problem to be solved and suggesting new behaviors needed to solve the problem as a lever for changing family relationships, as in the following example:

> A mother may say that her nine-year-old son is afraid to go outside the house and clings to her all the time. In the room the therapist may see that he sits beside her and holds on to her. She also may say he lies and will not do anything around the house, but that the problem is mostly that he is afraid and never leaves her side. He even sleeps with her so that the father has to sleep on the livingroom couch. The other children do not behave this way, but seem normal.
>
> This information from the mother does not tell the therapist what the problem is or what to do about it. He has only her version that the problem is inside the child and no one else has anything to do with it. To get more information and begin to make a change is the purpose of skillful family interviewing. After the mother has stated that problem the therapist needs to listen to the father and his views. Then he needs to listen to the brothers and sisters and what they say about it. After having spoken to each one, he will see disagreements appearing. For example, he will notice that the father does not quite agree with the mother and thinks she is taking care of the child too much and not letting him be on his own enough. He also does not like to be moved out of his own bed, he may say, although he is willing if it will keep the child from being afraid. Perhaps mother argues that father neglects the child. When mother and father talk about their disagreements, information may appear about how much the child is an issue between them.
>
> During this stage of the interview, it will probably become clearer how to think about this problem in terms of more than the child. The therapist may think of it as a peculiar relationship between mother and son; she has as much difficulty leaving him as he has leaving her. He may also be able to think in terms of three people and consider the possibility that the child is helping mother and father. If they cannot get together without fighting, particularly in bed, then the child is helping them by acting so fearful that they are kept more separate. They can then say it is the child who is the problem, and not bad feelings between them [Haley, 1976, p. 35].[8]

Notice in this example how Haley tries to define the family problem as carefully and fully as possible before treatment gets underway. He believes the responsibility for change rests entirely with the therapist. The therapist must use this family-focused information gathered during the initial interview to formulate ideas about how to bring

[8]From *Problem-Solving Therapy*, by J. Haley. Copyright 1976 by Jossey-Bass, Inc. Reprinted by permission.

about behavior change and, ultimately, problem resolution. Beyond the problem stage, there is an *interaction stage* in Haley's approach in which the family members are encouraged to talk to each other (rather than to the therapist). Finally, the *goal-setting stage* is reached and the family is asked just what changes they seek. In a sense this is similar to a therapeutic contract used by behavior therapists (see Chapter 5). The clearer the goal—the elimination of the problem or the alleviation of the symptom—the easier to evaluate progress and the greater the likelihood of therapeutic success.

By way of contrast, let us look at a sample of an interview by Kempler (1973), a gestalt family therapist. Kempler's approach is much more experiential[9] and spontaneous than Haley's, more confronting, more an encounter. His emphasis is on the here and now, on people becoming aware of, and reowning previously discovered parts of their personality in order to restore their wholeness or gestalt. Kempler presses for self-disclosure by family members, expecting they will have the courage to expose their vulnerabilities in the service of resolving their problems and improving their relationship. He shuns history-taking and discussions regarding "why" people behave as they do. Instead, he actively and directly insists that everyone, therapist included, become aware of "what" they do or say or feel. As a mechanic who would rather listen to a troublesome engine than hear a description of it, Kempler first starts up a family conversation:

MOTHER: Our 15 year old son Jim has been making a lot of trouble for us lately.

(The healthier the family, the more readily they talk to each other. For instance, should Jim respond immediately to his mother's charge with, "That's not true!", it would indicate that he has both self-confidence and the hope of being heard. Let's assume Jim doesn't leap in.)

THERAPIST (to Jim, evocatively): Do you agree that the number one problem in this family is that you are a trouble-maker?
JIM: Not really.
THERAPIST: Tell her what you think it is.
JIM: It's no use.

---

[9]**Experiential therapy** involves attention to the current interaction as the pivotal point for all awareness and intervention, as well as involvement of the therapist as a full and real person who makes a personal impact on the family with whom he works (Kempler, 1968). Carl Whitaker (Napier & Whitaker, 1978) also considers his work with individuals and families as "experiential." According to Whitaker, insight is not enough; the client(s) must have an emotionally meaningful experience in therapy, one that reaches the deepest levels. Like Kempler, Whitaker emphasizes personal encounter, with the therapist intuitively using his or her sense of self to help a family achieve a caring, person-to-person set of relationships between its members. More psychoanalytic than Kempler, however, Whitaker sees therapy as a chance to deliberately regress, an opportunity he too participates in, though not as profoundly as the client(s).

FIGURE 6-3. Walter Kempler, M.D. (Photo courtesy of Walter Kempler.)

THERAPIST (to Mother): Do you have anything to say to his hopelessness?
MOTHER: I think we've said all there is to say.

(Family members are often reluctant to engage one another, particularly initially. The therapist perseveres by offering himself, if necessary.)

THERAPIST (to Jim): I'd like to know what you think is the problem, Jim.
JIM: They're too rigid.

(The battlelines often have both parents on one side. It is better when it is a free-for-all.)

THERAPIST: Both of them identical?
JIM: Mother more than Father.
THERAPIST: Then, maybe you can get some help from him.
JIM: He's too weak. He always gives in to her.
THERAPIST (to Father): Do you agree with Jim?
FATHER: Of course not.
THERAPIST: You didn't tell him.

[Kempler, 1973, pp. 27–28][10]

[10]From *Principles of Gestalt Family Therapy*, by W. Kempler. Copyright 1974 by the Kempler Institute, P.O. Box 1692, Costa Mesa, CA 92626. Reprinted by permission.

Like Haley, Kempler is interested in what each person wants and from whom, expressed in as specific terms as possible. Participants are forced to talk to each other. If a wife complains to Kempler that her husband lacks understanding or sensitivity, he tells her to tell that to her husband and not the therapist, and to be specific in her complaint. If she argues that it will do no good, Kempler insists she tell that to her husband. If she then breaks down, admits her feelings of hopelessness, and begins to cry, all without a response from her husband, Kempler will point out his silence and invite him to anwer to her. Notice how, from the initial interview onward, the focus stays on the immediate; engagement and self-disclosure are basic ground rules as Kempler guides a family into understanding that they must face each other squarely if they are to untangle a family problem or overcome an impasse.

The Middle Phase

The middle phase of family therapy comprises the heart of the therapeutic process (Framo, 1965). Let us assume that, on the basis of the initial interview or brief series of interviews, the therapist and the family agreed to meet regularly, usually once a week for an hour to an hour and a half. It would be rare indeed for the members to unanimously express the need for help as a family; much more likely, some family members will be far more strongly motivated than others, some will express a willingness to participate if it will help the "sick" family member, all will be to a greater or lesser extent resistant to self-exposure or revealing family "secrets." Both conscious resistance (expressed as fear of rejection, shame, distrust of the therapist) and unconscious resistance (expressed through silences or too much chatter, lack of **affect** or too much intensity of affect, intellectualizations and clichés about family problems and their solutions, **acting-out** behavior, regression in various family members) are operating here. Haley (1976) has found it helpful to set a fixed number of family interviews (say, six times) if he finds the family particularly resistant or doubtful about continuing after the initial interview, with the proviso that they can all decide at the end of that time if more sessions are necessary.

Emotionally disturbed children, often the identified patients, usually reflect disturbed marriages and often cover up deeper family splits. When such families are told the entire family will be seen together,

> they initially accept the idea with equanimity, saying, "Yes, doctor, we understand. We want you to know that we will do everything in our

power to cooperate to get our daughter well. No sacrifice is too great."
In our early years of operation we used to allow discussion about the
designated patient to go on for a number of sessions; our rationale was
that the sessions should begin with what most concerned the family,
which obviously would be the illness of a member of the family. A typical exchange at that time was as follows: The parents would turn to the
patient with the words: "Tell us what is wrong, dear. Why don't you talk
to the doctor? Don't be afraid to say anything; we can take it. Would you
like to tell us off or hit us? Will that make you feel better?" The majority
of the time the patient, sensing the concealed injunction that she'd better say the right thing or at least avoid self-incrimination, would respond, "Nothing's bothering me," or she would behave in some irrational way to confirm the view of her as a demented or inept person. If
the patient, particularly if she has undergone individual psychotherapy
and feels the support of her therapist, actually reveals what's on her
mind, for example, in the form of "disloyally" commenting on the parents' unhappy marriage or angrily passing a judgment on mother (thus
violating family dictum number one) a series of events follows very
quickly. Father quickly changes the subject, a sibling begins to laugh,
and mother, after a dumbfounded look, hits her hand on her thigh,
turns to the doctor, and says, "See, doctor, this is what I mean. She's getting sick again." We have repeatedly noticed in most families that the
mother can never consider her daughter well until the patient no longer
manifests anger or deep resentment toward her [Framo, 1965, p. 162].[11]

More recently, Framo has begun directing attention to the entire
family instead of the designated or identified patient, asking each
member to reveal his or her experiences in the family as well as their
views about each other. A great deal about the family's underlying
problems and concealed areas of stress and conflict are often revealed
in this way.

As the entire family becomes oriented to therapy, they learn
what the role of the therapist will be (for example, the therapist will
offer guidance and direction but will not take over the parental functions, will not take sides with certain family coalitions against others
within the family, will not meet privately with one member, will try
to facilitate open and honest communication among family members,
will insist all members, children included, participate). At the same
time, the family learns its obligations: all members must attend unless
agreed otherwise beforehand, they must all be available at the agreed
upon time, they should be prepared for a possible increased strain and

[11]From "Rationale and Techniques of Intensive Family Therapy," by J. L. Framo.
In I. Boszormenyi-Nagy and J. L. Framo (Eds.), *Intensive Family Therapy: Theoretical and
Practical Aspects.* Copyright 1965 by Harper & Row, Publishers, Inc. Reprinted by per-
mission of the author and publisher.

FIGURE 6-4. James L. Framo, Ph.D. (Photo courtesy of James L. Framo.)

expressions of open hostilities for a while within the family as underlying sources of conflict are revealed, and so on.

During the middle phase of therapy, families begin to consider that relationships can change and that destructive alliances within the family (for example, between one parent and a child against the other parent) can be broken. The following case illustrates just such a situation in which a variety of therapeutic techniques were undertaken simultaneously.

Lisa Ash, a 5-foot-tall, 260-pound, 13-year-old girl, was brought to a mental hospital by a distraught mother who complained that she couldn't control her daughter's eating habits and was alarmed about the danger to her health. Lisa, a junior high school student, was the oldest of three daughters in a middle-class Jewish family. Both the father, a moderately successful shoe-store owner and his wife, a housewife, were overweight, as were various other uncles, aunts, and to a lesser extent, Lisa's two younger sisters.

The mother/daughter conflict was evident from the intake interview. In particular, both agreed that they battled frequently over discipline or any restrictions imposed by Mrs. Ash on Lisa's eating behavior. Whenever this occurred, the mother complained. Lisa would lock herself in her room, wait for her father to come home, and then tell him how "cruel" the mother had been to her. Usually, without inquiring further or getting the mother's story, he would side with Lisa and countermand the mother's orders. Occasionally he would even invite Lisa out for a pizza or other "snack."

Needless to say, the mother/father relationship was poor. They had not had sexual intercourse for several years, and Mrs. Ash assumed that her husband was impotent, although she was too embarrassed to ask him. She had become increasingly unhappy and had seen a psychiatric social worker a year earlier for several sessions, although then, as now, her husband refused to participate in therapy. He also opposed Lisa's hospitalization and for several months would not speak to any member of the hospital staff about his daughter's progress.

Lisa was placed on the adolescent open ward of the hospital and attended the special school within the hospital complex, remaining there for 12 months. During that period, four coordinated therapeutic programs were introduced: nutritional control (including a careful watch on calorie intake), individual psychotherapy twice weekly, family therapy (after much resistance, Mr. Ash agreed to attend), and ward milieu therapy. The picture that emerged was of an emotionally intense and chaotic family existence in which Lisa often screamed, hit, swore, and threatened to break household objects if she didn't get her "sweets." There was no regular mealtime at the Ash house; each member ate when and what he or she wanted. Lisa would regularly visit her father's store after school, and they would go out together for an ice cream soda or sundae. Finally acknowledging, during one family-therapy session, that the situation had gotten out of hand, Mr. Ash defended his actions by saying that he could never get himself to say "no" to Lisa for fear of losing her love. Mrs. Ash quickly conceded her resentment about her husband's relationship with Lisa, her own feeling of isolation, and her sense of helplessness; she was finally able to separate the two only by hospitalizing the daughter.

The program of calorie restriction was immediately successful. After 2 months, Lisa had lost 35 pounds; after 7 months, 80 pounds; and by 10 months, a full 100 pounds. Family therapy was less immediately successful. Mr. Ash and Lisa continued to play seductive games with each other: he called her on the telephone frequently, sent her flowers, and even visited her with a box of candy on her birthday, and she deliberately delayed coming to the telephone or lobby, to make her ultimate appearance more appealing. Finally, Lisa put an end to this kind of transaction, to Mrs. Ash's relief; Lisa learned limits on her own behavior largely from milieu therapy on her ward. Eventually, Mr. Ash was able to give up his seductive and overprotective behavior, realizing that if he really wanted to help his daughter, he should limit her self-indulgent, self-destructive behavior rather than encourage it.

Upon her discharge from the hospital, Lisa weighed 140 pounds, had some insight into her eating behavior, and had dealt with a number of other preadolescent problems. She agreed to undergo weekly individual psychotherapy for a while so that she would not regress to her former ways once she was home. A two-year follow-up found her able to control her eating and generally proud that she could take care of herself successfully [Goldenberg, 1977, pp. 350–351].[12]

As families become involved in treatment, if it is successful,[13] reorganizing of the family structure starts to take place. Increased autonomy for all members becomes more possible, roles within the family may become less rigid, previously hidden experiences may be shared and accepted by others, family members may begin to receive feedback, sometimes for the first time, regarding the reactions of others to their behavior. While some old interaction pattern may be highly resistant to change, and weekly therapy sessions do not produce steady progress but may even occasionally show regression in family relationships, the overall result to this middle phase of family therapy is a family better prepared to accept change and more willing to work to achieve its potentially positive benefits.

Termination

Generally speaking, family therapy is of shorter duration than individual therapy, especially because it focuses so precisely on eliminating a specific problem or alleviating a presenting symptom, making it clear to all when the goal has been achieved. Although the process may last anywhere from several weekly sessions to several months (or

[12] From *Abnormal Psychology: A Social/Community Approach*, by H. Goldenberg. Copyright © 1977 by Wadsworth, Inc. Reprinted by permission of the publisher, Brooks/Cole Publishing Company, Monterey, California.
[13] We will present a detailed discussion of the effectiveness of family therapy in Chapter 9. Comments here are intended to be generalizations only.

in rare cases, even years), Bell (1975), an experienced family therapist, estimates that eight to twenty sessions are a reasonable expectation.

No family leaves treatment problem-free, nor have all members progressed to the same point by termination time. Several members may be ready to move into new kinds of relationships, but one member may continue to obstruct the process, or a combination of two may retard a third (Framo, 1965). Nevertheless, families and therapist alike are apt to sense at about the same time that the family is ready to go off on its own, not without trepidations about the forthcoming loss of support from the therapist, but eager to function independently.

Most therapists agree that termination is easier in family therapy than in individual treatment. The family, now accustomed to working as a unit in solving its own problems, has developed an internal support system and is not usually overdependent on an outsider, the therapist. Family members have usually had considerable practice together during family sessions in solving family relationship problems and have verified that they are able to work on their problems together. Clearer and less veiled ways of communicating with each other have probably developed, roles have been reassigned to some degree, power redistributed.

Families may or may not announce that they are ready to conclude the therapy, but the signs are apparent in either case. For example, they now resolve interpersonal conflicts at home rather than bring them to the therapist. Having entered therapy with a specific problem, their subsequent behavior changes indicate the problem is resolved. The presenting complaint or symptom has usually disappeared, the family engages in more mutually satisfying activities, independent activities outside the family bring new satisfactions, the family has developed through their own efforts effective ways of solving their problems. It is time for disengagement from family therapy.

SUMMARY

Family therapy aims at alleviating the interlocking emotional problems that develop within any type of family organization. A family-oriented therapist may choose to work with entire families, subsystems within the family, or individual family members in order to help change the family social system. Family therapy is indicated especially for marital conflict, severe sibling rivalry, intergenerational conflict, or for clarifying and resolving relationship difficulties within a family, but contraindicated when one or more grossly disturbed family member(s) may be too destructive, violent, or too psychologically fragile.

Family therapists differ in their views regarding family diagnosis. Detractors find the process unproductive and distracting, while proponents argue that it is a necessary and useful guide to treatment planning. The latter group may rely on systematic observation of the family functioning together, on interviews, or on psychological assessment techniques in their evaluation of a family. Therapist values, such as the belief in marriage and family life, tend to be largely middle class in origin, and affect the therapy process and choice of therapeutic goals. The main goal appears to be in improvement in the family's functioning as a working, interdependent group.

Family therapy proceeds in stages beginning with the first contact with the family, which is usually by telephone. Most therapists will insist on seeing the entire family or as many members as possible, although children (especially young children) may be excluded in certain cases. There is no single way of conducting initial interviews; they range from a preplanned series of stages (Haley) to a spontaneous encounter in which self-disclosure is expected (Kempler). During the middle phase of family therapy, families are encouraged to look at their relationships, work on specific problems that brought them into treatment, and attempt to reorganize the family structure. If successful, usually after several months, families are ready to terminate treatment, now better able to work as a group on their problems and change destructive behavior patterns.

7

MODELS OF
CLINICAL PRACTICE

Although family therapy has come to be viewed as a major treatment modality in recent years, there still are no agreed on set of procedures followed by practitioners. Theoretically, most family therapists accept certain premises, such as the necessity of altering the context in which an individual lives and functions if that person is to change. All family therapists agree further that the area of treatment should be the relationships in which that person engages and is imbedded rather than an analysis and dissection of intrapsychic conflicts. They all assume that an individual's symptoms, presenting problems, or complaints are an expression of a family's dysfunction, and appear in one member in an effort to maintain homeostasis, to hide, obscure, or distract the family from that dysfunction. All view change in the individual as a result of changing the family system.

Beyond these axioms, there is considerable disagreement about how family therapy can most effectively be carried out. That should not be too surprising a statement, considering the fact that there is as yet no conceptual central core to a family theory. How, then, to convey to the reader a sense of the great diversity of therapeutic approaches currently existing side by side? One way chosen by some family therapists is to videotape their sessions for demonstration purposes later before professional audiences. This willingness to make their work public is highly commendable and quite useful for training purposes, as we shall discuss further in Chapter 9. However instructive, this approach may also prove frustrating and bewildering to the beginning therapist who attempts to emulate the seasoned and polished clinician but achieves poor results, since it is not always clear why the master therapist chose to intervene when he or she did, with what kind of intervention, by choosing what procedure or language, and so on.

One solution is to transcribe an interview with the therapist along with a verbatim account of a family therapy session in order for him or her to discuss the purposes and timing of interventions, assuming they were not carried out simply because they "felt right" at the moment. An example of this device is Haley and Hoffman's *Techniques of Family Therapy*, published in 1967. A more recent teaching technique has been developed by Papp (1977), who has asked some leading practitioners to reproduce and then discuss an entire case from beginning to end. This gives the reader the sense of a case as it develops and the therapist is asked to deal with new crises or handle new problems produced by the changes taking place in the family system.

We have chosen a third device, tying together the theories presented in Chapter 5 with examples of therapeutic techniques based on those theories. In this chapter we hope to give the reader a brief picture of how various therapists work, what they look for, and why they do what they do. Nine family therapists will be presented, sometimes with samples of their interviews. Therapies influenced by psychodynamic theories (Ackerman, Bowen), communications theories (Satir, Haley), structural theory (Minuchin), and behavioral theory (Stuart, Liberman) will be presented. In addition, the work of two independents (Zuk, Bell), somewhat outside the mainstream of most family therapy, will be discussed.

THERAPIES INFLUENCED BY PSYCHODYNAMIC THEORIES

Nathan Ackerman's Biopsychosocial Therapy

Ackerman's broadly based therapeutic approach, utilizing principles from biology, psychoanalysis, social psychology, and child psychiatry, was active, dynamic, courageous, and direct. Unaffected and deceptively casual in manner, Ackerman tried through a series of office interviews and home visits to obtain a firsthand diagnostic impression of the dynamic relationships among family members. Hearty, confident, crafty, unafraid to be himself or to disclose his own feelings, he was apt to bring out these same qualities in the family. Soon the family was dealing with sex, aggression, and dependency—areas they previously avoided exposing as too threatening and dangerous.

To watch Ackerman on film or videotape is to see an honest, warm, straightforward, charismatic person moving to the center of the family's star-shaped communication pattern, here challenging a prejudice, there coming to the aid of a scapegoated child, now helping expose a family myth or hypocrisy, vigorously supplying the emotional ingredient necessary to galvanize a previously subdued family. No topic is taboo or off limits, no family rules so sacred they cannot be broken, nothing so shameful as to be unmentionable. Labeled as a "conductor" type of family therapist by Beels and Ferber (1969), Ackerman is said to loan the family "his pleasure in life, jokes, good sex and limited aggression."

The following brief excerpt of a therapy session is with a family in crisis, brought on when the 11-year-old daughter threatened to stab her 16-year-old brother and both parents with a kitchen knife. This explosive attack was precipitated by the girl's discovery of a conspiracy among the others to lie to her, telling her that her dog had died when in reality the mother had brought him to the dog pound. The family indulges in many small lies and then covers up and denies feeling what they are feeling. Note how Ackerman will have none of this and persists, revealing his own feelings, in order to cut through the denial and open up the family encounter. The left hand column is the verbatim account, the right hand column is Ackerman's analysis of what is taking place:

DR. A.: Bill, you heaved a sigh as you sat down tonight.	Therapist instantly fastens on a piece of nonverbal behavior, the father's sigh.
FATHER: Just physical, not mental.	
DR. A.: Who are you kidding?	Therapist challenges father's evasive response.
FATHER: I'm kidding no one.	
DR. A.: Hmmm . . .	Therapist registers disbelief, a further pressure for a more honest response.
FATHER: Really not. . . . Really physical. I'm tired because I put in a full day today.	
Dr. A.: Well, I'm very tired every day, and when I sigh it's never purely physical.	An example of therapist's use of his own emotions to counter an insincere denial.
FATHER: Really?	
DR. A.: What's the matter?	
FATHER: Nothing. Really!	

DR. A.: Well, your own son doesn't believe that.

Therapist now exploits son's gesture, a knowing grin, to penetrate father's denial and evoke a deeper sharing of feelings.

FATHER: Well, I mean, nothing . . . nothing could cause me to sigh especially today or tonight.

DR. A.: Well, maybe it isn't so special, but . . . How about it, John?

Therapist stirs son to unmask father.

SON: I wouldn't know.

Now son wipes grin off his face, and turns evasive, like father.

DR. A.: You wouldn't know? How come all of a sudden you put on a poker face? A moment ago you were grinning very knowingly.

Therapist counters by challenging son, who took pot shot from sidelines, and then backed away.

SON: I really wouldn't know.

DR. A.: You . . . Do you know anything about your pop?

SON: Yeah.

DR. A.: What do you know about him?

SON: Well, I don't know, except that I know some stuff.

Dr. A.: Well, let's hear.

[Ackerman, 1966, pp. 3–4] [1]

Ackerman, trained as a psychoanalyst, remained interested in each family member's personality dynamics. However, also influenced by social psychology, he was impressed by how personality is shaped by specific social roles people are expected to play. It is within the family that it becomes possible to observe static, repetitive forms of role relationships. In his approach to families, Ackerman was always interested in how people define their own roles ("What does it mean to you to be a father?") and what they expect from other family members ("How would you like your daughter to react to this situation?"). When all members clearly delineate roles, family interactions proceed more smoothly. Old alignment patterns are then broken and new family transactions are possible as the family learns to accommodate to new experiences and cultivates new levels of complementarity in family role relationships.

According to Ackerman (1966), a troubled, perplexed, frightened family comes for family therapy; they know something is wrong but they don't know how or why or what to do about it. By tradition, they push one member forward as "sick," although several if not all are disturbed in various ways and degrees. They are there now because their previous equilibrium or homeostasis has been upset. The therapist tries to nourish hope, to keep them from feeling defeated. Generally speaking, Ackerman sees the therapist's role as offering *reeducation, reorganization* through a change in the pattern of communication, and *resolution* of pathogenic conflict as an avenue for inducing change and growth as a family.

As we have seen in Chapter 6, diagnosis and treatment are interwoven in Ackerman's approach. Rather than follow a formal intake procedure, the therapist watches as the family becomes engaged in the therapeutic struggle and relevant historical facts emerge (for example, mental hospitalization of a member, a daughter's abortion never told outside the family circle before, a suicide). The therapist observes the family's outer protective mask, their secret pact to avoid discussing certain subjects, the personalities of each member, their adaptation to family roles, the family emotional climate. Families are usually seen once a week for about an hour each session. According to Ackerman (1966), therapeutic change is often achieved within a period of six months to two years.

Ackerman believed the family therapist's principal job is that of a catalyst, moving into the "living space" of the family, stirring up interaction, helping the family have a meaningful emotional exchange, and at the same time nurturing and assisting members to come into better touch with themselves through contact with the therapist. With typical fluidity, he moved directly into the path of family conflict, helping influence the interactional process, supporting positive forces and counteracting negative ones, withdrawing as the family attempted to deal more constructively with its problems. Diagnostically, he attempted to assess a family's deeper emotional currents—their fears and suspicions, their despair, the urge for vengeance—using both his personal emotional responses as well as his psychodynamic insights to gauge, intuitively, what the family was experiencing, the patterns of role complementarity, and the deeper, more pervasive family conflicts. As noted earlier, by "tickling the defenses," he caught members off guard and exposed their self-justifying rationalizations. In due course, he was able to trace significant connections between the family dysfunction and the intrapsychic anxieties of various family members. Finally, as each member was helped to get in touch with what he or she was feeling, thinking, and doing, Ackerman helped them expand their awareness of alternate patterns of family relationships and discover new levels of intimacy, sharing, and identification.

Overall, Ackerman was aware that the family therapist must play a wide range of roles—activator, challenger, supporter, confronter, interpreter, and reintegrator. Unlike the orthodox psychoanalyst who chooses to remain a neutral, distant, mysterious **blank screen,** Ackerman as family therapist was a real, vigorous person who engaged a family in the here and now and made his presence felt. Unlike the psychoanalyst, who must deal with one isolated personality, the family therapist assumes that the forces of the individual and of the family are interdependent, and, further, that these relations are relevant to the causation of a disorder or dysfunction and their amelioration is through treating the entire family (Ackerman, 1970a).

Murray Bowen's Family Systems Therapy

A recent collection in one volume of papers by Bowen (1978) affords the reader an opportunity to study the evolution of Bowen's theories and techniques over 20 years. Initially concerned with families with a schizophrenic member, Bowen became increasingly interested in developing a broader family theory of emotional disorders and a method of family intervention developed from the theory. Up until the present time, he has continued to be concerned with the parallel activities of theory-building and family therapy techniques.

Like Ackerman, Bowen began his professional career with a psychoanalytic orientation, and, as we have noted in an earlier chapter, many of his early theoretical concepts (for example, undifferentiated family ego mass) reflect that viewpoint. However, unlike Ackerman, who attempted to straddle a psychoanalytic, individual-focused and a family systems-focused fence throughout his career, Bowen seemed to move more steadily in the systems direction (Bowen, 1975). Many of his later concepts (for example, interlocking triangles, multiple generation transmissions of dysfunction) reflect this later development in his thinking.

Bowen's standard method of family therapy is to work in a triangle situation consisting of two adults and himself. Even in those cases where the identified patient is a symptomatic child, Bowen asks the parents to accept the premise that the basic problem is between them. In such a situation, Bowen may never see the child at all. The terms "diagnosis" and "treatment" are shunned in order to avoid the implication that someone is "sick," and dependent on another to be made well. Bowen prefers to present himself as a researcher helping the family become researchers into their own ways of functioning. The term he seems to prefer is *coach* (having moved during his career, in his own words, from "couch" to "coach")—an active expert helping individual players and the team (family) perform to the best of their abilities.

Bowen (1976) takes the position that the successful introduction of a significant other person (a friend, teacher, minister) in an anxious or disturbed relationship system can modify all relationships within the family. The family therapist can be just such a person, if he manages to stay in emotional contact with the two most significant family members, usually the parents, but still remains relatively outside the emotional activity of this central triangle. Bowen's system of therapy is designed to modify the family's customary triangular emotional system. He insists that the therapist disengage from the system—a far cry from Ackerman's determination to dive in! He remains uninfluenceable, calm, low-keyed, neutral, detriangulated from the emotional entanglements between the spouses. If he can maintain that stance—despite pressures to be triangled into the conflict—Bowen contends that tensions between the couple will subside, the "fusion" between them will slowly resolve, and other family members will automatically change in relation to the parents. To reduce "fusion" is to help each partner distinguish between emotions and intellect. People who fuse emotions and intellect lead lives dominated by their emotional responses, according to Bowen. They are less flexible, less adaptable, more emotionally dependent on others, more easily stressed into dysfunction. The more differentiated their emotional and intellectual functioning becomes, the better they are able to cope with stress and the more orderly and successful their way of life. A well-differentiated person is not without feeling, but rather can freely experience and express feelings without becoming overinvolved emotionally with others.

The overall goal of Bowen's approach to family therapy is for each member to achieve a better level of differentiation of self, a disengagement from the undifferentiated family ego mass. When one member achieves this, others will automatically take similar steps (Bowen, 1976). A common Bowen technique is to choose one partner, usually the one who is more mature and closer to differentiating, and work with that one person for a period of time. The assumption here is that such a person is the one in the family most capable of breaking the old emotionally entangling patterns. When that person succeeds in taking an "I-stand," the others will shortly be motivated to do the same, moving off in their own directions. While a stormy period may follow before a new equilibrium is reached, the former pathological ties are broken, and each person achieves a greater sense of individuality.

Family therapy as directed by Bowen (1975) is calm, direct, and without emotional intensity. Each partner talks to him rather than directly to each other. Confrontation between the partners is avoided in order to keep down any possible emotional tensions between them. In this way, what each partner is thinking is externalized in the presence of the other, with Bowen careful not to be caught up in an effort by either (or both) to triangle him in. Interpretations are avoided. Instead, calm questioning defuses any emotions and forces the partners to think about the issues causing their difficulties. Instead of blaming the other or rushing toward togetherness as a solution, Bowen forces each to focus on the part his or her self plays in the relationship problems.

In Bowen's experience, some families may need as little as 5–10 sessions for achieving good results. Others may require 20–40 sessions until symptoms subside. He claims (Bowen, 1975) that no other approach has been as effective in producing good long-term results.

THERAPIES INFLUENCED BY COMMUNICATIONS THEORIES

Virginia Satir's Conjoint Family Therapy

An early advocate of working with entire families, best known for her family therapy demonstrations around the world as well as her numerous influential writings (Satir, 1967; Satir, 1972; Satir, Stachowiak, and Taschman, 1975; Bandler, Grinder and Satir, 1976), Satir is today a much-celebrated authority on helping families to transform themselves through the process of communication. In all of her work, Satir never loses sight of the family unit—how it deals with pain and suffering, the methods by which it tends to stabilize itself and achieve homeostasis, and especially the ways it has evolved for communication among its members. Early on in family therapy, she presents herself as a teacher introducing the family to a new language, helping them to understand their communication problems, which she sees as the root of their troubles. Basically, Satir is a teacher of a method of communication (Beels & Ferber, 1969). Treatment is completed when the family has learned and applied her method, resulting in a deepening of their relationships.

Satir's primary talent is as a therapist, in her own ability to communicate clearly and perceptively. She speaks simply and directly, keeps up a running account of what she is doing with the family, tries to pass along her communication skills to family members, then arranges encounters between members according to the rules she has taught them. In the following example of an early session (Satir, 1967) the parents and their children, Johnny, aged 10, and Patty, aged 7, are being seen together as a family although the identified patient is Johnny, who is having behavior problems at school. Satir wants to clarify what ideas each member has about what to expect from therapy and why each is there. Note how she tries to help the family: (1) to recognize individual differences among its members by having each member speak for himself or herself, (2) to accept disagreements and differing perceptions of the same situation, and (3) particularly to say what they see, think, and feel in order to bring disagreements out into the open.

PATTY: Mother said we were going to talk about family problems.
THERAPIST: What about Dad? Did he tell you the same thing?
P: No.
T: What did Dad say?
P: He said we were going for a ride.
T: I see. So you got some information from Mother and some information from Dad. What about you, Johnny: Where did you get your information?
JOHNNY: I don't remember.
T: You don't remember who told you?
MOTHER: I don't think I said anything to him, come to think of it. He wasn't around at the time, I guess.
T: How about you, Dad? Did you say anything to Johnny?
FATHER: No, I thought Mary had told him.
T: *(to Johnny)* Well, then, how *could* you remember if nothing was said.
J: Patty said we were going to see a lady about the family.
T: I see. So you got your information from your sister, whereas Patty got a clear message from both Mother and Dad.

(Shortly, she asks the parents what they remember saying.)

T: How about that, Mother? Were you and Dad able to work this out together—what you would tell the children?
M: Well, you know, I think this is one of our problems. He does things with them and I do another.
F: I think this is a pretty unimportant thing to worry about.
T: Of course it is, in one sense. But then we can use it, you know, to see how messages get across in the family. One of the things we work on in families is how family members communicate—how clearly they get their messages across. We will have to see how Mother and Dad can get together so that Johnny and Patty can get a clear message.

(Later, she explains to the children why the family is there.)

T: Well, then, I'll tell you why Mother and Dad have come here. They have come here because they were unhappy about how things were going in the family and they want to work out ways so that everyone can get more pleasure from family life.

[Satir, 1967, pp. 143–145.][2]

[2]Reprinted by permission of the author and the publisher from Virginia Satir, *Conjoint Family Therapy* (Rev. ed.). Palo Alto, California: Science and Behavior Books, 1967.

In this brief excerpt we also see Satir's effort to build self-esteem in each family member and to emphasize that each person is unique and must express his or her own views without another person (for example, a parent) answering for him or her. Warm and caring, with a strong set of **humanistic** values, Satir stresses the role of intimacy in family relationships as a vehicle for growth among all family members. The family should be the place where members can ask for what they need, where needs are met and individuality is allowed to flourish. Dysfunctional families do not permit individuality and members fail to develop a sense of self-worth. If parents are poor models of clear and unambiguous communication, Satir believes the therapist must show them how to change, how to get in touch with their own feelings, how to listen to others, how to ask for clarification if they do not understand another person's message, and so on. Through her gentle, matter-of-fact questioning, Satir may help some families for the first time to listen to their children's statements and opinions, and for the children to understand their parents' views and behavior. The process of feedback in an open system flows in both directions. Congruent ways of communicating, expressing genuine feelings to each other, replace the blamer/ placater/ super-reasonable/ irrelevant combinations of family communications styles described on page 117. The ultimate result is more functional family behavior.

Satir is a vigorous, down-to-earth sort of person who engages a family directly and authoritatively from the first session onward. Whatever the content of the session—child-rearing practices, sex, money, discipline, in-laws—Satir tries to aid the family to expand their choices of expressing congruent communication and of coping as a family (Bandler, Grinder, & Satir, 1976). In some cases, she may begin by compiling a family life chronology, to understand better how the family got to their present place. More generally, she begins to gather information in the first phase of therapy in order to identify the way the family members themselves want their family experience of living together to be. Specifically, what desired state do they seek and what resources have they presently developed to achieve it? Such information is the first step in the process of opening up the family system to the possibilities of growth and change and preparing them all for actively participating in creating that state.

For Satir, the therapist's chief role is to be a model for what she expects the family to change. The therapist's messages must be congruent; movement and sound of voice must match the words. Information gathered early in therapy is shared with the family, helping them understand the process that brought them to where they are now as well as what steps in the process must occur to allow them to make the changes they desire. As they learn to understand and trust one another, past miscommunications may be uncovered and corrected. Verbal communications by family members begin to match up with their nonverbal behavior. The therapist is a facilitator, helping the family to appreciate the skills it possesses within itself to change. Change is simply a step in an ongoing process over which the family learns to exercise control. The family learns to make new choices instead of rigidly adhering to old patterns. In the final phase of treatment, the therapist assists the family to solidify the changes and gains. In effect, a new family history becomes the base for new confidence in taking risks to change and grow.

Long known for her clinical sensitivities and therapeutic skills with families rather than for any comprehensive theoretical formulations, Satir has now begun to supply a systematic rationale for her interventions. Teaming with two colleagues (Bandler, Grinder, & Satir, 1976), she has begun to identify the key elements in her therapeutic approach: breaking the calibrated loops (expectations) in the communication patterns existing among family members, helping the family work together to understand what they want, preparing them for a new growth experience, helping them learn a new family process for coping and communicating, and making explicit the tools and skills they will need to continue the change process after therapy. Most specifically, she teaches the family explicit skills to give them new ways of communicating as a family. Presumably, having learned these skills, they are ready to move on to a truly open system, one where they now have the tools to cope creatively and effectively, regardless of the content of any new problem or crisis, using the coping strategies they themselves have established during family therapy. Specific techniques are elaborated in her latest writings, tied to the underpinnings of communication theory. Through it all emerges Satir the humanist, the communications teacher, the model of congruent behavior, believer in fostering individuality for children and adults alike and in the possibilities of family change and growth.

Jay Haley's Problem-Solving Therapy

Haley was an early worker in family research, particularly significant for his part in developing the "double-bind" concept (see Chapter 3) to account for the effect of a family's pathological communication patterns in the development of schizophrenia in a family member (Bateson, Jackson, Haley, & Weakland, 1956). A pioneer in family therapy, first editor of the journal *Family Process*, Haley has continued to publish widely in the field, editing some noteworthy volumes (for example, Haley & Hoffman, 1967; Haley 1971c) and presenting his own contributions to technique in others (for example, Haley, 1963; Haley, 1976). Now affiliated with the Family Therapy Institute in Washington, D.C., Haley spends a great deal of his professional time training teachers of family therapy in his direct, active, highly focused therapeutic techniques, which are largely based upon communications theory with some behavioral procedures recently added.

Fundamental to communication theory is the idea that communication defines the nature of the relationship one is having with a partner. If a husband is willing to discuss only the weather with his wife when they are together in the evening, he may be defining the relationship as one where they will only talk about conventional matters. If she refuses to comment on tomorrow's forecast but instead expresses the idea that they seem distant from one another this evening, she is attempting to redefine the relationship on more personal and intimate terms. Implicit in every relationship, according to Haley (1963), is a maneuver for power, a struggle over who defines the relationship two people are having together. As we noted in Chapter 5, in some marriages a partner's symptoms (for example, anxiety attacks, phobias, depressions, heavy drinking) may control what takes place between the mates—where they go, what they do together, whether one can leave the other's side for any length of time, and so on. Traditionally, such symptoms have been explained as expressions of intrapsychic conflict and therefore as involuntary aspects of one partner's "illness." Haley, strongly opposed to intrapsychic explanations, defines symptoms as interpersonal events, as tactics used by one person to deal with another. The emphasis is not on the struggle to control another person but rather on the struggle to control the definition of the relationship. If symptoms are a strategy for dealing with people—as Haley (1963) has relabeled them—then the therapist must devise methods for encouraging the patient to develop other ways of defining relationships so that the symptomatic methods will be abandoned.

Haley (1963) points out that psychotherapists and patients continually maneuver each other in the process of treatment. Elements of a power struggle exist in psychoanalysis, hypnosis, behavior therapy, family therapy, and all other treatment forms. Families may try to manipulate, deceive, exclude, or subdue a therapist in order to maintain the homeostatic balance they have achieved, even if it is at the expense of symptomatic behavior in one of their members. Therapists too must devise strategies for staying in charge and directing what is happening. Haley (1976) sees his task as taking responsibility for changing the family organization and resolving the problem that brought the family to see him. He is highly directive, he gives the family precise instructions and has them carry out tasks. Thus, he is highly manipulative in his procedures. For example, he cites the case

(Haley, 1976) of a grandmother siding with her grandchild (aged 10) against the mother. He saw the mother and child together, instructing the child to irritate the grandmother and instructing the mother to defend her daughter against the grandmother. This task forced a collaboration between mother and daughter and helped detach the daughter from her grandmother.

As we can see from this example, Haley is an active, take-charge family therapist. Artfully gaining the position of family change-maker, he intervenes when he chooses (rather than at those times when the family requests his participation), comments openly about the family's efforts to influence or control him, gives directions and assigns tasks, and assumes temporary leadership of the family group. He avoids getting enticed into coalitions within the family; adroitly, he alternately takes sides to overcome an impasse, but quickly disengages from becoming allied with one or another family faction.

Another Haley (1963) tactic is to emphasize the positive, usually by relabeling seemingly dysfunctional behavior as reasonable and understandable. In one often-quoted example, he boldy and somewhat outrageously told a husband who had chased after his wife with an axe that the man was simply trying to get close to her! Pollyannaish as this may appear to be, Haley is simply following a principle of communication theory described earlier—that all communication occurs at two levels, and that the message at the second level (metacommunication) qualifies what takes place on the surface level. Thus, the significance of any behavioral event changes depending on the class to which it is assigned. (The same remark by a sender in normal conversation can be taken as a joke or an attack, as praise or blame depending on the context in which the receiver places it.) By relabeling or reframing, Haley changes the context, freeing the participants to behave differently in the new context.

Haley's use of **paradoxical intervention** represents a particularly ingenious way of forcing a person to abandon old dysfunctional behavior. Most directives Haley issues to a family are those he wants and expects them to follow in order for them to change. However, there is another kind of directive in which he wants the family members to resist him so they will change. These are called paradoxical tasks, because it seems to the family that through his assignment he is asking them not to change at the same time that he tells them that he wants to help them change. Haley (1976), the strategist, assumes families who come for help are also resistant to any help being offered. The result may be a power struggle, with the therapist trying to help them to improve, but unstabilizing their balance in the process, and the family trying to get the therapist to fail but to go on trying because they realize something is wrong.

After setting up a benevolent framework in which change is expected, he carefully encourages the member(s) with the behavior to be changed to continue that behavior unchanged[3]—a domineering wife to continue to run everything in the family; a daughter refusing to attend school to stay home; an adolescent boy masturbating in public to continue doing so, only to keep a chart of how often, what days he enjoyed it most, and so on. Haley might tell a couple who always fight unproductively to go home and fight for three hours. The issue becomes one of control. The domineering wife no longer runs everything if the therapist is telling her what to do and if she resists his directive she will become less domineering. Similarly, he assumes in the other cases that the symptom presented, originally a way of gaining an interpersonal advantage, will resolve if the symptom now places the person at a disadvantage. In the case of the couple, Haley expects them to stop fighting; people do not like to make themselves miserable because someone else tells them to do so. Haley is a master at bringing out change through the use of therapeutic paradox.

Active, goal-directed, manipulative, and a brilliant strategist, Haley concerns himself with changing problem behavior and eliminating symptoms. While he shares Satir's concern with effective communication, his approach is not like hers in that his is not intended to offer insight, resolve intrapsychic conflicts, or provide a growth experience. He is concerned with the power alliances and coalitions within a family and with the metacommunicative aspects of family relationships. As we indicated in the previous chapter, Haley (1976) sees family therapy as going through formal stages during which a problem in the present situation is defined and new behavior is encouraged or sug-

---

[3]Although we have chosen to describe Haley's use of paradox as an intervention technique, the reader should be aware that this same approach is employed by many family therapists. We have included it here in our discussion of those therapies that emphasize clear communication because a paradoxical injunction (for example, "Be spontaneous.") is a prototype of a double-bind situation. To command someone to be spontaneous is to demand behavior that by its very nature cannot be spontaneous because it is commanded! Thus, with seeming innocence, the message sender is trapping the receiver into a situation where rule compliance entails rule violation (Watzlawick, Weakland, & Fisch, 1974). The receiver is faced with two conflicting levels of messages, is bewildered, and cannot make an effective response. As Haley, Milton Erickson, Watzlawick, and others use the paradox therapeutically, the family is directed in effect to "disobey me." As in the case of commanding someone to be spontaneous, instructing that person to disobey what you are saying is to produce a paradox. Thus, the family told not to change in effect defies the therapist's injunction; the family begins to change to prove the therapist wrong in assuming they could not change. If the therapist allows himself to be put down as wrong and even suggests the change is very likely to be temporary and a relapse probable, the family will resist relapse and continue to change to prove him wrong again. It is essential that the therapist never claim credit for helping—indeed, that he be puzzled by the change—so as to preclude the family's need to disobey him by having a relapse.

gested to solve the problem, changing family relationships in the process. According to Haley, brief, intensive intervention with a family followed by rapid disengagement is preferable to long-term involvement.

THERAPIES INFLUENCED BY STRUCTURAL THEORIES

Salvador Minuchin's Structural Therapy

Born in Argentina, Minuchin received his medical training there and set out to practice pediatrics. When Israel declared itself a state in 1948, Minuchin volunteered his services as an army doctor in the war with the Arab nations. Later trained as a child psychiatrist in the United States, he returned to Israel to work with displaced children from the Holocaust and then Jewish immigrants from the Arab countries. It was at this point that he became interested in working with entire families. Back in the United States, he started developing a theory and set of special techniques for working with poor families at the Wiltwyck School where many delinquent Black and Puerto Rican children from New York City were sent. Many of the direct, concrete, action-oriented intervention procedures he developed there he later brought to the Philadelphia Child Guidance Clinic, where he was director from 1965 to 1975. Originally a small clinic with a staff of ten located in the heart of the Black ghetto, the clinic blossomed under Minuchin's boldly imaginative leadership until it has become the largest facility of its kind known. It has 225 members and is part of the Children's Hospital on the campus of the University of Pennsylvania. It remains one of the few clinics where ghetto families are in the majority. Minuchin now spends most of his professional time teaching, supervising, writing, and demonstrating his dramatic techniques with local families he has never met before in front of professional audiences around the world.

Minuchin is a compelling presence, a colorful and somehow larger-than-life therapist who enters a family, adapts to the family organization, refuses to be ignored, and forces the family members to accommodate to him in ways he decides will facilitate movement toward the goals of treatment. He adopts the family's affective style; in a constricted family he is undemonstrative; in an expansive family he is jovial and uses expressive movements. He quickly assimilates the family's language patterns and commonly used terms. He tells anecdotes about his own experiences when he feels they are relevant to the family discussion. As a therapist, he describes himself (Minuchin, 1974a)

as acting like a distant relative, joining a family system and accommodating to its style. As he blends into the family, he begins to understand family themes and family myths, to sense a member's pain at being excluded or scapegoated, to distinguish which persons have open
communication pathways between them and which closed, and so on,
as he intuitively gets a picture of the family structure in operation.

Minuchin (1974b) conceives of family pathology as resulting
from the development of dysfunctional sets. These family reactions,
developed in response to stress, are repeated without modification
when there is conflict. A father experiencing stress at work comes
home and shouts at the mother. She counterattacks, escalating the conflict, which continues without change until one member abandons the
field. Both parties experience a sense of nonresolution. Or in another
example, a mother verbally attacks an adolescent, the father takes his
child's side, the younger children seize the opportunity to join in and
pick on the adolescent. All family members become involved, various
coalitions develop, but the family organization remains the same and
the dysfunctional sets will be repeated in the next stressful situation.
Minuchin believes restructuring is necessary—confronting and challenging the family, opening up for view their repetitive pathogenic
sets, bringing about changes in family rules and realignments. By
changing the patterns that support certain undesirable behaviors, by
rearranging sequences between people, restructuring of the family can
take place.

Innovative, unconventional, deliberately manipulative in calculated interventions he makes into the family's organization, Minuchin
concerns himself with changing the dysfunctional aspects of a family
system. He assumes that a family coming to see him is experiencing
some stress that has overloaded the system's adaptive and coping
mechanisms, handicapping the optimal functioning of its members in
the process. Minuchin sets himself the task of rearranging the family
organization—restructuring the system which governs its transactions—so that the family will function more effectively and the
growth potential of each member will be maximized (Minuchin,
1974b).

Minuchin's therapeutic approach with families follows a carefully laid out set of plans and intervention procedures. Speaking generally, he advocates that the therapist begin by affiliating with the family
in order to experience firsthand the pressures of the family system. He
acts and reacts as a subsystem of that overall family system. Once he
has gained entrance, he begins to probe the family structure, looking
for areas of flexibility and possible change. For example, if a family
has come for therapy because the teenage daughter is shy, withdrawn,

and has difficulties in her social life, he may observe for diagnostic purposes how they enter the therapy room. Quickly, he notes that the girl sits next to her mother and moves their two chairs close together. When the therapist asks what the problem is, the mother answers, ignoring her daughter's attempt to add her thoughts on the matter. The mother seems to have too intimate a knowledge of her adolescent daughter's personal life, more than is usual. Within a few minutes after starting, Minuchin makes his first intervention, asking the mother and father to change chairs. Structural therapy has begun—the father is brought into the picture, the family flexibility is being tested, there is an implication of pathology in the mother/daughter dyad, the family's reason for seeking therapy for the teenager has been relabeled as a problem with a larger focus (Minuchin, 1974b).

Minuchin's interventions very likely increase the stress on the family system, perhaps even create a family crisis, unbalancing family homeostasis, but they open the way for transformation of the family structure. He recognizes that in an enmeshed family system, as in the example just discussed, members of the family often feel the family as a whole can neither withstand change nor adapt to it; as a consequence, the system demands certain members change—develop symptoms—in order to maintain the malfunctioning homeostasis. When the danger point of family stress is approached, the symptom bearer will be activated as part of a conflict-avoidance circuit. The family system reinforces the continuance of the symptoms because such conflict-detouring sequences maintain the system's balance and status quo. It is the therapist's job to make everyone aware that this is a family problem and not an individual one and to change the family organization so it will continue with new functional sets rather than slavishly repeating dysfunctional ones.

The therapeutic tactics employed by Minuchin are often dramatic and at times theatrical. He enjoys setting up situations, functioning like a stage director, creating a scenario, assigning a task to the family and requiring them to function with the new sets he has imposed. For example, in treating an anoretic child, self-starving but refusing to eat, Minuchin arranges for the first session to meet the family for lunch (Minuchin, Rosman, & Baker, 1978). He does so deliberately, in order to foster a crisis around eating and experience what the family members are experiencing. He observes the parents plead, demand, cajole, become desperate, and feel defeated. He watches the adolescent girl[4] demonstrate hopelessness and helplessness, pathetically asserting

---

[4]Although anorexia can occur in both boys and girls, it is extremely rare among boys. Thus, most discussions of anorexia deal with anoretic girls.

through her non-eating that she has always given in to them at the expense of her self, but will do so no longer. While the daughter is usually labeled as the problem, Minuchin helps them see that anorexia nervosa is a diagnosis of a family system, not simply the adolescent's symptomatic behavior. All the family is locked into a futile pattern of interaction that has become the center of their lives; each member has a stake in maintaining the disorder. A particular type of enmeshed family organization, in which the child learns to subordinate her sense of self, has been found by Minuchin and his colleagues to be related to the development and maintenance of psychosomatic syndromes in adolescent girls. In turn, the syndrome plays an important role in maintaining family homeostasis. Structural family therapy helps each person in the family recognize and be responsible for causing and maintaining the syndrome. By creating a family crisis, Minuchin forces the family to change the system, substituting more functional ways of interrelating.

The following is typical of Minuchin's directly manipulative, persistent, crisis-provoking approach. Demonstrating his technique with a family with an anoretic adolescent daughter, he insists that the parents force the emaciated girl to eat or she will die. They coax, cajole, threaten, yell, and finally stuff food down her throat until their daughter collapses in tears. Minuchin believes she will now eat. As he later explains it:

> "The anoretic is obsessed with her hopelessness, inadequacy, wickedness, ugliness. I incite an interpersonal conflict that makes her stop thinking about how terrible she is and start thinking about what bastards her parents are. At that demonstration, I said to the parents, 'Make her eat,' and when they did she had to deal with them as people. Previously, the parents had been saying 'We control you because we love you.' In the position I put them in, they were finally saying 'Goddam it, you eat! Let's stop this crap about love or no love, and you eat, goddam it!' That freed her. She could then eat or not eat; she could be angry at them as clearly delineated figures" [Malcolm, 1978, p. 78].

Through such an approach, Minuchin has been able to show that the anoretic symptom is embedded in the faulty family organization. Changing that organization eliminates that death-threatening symptom. Minuchin's data indicate an 86% success rate for anoretics with structural therapy. Psychosomatic disorders provide an area where cure of illness can be scientifically measured, not merely assumed or implied. Minuchin's success in this area suggests that further research may show that his form of calculated intervention may be similarly successful with other family problems.

THERAPIES INFLUENCED BY BEHAVIOR THEORIES

Richard Stuart's Operant-Interpersonal Therapy

Behaviorists have made a significant impact on the current practices of family therapy. Indirectly, we see their influence on therapists such as Haley and Minuchin, who, while not themselves strictly behaviorists, manipulate environments and attempt to change specific maladaptive patterns of interactive behavior. More directly, the behavioral approach is best articulated in the writings of Richard Stuart, who has published extensive research on work with marital-discord couples.

Stuart (1976) begins by assuming that every dimension of a marriage is subject to continued fluctuations, ranging from who is to provide which kinds of new stimulations, and in which ways, to how both old and new responsibilities should be allocated and reallocated over time. In the same way, he recognizes that each spouse's commitment to the marriage varies over time, depending on his or her experience within the marriage or outside of that relationship. Stuart makes the further assumption that at least one of the spouses has doubts about remaining married, and that is why the couple has sought treatment or counseling. Therefore, he views the therapist's task as helping both spouses create the best possible relationship they can at this point. Then, he reasons, if even at its current best it is not enough (that is, in behavioral terms, the marriage offers insufficient reinforcements relative to the rewards they expect to earn living alone or with another partner), they can decide to end their marriage. On the other hand, if having changed their behaviors toward each other, the husband and wife evaluate the changes positively, they can recommit themselves to maintaining the marriage.

Orderly and precise in his approach, Stuart has developed an eight-stage model (see Figure 7-1) with the central theme of accelerating positive behavioral change. After each spouse independently completes a lengthy Marital Pre-Counseling Inventory (for example, detailing daily activities, general goals, satisfactions and targets for change, and level of commitment to the marriage), the therapist can plan an intervention program in an organized and efficient manner. The couple then agrees by telephone to a treatment contract: joint sessions, a willingness to have the therapist reveal to both all information each has provided, a commitment to six sessions, after which a decision about further treatment can be made. At this point, Stuart has thus made clear he will not enter into collusion with one spouse (for example, keeping a secret) against the other, that he expects both of

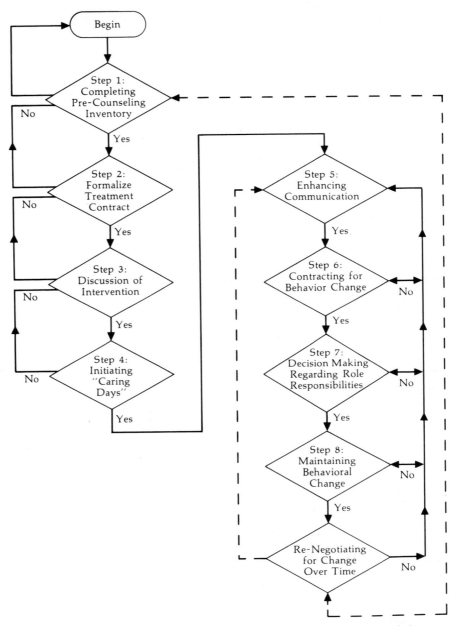

FIGURE 7-1. Flow chart of a behavioral treatment process for marital discord. (From "An Operant Interpersonal Program for Couples," by R. B. Stuart. In D. H. L. Olson (Ed.), *Treating Relationships*. Copyright 1976 by Graphic Publishing Company. Reprinted by permission.)

them to become involved in the process, and that he expects them to initiate change within a finite period.

During the first conjoint session (step 3), in which Stuart discusses the rationale of this therapeutic approach, he especially attempts to indoctrinate them with the idea that the most effective way to initiate change in a troubled marriage is to increase the rate at which the partners exchange positive behavior.[5] The fourth step, creating "caring days," is consistent with the notion of motivating both partners to achieve their treatment objectives. As seen in Figure 7-2, each person lists specific desirable behaviors from the other and is asked to emit from eight to twenty of the behaviors requested by the partner each day. Each partner is to emit caring behaviors independently of the other's actions, as a demonstration of commitment, which is consistent with Stuart's idea of "positive risks" described in Chapter 5. Each partner records the number and type of caring behavior given and received each day, achieving a "commitment index" and "pleasure index" for the total of that day's caring behavior offered or received, respectively.

The remaining four steps in Stuart's approach are tailored to the unique needs of each couple. Step 5 is devoted to training them to accurately communicate honest, timely, and constructive messages, without subterfuge, misinterpretation or superfluous innuendo. A behavioral contract can then be negotiated (step 6).[6] Here, for example, efforts might be made to change ritualized role responsibilities, such as a wife asking her husband to babysit so that she might attend an evening class or a husband asking her to take over responsibility for balancing a checkbook. They might also work on developing specific

[5] We discussed Stuart's use of the exchange or mutual reinforcement of desired behaviors between spouses in Chapter 5. Stuart (1971) has also applied the exchange model of behavioral contracting in working with families in which a young member is delinquent.

[6] Elaine Blechman (1974) at Yale has developed a "contracting game" to teach families negotiation and problem-solving skills. Although reluctant to confront their problems directly, families in conflict must be helped to strengthen such abilities and decrease their aversion to solving problems, according to Blechman. She utilizes a game board with 14 squares. Each square makes a statement (for example, "Red, tell Blue what to do more of and when") or asking a question (for example, "Blue, ask Red if he agrees to the reward you choose"). The game involves participants (family members) going around the board through each step, selecting target behavior they have programmed to negotiate (for example, "Red, draw a problem card"), agreeing on more pleasing behavior to replace problem behaviors, deciding on rewards—such as play money or humorous bonus cards for pleasing behavior—and, finally, writing out and signing a contract together (for example, how to deal with clothes left on the floor). The Family Contract Game is designed to provide powerful antecedents and consequences for effective problem-solving behavior; learned problem-solving skills presumably will transfer from the game to use at home as needed, ultimately becoming a useful family tool for negotiating problems.

Wife's Requests

1. Greet me with a kiss and a hug in the morning before we get out of bed.
2. Bring me pussywillows (or some such).
3. Ask me what record I would like to hear and put it on.
4. Reach over and touch me when we're riding in the car.
5. Make breakfast and serve it to me.
6. Tell me you love me.
7. Put your things away when you come in.
8. If you're going to stop at the store for something, ask me if there is anything that I want or need.
9. Rub my body or some part of me before going to sleep, with full concentration.
10. Look at me intently sometimes when I'm telling you something.
11. Engage actively in fantasy trips with me—e.g., to Costa Rica, Sunshine Coast, Alaska.
12. Ask my opinion about things which you write and let me know which suggestions you follow.
13. Tell me when I look attractive.
14. Ask me what I'd like to do for a weekend or a day with the desire to do what I suggest.

Husband's Requests

1. Wash my back.
2. Smile and say you're glad to see me when you wake up.
3. Fix the orange juice.
4. Call me at work.
5. Acknowledge my affectionate advances.
6. Invite me to expose the details of my work.
7. Massage my shoulders and back.
8. Touch me while I drive.
9. Hold me when you see that I'm down.
10. Tell me about your experiences at work every day.
11. Tell me that you care.
12. Tell me that I'm nice to be around.

FIGURE 7-2. A sample request list for caring days, a crucial aspect of Stuart's "operant-interpersonal" approach for couples. (From "An Operant Interpersonal Program for Couples," by R. B. Stuart. In D. H. L. Olson (Ed.), *Treating Relationships*. Copyright 1976 by Graphic Publishing Company. Reprinted by permission.)

strategies for dealing with arguments, perhaps even arranging signals to alert each other of their willingness to end the argument. Changes oriented toward producing greater trust in each other are also negotiated at this point. A behavioral contract, implicit and explicit, is entered into, based on the quid pro quo ("something for something") exchange of desirable behaviors.

In the final two steps, the couple learns more effective decision-making strategies (that is, formulating a goal and problem solving set, assembling facts, and so on), particularly regarding who will take major responsibilities for what areas of their lives. In the eight steps, they are helped to maintain the changes they have made by learning specific "relationship rules" summarizing what they have agreed are, for them, the best ways of continuing communicational, behavioral, and decision-making changes. Stuart insists on periodic self-assessments at four-month intervals, by completing the Marital Pre-Counseling Inventory, so that they might gauge their progress and plan new objectives for further relationship change.

Confident, thorough, and well-planned in his approach, Stuart has treated over 750 couples with this technique over a ten year period. Results of the first 200 couples, comparing pre- and post-therapy inventory responses, indicate an increased commitment to the marriage by one spouse in 84% of the couples and by both in 77%. One year later, 84% were still married and revealed a high level of continued commitment to the marriage. Despite some criticism that his approach is somewhat mechanical, Stuart helps couples improve their problem-solving and decision-making ability, clean up their indirect, disruptive, or confusing communication patterns, learn to give and receive pleasure and caring, and function more effectively and happily as a working marital unit.

Robert Liberman's Contingency Contracting

Generally speaking, behavior therapists tend to systematically analyze precisely what observable behaviors need to be changed and what environmental contingencies seem to be supporting (and thus reinforcing) the undesired maladaptive behaviors. They then choose reasonable and achievable goals for the family that call for alternative, adaptive behaviors. Finally, they guide the family to change the contingencies of their social reinforcement patterns from maladaptive to adaptive target behaviors (Liberman, 1970). Success is measured by the extent to which the specified goals are reached. We presented a case in Chapter 5 in which Liberman successfully treated a couple with a long history of marital disharmony through the use of behavioral techniques, especially the operant-conditioning procedure called *shaping*.

When any form of family therapy is successful, it is because the therapist has successfully guided the family members into changing their ways of dealing with each other. In behavioral terms, each family member has learned to change his or her responsiveness to the other; what has changed are the consequences of behavior or contingencies of reinforcement. The therapist uses his positive relationship with the family, according to Liberman (1972), to reprogram the contingen-

cies of reinforcement operating in the family system. Unlike other behavior therapists, who minimize the importance of their relationships
with a family in treatment, Liberman stresses the role of a therapeutic
alliance and positive relationship so that he can use himself as a lever
to generate change in the family system of reinforcement contingencies. He sees himself as an educator, initiating changes through direct
guidance but also partly through his capacity to show empathy,
warmth, and concern for those with whom he is working.

Liberman is a behavior therapist with a systems outlook. That
means that, while he never loses sight of the target behaviors to be
achieved, he recognizes that behavior therapists cannot restrict their
work with families to weekly office therapy sessions. Home visits and
involvement with other agencies or systems impinging on the family
members (for example, schools, work settings) are part of his effort.
Experimental research on the effectiveness of various treatment approaches (Liberman, Levine, Wheeler, Sanders, & Wallace, 1976) is also
a part of his determination to develop brief and inexpensive treatment
programs for couples and whole families.

In recent years, Liberman, a California psychiatrist affiliated with
UCLA and Camarillo State Hospital, has elaborated on a popular behavioral technique called **contingency contracting** as a family-based
intervention strategy for harnessing natural reinforcers present in the
family milieu (see Figure 7-3). A contingency contract is a means by
which two or more family members exchange positively rewarding,
desired behaviors in each other. A contract, simple and easy to understand by all family members over the age of ten, is negotiated wherein
each participant specifies who is to do what, for whom, under which
circumstances, times, and places. Negotiations are open and free from
coercion; the terms of the contract are expressed in explicit and clearly
understood words. For example, negotiating with an adolescent over
poor grades, part of the contract reads "a C grade or better on the
weekly quiz" rather than "do better in school." The latter is too vague
and open to different interpretations by the participants, so that the
adolescent may believe he or she has done better and fulfilled his or
her part of the agreement, while the parents believe the gain is insignificant, and the conflict between them over school performance remains unresolved. By the some token, the parents must be specific
("We will give you $5 toward the purchase of new clothes for each
week your quiz grade is C or better") and not general or ambiguous
("We'll be more generous about buying you clothing if you get good
grades"). The point here is that each participant must know specifically what is expected of him or her and what may be gained in return.

A contract is an opportunity for success, accomplishment, re-

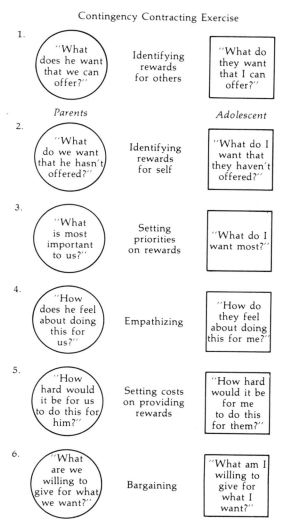

Contingency Contracting Exercise

1.
"What does he want that we can offer?" — Identifying rewards for others — "What do they want that I can offer?"

Parents — *Adolescent*

2.
"What do we want that he hasn't offered?" — Identifying rewards for self — "What do I want that they haven't offered?"

3.
"What is most important to us?" — Setting priorities on rewards — "What do I want most?"

4.
"How does he feel about doing this for us?" — Empathizing — "How do they feel about doing this for me?"

5.
"How hard would it be for us to do this for him?" — Setting costs on providing rewards — "How hard would it be for me to do this for them?"

6.
"What are we willing to give for what we want?" — Bargaining — "What am I willing to give for what I want?"

FIGURE 7-3. Steps in a contingency contract negotiated between parents and an adolescent. The Family Contracting Exercise is a structured learning experience conducted by the behaviorally oriented family therapist to help family members, stepwise, to identify their needs and desires (rewards) for themselves and each other, to set priorities for rewards for self, to empathize with the other, to set costs on providing rewards to others, and finally to bargain and compromise. This sequence is outlined for the parents in circles and for the adolescent in squares. (Reprinted with permission from *Journal of Behavior Therapy and Experimental Psychiatry, 6,* L. Weathers and R. P. Liberman, "The Family Contracting Exercise." Copyright 1975, Pergamon Press, Ltd.)

ward. However, the target behaviors, such as a C grade, must be realistic and within the grasp of the contractor. Each member must accept the idea that privileges are rewards made contingent on the performance of responsibilities. In such cases, Liberman believes a family member will exchange maladaptive behavior for adaptive behavior in anticipation of a positive consequence, a desired change in the behavior of the other. The child's responsibilities (that is, better grades) are the parents' reinforcers and the parents' responsibilities (money) are the child's reinforcers. Liberman helps a family set up a monitoring or record-keeping system that enables the contractors and the therapist to assess their reciprocal fulfillment of the terms of the contract. Bonuses are given for consistent fulfillment of the terms and penalties imposed for failure to adhere to them. Note that, as in all behavioral procedures, the success of treatment can be measured by the success to which the contract works for all parties.

Contingency contracting is not an end in itself, but merely one motivating and structuring device among a variety of family intervention techniques (for example, modeling, shaping) used by Liberman. Contracting may open up communication within a family and help members express for the first time what each would like from the others. In some cases, the act may force the member to state what he or she wants, and in doing so make that member aware of wishes he or she did not previously recognize. Finally, an important by-product of this approach is to focus family attention on goals and accomplishments. Liberman, practical, humane, and down-to-earth in his clinical approach, believes that contingency contracting formalizes the family's natural expectations into concrete behaviors. By giving recognition for achievement, he believes the family becomes more positive in its future interactions.

TWO INDEPENDENT THERAPIES

Gerald Zuk's Triadic-Based Family Therapy

An early critic of the psychoanalytic influence on the then newly emerging field of family therapy, Zuk, a psychologist affiliated with the Eastern Pennsylvania Psychiatric Institute in Philadelphia, was among the first to offer a systems-oriented vewpoint that departed from the traditional view of helping patients develop insights into and work through their unconscious resistance to change. According to Zuk (1971a), much of what transpires in family therapy is a carry-over from the individual-focused psychoanalytic view, which emphasizes a dyadic interaction. He believes that when therapists, trained in this approach, shift to working with families, they nevertheless treat dyadic relationships (for example, mother/father, father/child) in the family. Instead, Zuk argues that family therapy should be **triadic-based**. That is, it must be based on the interactions of three or more persons in the family.

FIGURE 7-4. Gerald H. Zuk, Ph.D. (Photo courtesy of Gerald H. Zuk.)

Zuk contends that families may develop pathogenic relationships (see discussion below) largely over issues of power and control, and that they attempt conflict resolution by developing go-between processes that are triadic in nature. For example, a woman may pit her husband and the children against each other so that she can reserve for herself the role of benevolent go-between in the family. Although she may complain bitterly that someone has to keep them apart and the role has fallen on her by default, Zuk believes the woman may be employing the go-between process to control relationships with both her husband and the children. In family therapy, she may assume the same role between the therapist and her family. While ostensibly helping the therapist, she channels all messages through herself and in the process may alter or rearrange them, thus undermining the therapist's efforts. Zuk believes triadic-based transactions, involving family coalitions, alliances, or efforts at negotiation, may become pathogenic, leading to dysfunction among one or more family members. His triadic-based system of family therapy may parallel the triadic-based pathogenic relationships in the family, except that the therapist gains control of the go-between process. With this leverage, says Zuk (1971a), he is able to shift the balance of pathogenic relating among family members so that new forms of relating will emerge.

What are pathogenic ways of relating? They are destructive, inflammatory, malevolent processes seen in family interviews, ways used within the family to systematically control or manipulate a member's behavior (Zuk, 1976). Silencing strategies used to isolate a member into silence for some transgression are a common example; scapegoating a member is another. In the former case, a coalition among members is formed to shut another member up, punishing him or her through use of the silent treatment (using silence to induce silence), changing the subject when that person brings up a "sensitive" topic, laughing or coughing or grimacing as a signal to change the subject, and so on. The clear message is to comply or fall out of the good graces of the family. If successful, silencing strategies may actually induce silence or they may induce babbling, a form of communication that makes no verbal sense and is often seen in schizophrenics. The family therapist must intervene directly to break up the power struggle that often ensues between silencers and silenced (or babbling) ones within a family.

Scapegoating, in a sense, is a kind of silencing strategy aimed at isolating a victim within the family. All of the inadequacies of the family members are heaped on the scapegoat, who is held responsible for family failures or shortcomings in functioning. The scapegoat usually accepts the role by absorbing the inadequacies of the family, and develops a self-image and way of relating to others that reflects this role. Other examples of pathogenic relating offered by Zuk are overt or covert threats of physical or psychological violence made by a coalition of family members against another member, selective inattention by the family to the intense emotions of a member, resorting to unfair or inappropriate labeling ("wild," "bad," "stupid") of a member, or maintaining certain family myths and rituals despite their uncertain origin ("insanity runs in the family"). Zuk (1971a) sees the therapist's go-between process in family therapy as aimed primarily at undermining pathogenic relating in families and replacing it with more productive alternatives. To bring about change, he believes, the therapist must pressure family members into redefining and restructuring their relationships.

Advancing the unorthodox (and somewhat risky) notion that to be effective the therapist must be an active and judicious side-taker, Zuk (1967) intentionally casts his weight to one side or the other in order to tip the balance in favor of more productive relating, or at least disrupt a chronic pattern of pathogenic relating. In the following example, a fifth session with the family, three people—Zuk, a 40-year-old woman with a drinking problem attending Alcoholics Anonymous meetings, and her 56-year-old husband, who accuses his wife of sexual promiscuity—are discussing the man's alleged feelings of anger and jealousy. The man denies having these feelings at first, but Zuk seems to implicity side with him against the wife, suggesting his feelings are genuine and valid and call for a response from his wife.

THERAPIST: The question is . . . your husband is showing jealousy.
MOTHER: Right. I've said this from the beginning.
THERAPIST: And you are responding in a funny kind of way. I don't know whether you're encouraging it or discouraging it.
MOTHER: You would have to understand AA. I don't know if you do. But each and every one of us help each other out in maintaining sobriety.
FATHER: But a man don't help no woman, and the woman don't help no man! A man helps a man and a woman helps a woman!
THERAPIST: Yes. Your husband is raising the question of men in particular; jealousy of the men. And you are not responding to that. You're putting it in terms of humanity . . .
MOTHER: I've given in to every whim about jealousy. I've stopped kissing my kids and stopped hugging them.
THERAPIST: But you're still sleeping with your son.
MOTHER: He's in my bedroom, yes . . .
THERAPIST: Maybe you've stopped kissing him, but you haven't stopped sleeping with him.
FATHER: Her son is not sleeping with her; he's sleeping in a twin bed.
THERAPIST: Are you defending her too now? (laughs) Whose side are you on? I'm not implying anything. . . . This has been something that you brought up here today.
FATHER: That's right.
THERAPIST: You're angry about it.
FATHER: I'm not angry about it.
THERAPIST: You say you're not and I say you are.

Shortly after this exchange in which, by encouraging the husband to express his jealousy and by confronting the wife with her evasiveness, the therapist appears to side with the husband, the therapist then turns the tables: He now confronts the husband in such a way as to appear to side with the wife.

THERAPIST: . . . Is that what you're saying to him: "I need companionship. I need somebody?"
MOTHER: I certainly do need somebody . . .
THERAPIST: "I need my son close to me because I get something from him that I don't get from somebody else." This I think is what your wife

seems to me to say. She says, "I need something too. And whether you're jealous about it—well, that's just too bad. I need those things." That's what she's saying . . .

FATHER: Well, I understand that and I want to try my best to give her what she wants!

[Zuk, 1971a, pp. 74–75.][7]

By siding alternately with one and then the other, Zuk hopes to facilitate an open expression of their underlying feelings and conflict with each other, rather than allowing them to use their customary tactics for avoiding confrontation. By acting as go-between, or broker, he tries to help them negotiate and resolve conflicts. As he moves from one side to the other and back again, he exerts the critical leverage on their fixed pattern of relating.

Zuk views the therapist and the family as adversaries. The family will try to convince the therapist at the onset that nothing is wrong; paradoxically, in the process they may improve their relationship just enough to try to change the therapist's position. Beneficial change for most families, however, as Haley has also suggested, comes out of the struggle for control between the therapist and the family (Zuk, 1967). As the therapist probes for conflict, encourages the open expression of conflict, and exposes the family's efforts to deny or cover up disagreements, he begins to zero in on specific disagreements he considers significant. He resists efforts by the family to control the situation by establishing their own rules. In this way, he establishes his authority and go-between role, resisting all efforts to displace him. His style of relating to them may be bold and confrontational, or reserved and nondirective, depending on his view of the family background, their expectations about therapy, the nature of the pathogenic relating that exists, and the therapeutic progress that has been made previously (Zuk, 1976). Whatever the strategy, Zuk as artful therapist is constantly structuring and directing the therapy. Change in both individual and family functioning as a whole, according to Zuk, come from the bargaining or negotiation that has gone on between the therapist and family members.

John Bell's Family Group Therapy

A lone figure in the field of family therapy, Bell seems to have developed principles and technical skills for working with families that are independent of the theories and techniques we have discussed

[7]From *Family Therapy: A Triadic-Based Approach*, by G. H. Zuk. Copyright 1971 by Human Sciences Press. Reprinted by permission of the author and publisher.

thus far. In one sense, he is an unsung hero of the field, an actual founder of family therapy, but one who has gone off in his own direction, an inductive action researcher and innovator more interested in new ideas and practices than in laying claim to territory.

As Bell himself tells the story (Bell, 1975), a casual remark he overheard while visiting the Tavistock Clinic in London in 1951, to the effect that Dr. John Bowlby was experimenting with group therapy with families, stimulated Bell's interest in applying the technique to treat behavior problems in children. Bell assumed Bowlby, a distinguished British psychiatrist, was treating the entire family, although this later proved to be an erroneous assumption; actually Bowlby only occasionally included family conferences as adjuncts to working with the problem child. On the basis of this misinformation, Bell began to think through the technical implications of meeting with an entire family on a regular basis. Once back in the United States, a case came to his attention that gave him the opportunity to try out this method as a therapeutic device. As a result, family therapy was officially underway, although Bell's description of his work did not receive widespread dissemination until a decade later (Bell, 1961). That groundbreaking monograph is often considered, along with Ackerman's text (Ackerman, 1958), as representing the founding of family therapy as practiced today.

Bell, a California psychologist affiliated with the Palo Alto Veterans Administration Hospital, Stanford University, and the University of California, calls his form of intervention "family group therapy" in order to emphasize that he is applying the social psychological theories of small-group behavior in relating to the natural group that is a family. His practical and simple purpose is to aid the family group, ultimately independently of the therapist, to function more effectively, with fewer constrictions to bind them into nonfunctional activities and relations, with less tension, with more efficient use of their problem-solving skills, and with expanded and improved communication between family members so that they can reach their goals. To do this, Bell encourages the family to structure itself into a conference where unsatisfactory relationships between members are faced, family problems are worked on together, family goals are clarified, decisions are reached for achieving those goals, and proposed methods are tried until mutually satisfactory problem-solving has been successful. Bell remains the facilitator, the process leader, staying outside the family rather than joining it, but helping it to determine its own family-directed goals and move toward them as a group.

To achieve his objectives, Bell (1976) works on process interventions that have the effect of engaging the family and moving them through the natural stages of small, task-oriented group development.

FIGURE 7-5. John E. Bell, Ed.D. (Photo courtesy of John E. Bell.)

As the therapy group—now the therapist plus the family—develops, it progresses through these stages, as does any ongoing group brought together to engage in some common project. Initially, the family group is helped to explore the expectations of its members as they begin to form relations with the therapist, who carefully defines the therapy rules. If they make a commitment to proceed as a group, they nevertheless test the firmness of the rules, the commitments each has made, and in what ways each member will participate. Inevitably, a power struggle with much hostility begins to develop, as individuals and coalitions within the family fight to protect their own interests and for dominance. Rather than an end in itself, exorcising some family demons, the struggle is instrumental to group development and consolidation, and to the ultimate emergence of consensus within the family about the problems on which to work. In Bell's view, they are then a group that has become functional toward selecting and reaching the family goals. In the next stage, the family group concentrates its energies on selecting a common task to undertake (for example, getting rid of a particular family annoyance or dealing with an acute family crisis). Bell keeps them all engaged in the task, as they now begin to struggle toward a livable resolution that will accommodate the respective goal-demands of each group member or family subgroup. This is the heart of the treatment, releasing the creativity of each member, overcoming lassitude or withdrawal over failure, removing blocks to action, reopening and widening communication patterns, redefining expectations and holding a fracturing family together. The goal of therapy is reached as conciliation is achieved among the group participants, other pressing problems are resolved, and the group separates from the therapist. In Bell's experience, family members then typically tighten the boundaries around their family "by accentuating the strengths and importance of family initiatives, communication, decisions, and other actions" (Bell, 1976, pp. 138–139). Throughout all stages of his work with a family, Bell continues to stress that the locus of the problems amenable to family therapy is in the family and not separately in individuals. The outcomes must be evaluated in terms of family well-being according to the family's united opinion.

Bell as process leader works actively to help family members close gaps between themselves, should any member seek to withdraw from the family action. He provides a model of himself as the listener for others to emulate. He distributes opportunities for family members to speak, mirroring back to them the interactions he is observing. He confines the content to family interactions, refusing to allow a member to escape by introducing extraneous matters. He adapts to a particular family's pace of development as a group. He encourages exploring and trying out new ways of interacting. As we noted in Chapter 6, Bell insists that the entire family be present for each session, even postponing meetings if any one member cannot attend. After the initial contact he refuses to see or talk by telephone with one member only. All of this is done to emphasize that they are dealing with a family problem and the group as a whole cannot resolve a family problem unless all work together. An excluded person may work against any change brought about by the remainder of the family group.

Bell's leadership is gentle, polite, sympathetic, respectful, and unemotional. He does not join in or intrude on a family but rather affirms their ability to develop strategies to solve their own problems and attain their own goals. Far less dramatic in style than family therapists such as Ackerman, Satir, or Minuchin, Bell nevertherless has definite ideas on how a family can go about solving its problems and reaching its goals. By remaining outside the family, he does not take over another person's roll or authority (for example, a father to a child) or make decisions for the family on how it should function. Bell works with a family as a natural group, persons in relation to one another who have shared experiences and will continue to live together after family therapy is terminated. He sees the family group therapist as an agent of change, helping both the family as a whole and its individual members to initiate, accomplish, and consolidate changes. In a sense, Bell's part in the process is to help initiate and monitor the chain reaction as the family transforms itself into a more perfectly functioning group.

Bell, himself, is the first to admit that his therapy cannot solve all family problems. In recent years he has concentrated his attention on developing methods to help families whose problems are beyond interactive relations—such as families that include a hospitalized patient, are affected adversely by large social problems such as unemployment and poverty, are alienated from the mainstreams of society, are battered by inhumane work settings, are deprived of adequate support networks, or are disturbed by psychosis, character disorders, developmental problems, or physical or mental deterioration. In this work he is moving to create family-enhancing environments—a treatment program he calls Family Context Therapy.

SUMMARY

Since there are as yet no agreed-on techniques of family therapy, we have endeavored in this chapter to present a variety of intervention strategies used by nine leading therapists. Therapies influenced by psychodynamic theories (Ackerman, Bowen), communications theories (Satir, Haley), structural theory (Minuchin), and behavior theories (Stuart, Liberman) are included, along with the practices of two independent family therapists (Zuk, Bell).

Ackerman's approach is active, dynamic, and direct, as he proceeds in a warm and straightforward manner to the heart of the family's problems, helping the family have a meaningful emotional exchange. Bowen is more restrained, more neutral, more cerebral, as he focuses on the family system and attempts to modify its customary triangulations and help individual members develop a better level of differentiation of self. Satir, with a strong set of humanistic values, zeros in on a family's communications problems, teaching them new methods that are designed to deepen their relationships and prepare them for new growth experiences. Haley attends to the power elements of a relationship, devising strategies for staying in control and actively and deliberately directing families to change their behavior patterns.

Minuchin engages a family, accommodating to its style, then attempts to rearrange the family organization, restructuring the system that governs its transactions, so that the family substitutes more functional ways of interrelating. Stuart works to increase family members' problem-solving and decision-making abilities, and to help them learn

TABLE 7-1. A Summary Comparison of Models of Clinical Practice of Family Therapy

	Theory Base	Use of Family Diagnosis	Role of Therapist	Treatment Unit	Goals
Ackerman	Psychoanalysis; social psychology; child psychiatry	Yes	Active; catalyst; self-disclosing	Entire family	Clearer role differentiation; increased role complementarity
Bowen	Psychoanalysis; systems	No	Active; low-keyed; directive; coach	Triangle—therapist plus two adults	Reduce fusion; increase level of self-differentiation
Satir	Communication	Yes; family life chronology	Teacher and model of clear communication; facilitator	Marital couple plus children over 4 years old	Growth experience; development of open communication system
Haley	Communication; behaviorism	No	Directive; responsible for creating change; manipulative; use of paradox	Entire family	Change behavior to eliminate presenting problem or symptom
Minuchin	Systems; behaviorism	Yes; by observation	Stage director; active intervenor; manipulative	Entire family	Restructuring of family organization
Stuart	Behaviorism	Yes	Teacher or trainer of new behavior patterns	Marital couple	Learning "relationship rules"; exchanging positive behaviors
Liberman	Behaviorism; systems	Yes	Teacher; shaper of behavior; contract negotiator	Entire family	Reprogramming of contingencies of reinforcements
Zuk	Systems	No	Go-between; side-taker	Triadic—3 or more family members	Reduction of pathogenic relating in family
Bell	Social psychology	No	Facilitator; action researcher; process leader	Marital couple plus children over 9 years old	More effective family functioning

to give and receive pleasure and caring. Behaviorist Liberman tries to reprogram the contingencies of reinforcement operating in the family system by means of a contingency contract drawn up by two or more family members who opt to exchange positively rewarding behavior in each other. Zuk's approach with families is triadic-based, as he acts to control the go-between process among family members in order to disrupt chronic patterns of pathogenic relating and tip the balance in favor of more productive relating. Bell, basing his approach on the social psychology of small group behavior, acts as a process leader to facilitate problem solving and decision making in the family group.

Table 7-1 compares the various approaches of the therapists we have discussed in this chapter.

8

INNOVATIVE TECHNIQUES IN FAMILY THERAPY

A number of noteworthy forms of family therapy—in a sense, variations on the themes presented in the previous chapter—will be discussed now. Some, such as multiple family therapy or multiple impact therapy, represent well-established approaches to family treatment, while others, such as family sculpture or family choreography, are special techniques rather than full-fledged therapeutic approaches. The latter are useful supplements to various ways of conducting family sessions. Some are based on technological breakthroughs (for example, **videoplayback** techniques). Others represent the application of increased scientific knowledge regarding an important aspect of human behavior (for example, conjoint sex therapy) or the extrapolation to families of innovative individual clinical procedures (for example, **crisis intervention**), as in family crisis therapy. Family therapy in the home is also represented here in the form of **social network intervention.**

MULTIPLE FAMILY THERAPY

Developed originally from working with hospitalized schizophrenic patients and their families, Multiple Family Therapy (MFT) is an adaptation of group therapy techniques to the treatment of whole families. During the 1950s, Laqueur, a psychiatrist at a state hospital, made the observation that many of his patients improved steadily while receiving treatment in the hospital, only to return in worse condition after weekend visiting with their families. He orginally invited large groups of patients and their families to joint informational meetings, but later decided it was more workable to deal with groups of four or five families. Not only did this prove expedient, saving time and personnel, but the interaction between families seemed to bring about desired behavior changes more quickly than did working with the individual patient alone or with individual families. Such an approach also proved useful in helping the patient adjust later from a structured hospital milieu to an unstructured home situation (Laqueur, 1976). Since its introduction in the early 1950s, MFT has progressed to the point of being used now with a wide variety of dysfunctional families and in a great number of clinical settings (Strelnick, 1977).

Four to five randomly selected families meet with a therapist and (sometimes) cotherapist[1] weekly, for 60–75 minutes, during which they share problems with each other and help one another in the problem-solving process. The therapist(s) is likely to act as facilitator, guiding the discussion, pointing out transactional patterns he or she observes, and reviewing what took place at the close of the session. Group members do not necessarily sit clustered as individual families; movement and position changes are common as mothers may join together temporarily at one point or perhaps children group together as they learn of their common problems. Groups are open-ended, so that a family leaving the group for whatever reason is replaced by a newly referred family.

Apparently, the benefits of such an approach accrue from the combined benefits of family and group therapy. Group identification and support, easy recognition of, and quick involvement with, each other's problems, seeing one family's communication problems portrayed by another family, and learning how other families solve their relationship problems appear to be particularly valuable (Goldenberg & Goldenberg, 1975). Learning new patterns for resolving conflict may come from observing another family deal with an analogous conflict situation more successfully. For some children (often the identified patients), new experiences with parents other than their own may be less threatening and may prove enlightening and therapeutic. A therapist may use less-disturbed families to reach more-disturbed ones. In a sense the former serve as cotherapists, understanding the latter's problems as not totally different from their own, but offering suggestions or serving as models, through their family interaction, of better conflict resolution. This is particularly true in open-ended groups,

---

[1]The issue of the use of cotherapists is a controversial one in family therapy. It will be discussed in greater detail in Chapter 9.

where families new to the group may be helped by other families closer to successful termination.

What are the mechanisms of change in multiple family therapy? Laqueur (1973, 1976), adopting a general systems theory outlook, views each individual as a subsystem of a higher system, the family, which in turn represents a subsystem of the MFT group. The MFT group, then, receives input from its various subsystems, processes the information, and through its feedback loops provides output in the form of feedback information to the distressed family and its individual members. Through the circular interaction between the therapist and all group members, such insights may reverberate throughout the entire MFT system, speeding up progress for all the participating families. Secret codes for a disturbed family's internal verbal and nonverbal communications may be broken by other families. A signal from the therapist may be picked up by a sensitive family member, who amplifies it throughout his or her family and onto the entire MFT system. Because so many authority figures—therapists, fathers, mothers—are present, the young identified patient may feel encouraged to work out any problems over independence by the comparatively nonthreatening process of understanding through analogy and identification. Role-playing a son/father relationship with a father from another family may not only help the son learn new ways of coping with such a stiuation with his real father, but may provide the bonus of transmitting similar insights to all the sons and fathers present.

Over 25 years, Laqueur (1976) and his colleagues have treated over 1500 families in MFT groups, particularly families with hospitalized schizophrenic members. Only a handful have been considered unsuited for this form of family therapy, primarily because exposure of some vital secrets might lead to explosive consequences, according to Laqueur. However, even in these cases, he acknowledges that despite conspiracies of silence such secrets are usually common knowledge within the family; rather than true secrets, they are more accurately described as barriers to communication and the free sharing of experiences.

An interesting variation of multiple family therapy involves multiple marital couple therapy, usually consisting of three to five couples. Even in those cases where the identified patient is a child, the course of family therapy frequently evolves to an identification and consideration of parental conflict, as we have noted earlier. In such cases, family therapy becomes marital-couple therapy. Bringing together a number of couples so they may deal with common problems of marriage seems the next logical and efficient step. Framo (1973), Alger (1976b), and Liberman, Wheeler, and Sanders (1976) have all described their work with multiple-couple groups. In some instances, cotherapists who themselves are husband and wife (Low & Low, 1975) add greater personal involvement and authenticity to the group, serving as models in their ongoing demonstration of problem-solving as a couple.

Couples groups seem ideal for marriage partners to recognize that their problems are not unique, that some conflict is an inevitable part of a marital relationship, that all marital pairs have to work out accommodations in a number of areas (children, sex, money, and so on). Couples may learn from one another about how to negotiate differences and how to avoid the escalation of conflict. In one sense, a couples group provides a forum where each person can express his or her expectations of their marriage and of their mates, with feedback from others providing reality testing. Based on his work with over 200 couples, Framo (1973) considers such an approach the most effective therapy for marital couples. A positive support system of peers—other couples as much or more than the therapist—is a significant therapeutic plus for couples groups (Alger, 1976b). Liberman, Wheeler, and Sanders (1976), adopting a behavioral approach, train couples in communications skills and in learning to recognize, initiate, and acknowledge pleasing interactions. Their goal is to increase the range and frequency of positively experienced interaction between spouses, aided by the support and cohesiveness of the couples group. As a couple's behavioral interactions are better balanced, it is their contention that marital satisfaction will greatly increase.

MULTIPLE IMPACT THERAPY

With the goal of providing brief but intensive intervention for a family with a disturbed adolescent in crisis, MacGregor, Ritchie, Serrano, and Schuster (1964), of the University of Texas Medical Branch in Galveston, developed a unique, crisis-focused approach to family therapy. Psychologist MacGregor and his associates operate as a clinic team, devoting full time for two days or so to the study and brief treatment of a single family in crisis. Called Multiple Impact Therapy (MIT), this highly focused procedure is based on two assumptions: (1) that individuals and families facing a crisis are motivated to mobilize family resources to meet it, and thus are more likely to be receptive to professional help than at other times, and (2) that psychotherapy is likely to produce faster results in the early stages of treatment, so rapid intervention is highly desirable (Ritchie, 1971).

Essentially an expanded intake procedure, MIT involves an entire family in a series of continuing interactions with a multidisciplinary team of mental health professionals over the two-day period. Beginning with a diagnostic team/family conference, the team starts to gather information about the family's role in the social development of the adolescent in crisis. Following this first collective conference, private individual interviews are arranged, each family member with a different therapist. The venting of grievances, the presentation of each person's viewpoint, and self-justification are common here. Later, various combinations of team members and family members may hold joint sessions, as when the teenager and his or her interviewer join with one or both parents and their interviewer(s). Therapists may overlap in working with different individuals or combinations; multiple therapists may work with the same individual or same pair of family members; occasionally two family members (for example, father and son) may be left alone to work on their problems themselves. After the team has had an opportunity to discuss their findings at lunch—the family is also encouraged to talk together at this time—individual interviews resume but with switched interviewers (that is, the husband's interviewer in the morning may become the wife's interviewer in the afternoon, and vice versa). While the adolescent is being given psychological tests, joint sessions between the parents and their interviewers are held, as the team begins to close in on the dysfunctional aspects of the family's functioning that are being uncovered. At the end of the first day, the team and family reassemble for a group discussion of what they have learned.

The second day accelerates many of the first day's interviewing procedures, with family members likely to produce more emotionally charged responses to what is taking place. Overlapping interviews are more freely used; insights gained from one interview are shared in the next one. Factors interfering with family communication in general and intimate communication between the parents are likely to become the focus of interest. A final afternoon team/family conference is held, findings are reviewed, and specific recommendations made for dealing with "back-home problems." In some cases, an additional half day is needed. Before the family leaves, follow-up sessions several months later are arranged in order to evaluate the extent to which any gains made during the intensive two days are sustained (MacGregor, 1971).

During the course of two days, the team has examined the marital relationship closely and taken initial steps toward strengthening it. Parent/adolescent transactions are investigated, with the idea of clearing up clogged lines of authority. All members have undergone a powerful emotional experience and are oriented by the team to the future rather than the past. The team's solidarity, prior experiences with families, and sheer number have a positive impact on the family and its value system. More than simply providing insights, MIT aims to change the family from a relatively closed system to an open system conducive to growth. More open communication, greater acceptance of one another, clearer role differentiation between members, increased flexibility in attempting new ways of relating—especially to and by the disturbed adolescent—are all encouraged, so that family members can give up playing repetitive roles in a reverberating system and begin to explore new ways of growth.

FAMILY CRISIS THERAPY

Crisis intervention with individuals experiencing acute distress is characterized by being brief, promptly available, action more than insight oriented, and directed at here-and-now problems. As we saw in the previous discussion of Multiple Impact Therapy, crises occur not only to individuals but also to their families. Divorce, death, an alcoholic parent, a runaway or delinquent child, a heavy drug-using adolescent, and so on may cause multiple problems and stresses for all the family. Family crisis therapy, designed for emergency situations, seeks to help the family resolve such crises through a process of systems change and to restore its functioning to its previous adaptational level. In some cases, immediate aid to the family on an outpatient basis may prevent the hospitalization of one or more of its members.

Family crisis therapy aims to help a distressed individual and his or her family to actively define the family systems crisis and then utilize the family's combined coping skills to deal with the present, as yet unresolved, situation. It is time limited (typically up to six sessions) and highly focused on the management of the current crisis and the prevention of future crises. The therapist redefines the presenting problem as one involving the entire family, the solution to which calls for all members as a group to contribute whatever they can to help.

The first extensive and systematic treatment of families in crisis came with the establishment of the Family Treatment Unit at the Colorado Psychiatric Hospital in 1964 (Langsley & Kaplan, 1968). This unit was set up to offer outpatient crisis therapy to families where one member, usually diagnosed as schizophrenic, would ordinarily be hospitalized. Part of the rationale employed was the belief that removing a disturbed person from the home and placing him or her in a hospital has two drawbacks: it scapegoats that person as the cause of all family problems, and it thereby helps the family to avoid those very problems that may have precipitated the crisis that led to the person's disturbed behavior. Instead, in this approach, families in acute crisis situations remain together, receiving intensive family therapy on an outpatient basis. Usually, family crisis therapy averages about three weeks in duration and includes five office visits and one home visit. The latter is especially valuable in observing family interactions and ways of functioning in a natural environment, in addition to strengthening the family's commitment, involvement, and belief that the hospital team cares (Langsley, Pittman, Machotka, & Flomenhaft, 1968).

As practiced by the Colorado group, family crisis therapy consists of seven overlapping steps: (1) the therapist is immediately available on being contacted by a family member, thus acknowledging the family's concern and current helplessness; (2) the therapist insists on involving the entire family; (3) the family's attention is focused on the specifics of the current crisis; (4) the identified patient typically begins to experience some relief from anxiety and disabling symptoms; (5) each family member gains awareness of what changes he or she must make in attitude or behavior to assist in solving the problem; (6) the specific crisis is resolved as family members negotiate as a group and change to cope with new responsibilities; and (7) termination, as the family group takes on the responsibilities for what will occur, rather than scapegoating a member (Pittman, 1973). If necessary, referral for long-term therapy may be made for the disturbed individual or the entire family.

In a carefully designed experiment on the effectiveness of family crisis therapy (FCT) in avoiding mental hospital admission, Langsley and associates (1968) responded to the request for immediate hospitalization of a family member by assigning alternate applicants either to the outpatient Family Treatment Unit or to the university psychiatric hospital. In the former group, the patient and his or her family were seen together for crisis therapy for six visits over a three-week period. The latter group of matched patients received customary hospital treatment—individual and group psychotherapy, drugs, participation in the hospital's therapeutic community—for an average stay of slightly less than a month. In addition, their families were seen separately from them by the hospital's psychiatric social worker. A follow-up study showed that the FCT patients were less likely to be hospitalized within six months following treatment than the hospitalized patients were to be rehospitalized. A later study (Langsley, Machotka, & Flomenhaft, 1971), comparing 150 FCT patients and 150 hospitalized patients 18 months after treatment, showed similar benefits for FCT patients, although the differences in hospitalization rates between the groups tended to decrease with time. At both the six- and eighteen-month checkpoints, if hospitalization became necessary, the FCT patients were likely to spend considerably less time in the hospitals than did their previously hospitalized counterparts. Apparently hospital treatment encourages further hospitalization. Family crisis therapy can be an effective preventive measure in avoiding hospitalization, returning patients and families to a functional level, and helping them manage future hazardous events.

If a crisis period is an optimum opportunity for positive behavioral changes and rearrangements in the relationships between family members, as we have indicated, then why not therapeutically induce a crisis as a way of helping families to break old dysfunctional patterns

FIGURE 8-1. Family coalitions frequently introduce stress into a family system, handicapping the functioning of individual members as well as the family as a whole. In this simulated family scene, the mother and younger daughter sit separately from the father and older daughter, suggesting a division within the family. Mother's whispered secret further strengthens her alliance with one child, while the other members appear to be out of touch with what is going on. Successful family therapy may produce role changes, clearer communication patterns, and a restructuring of the family organization. (Photo © by Bruce W. Talamon/ People Magazine.)

and learn new ones? Minuchin and Barcai (1972) suggest doing just that—deliberately causing temporary upheaval in a family by intervening in ways that will produce unstable situations that require change and the restructuring of the family organization. We saw an example of the technique in Chapter 7, when Minuchin urged the parents to insist that their anoretic daughter eat, forcing them to change their ways of dealing with one another in order to cope with the situation. Particularly in very rigid families with seriously ill anoretic girls, Minuchin (Minuchin, Rosman, & Baker, 1978) pits the patient against the parents, reframing the issue as one of control versus disobedience rather than one in which the adolescent is treated as an incompetent and ineffective person, too sick to help herself. Her refusal to eat is voluntary, Minuchin points out to the parents, aimed at frustrating and defeating them, rather than being an involuntary symptom over which she has no control. She has won over them, unless they mobilize together to deal with her rebelliousness. At the same time, he shows the adolescent that she is not helpless as she feared, but actually, through her symptoms, demonstrating considerable power. The family, now placed in a crisis situation, must develop new ways of responding. By precipitating the crisis, Minuchin has maneuvered them into a position where they must change. There is considerable clinical evidence (Doyle & Dorlac, 1978) to indicate that the entire family unit is most receptive to change, restructuring previously maladaptive coping patterns, while the crisis is in progress.

SOCIAL NETWORK INTERVENTION

Some family therapists choose to work in a troubled person's home, assembling that person's entire social network, including his or her nuclear family as well as friends, neighbors, work associates, significant persons from school, church, various social agencies and institutions—in short, the sum total of human relationships that are meaningful in his or her life. Brought together and led by a team of therapists (here called "network intervenors"), such a group of interrelated people has within itself the resources to develop creative solutions to that distressed individual's current predicaments, according to Speck and Attneave (1973). Moreover, these family therapists contend that much of the behaviors traditionally interpreted as symptoms of **mental illness** derive from feelings of alienation from just such relationships and resources.

Social network intervention (sometimes referred to as Network Therapy), which attempts to mobilize 40 to 50 people who are willing to come together in a crisis to be forged into a potent therapeutic force, is particularly appealing in an age of increasing depersonalization. Orginally developed from work with schizophrenics in their homes, network therapy is based on the assumption that there is significant disturbance in the schizophrenic's communication patterns with all members of his or her social network, not just within the nuclear family. Consequently, this approach works at tightening the person's network of relationships, intimately involving the entire group as much as possible in one another's lives. Speck and Rueveni (1969) see such networks as analogous to clans or tribal units; their major benefit derives from offering support, reassurance, and solidarity to their members. No longer limited to schizophrenics and their families, this technique may be used with equal ease with all varieties of dysfunctional behavior (for example, drug abuse, depression following a suicide attempt) labeled as "sick" by society. In each case, social network intervention attempts to foster an emotional climate of trust and openness as a prelude to constructive encounters between the participants.

In such an assembly, tribal-like bonds can be created or revived not only to cope with the current crisis but also to sustain and continue the process long after formal meetings with a team of therapists are terminated. Benefits are said (Speck & Attneave, 1973) to derive from the "network effect"—a spirited and euphoric group phenomenon (seen in peace marches, revival meetings, tribal healing ceremonies, and massive rock concerts, as well as in the seemingly dissimilar Lions Clubs' group singing) in which the group takes on an affiliative life of its own and experiences a sense of union and oneness that is somehow larger than what each participant contributes. In the case of social network intervention, under the influence of the "network effect," the members may focus more energy, more attention, and more reality testing on the tasks to be carried out than could any therapist alone during the same brief period of time.

Therapeutic intervention usually gets underway when the network intervention team redefines the troubled person's "symptoms" as a natural reaction to an inadequate social structure, rather than a sign of mental illness or the like. Presented to his or her nuclear family and those people who are daily intimates, the person's present predicaments are further defined into two or three specific issues (for example, helping that person find employment, make more and better friends, move out of the house) that are potentially resolvable. This close group is then encouraged to assemble its social network to meet with the intervention team (usually two to five professionals, sometimes enhanced by nonprofessional "network activists" who can help mobilize group action and organize its execution). Invited people are told that they are coming together to help the nuclear family in its crisis and that a team of intervenors will provide leadership, at least at the start. Although the number and length of meetings varies, six evening sessions, each four hours in duration, at one- to four-week intervals, is most common. In rare cases, the network intervenors may be limited to only one meeting in which to produce the therapeutic "network effect." More commonly, several sessions will occur, and the team of intervenors can meet regularly between sessions to plan their strategy.

The goal of network intervention is to capitalize on the power of the assembled network to shake up a rigidified system in order to allow changes in the family system. It is hoped that some new bonds will be strengthened and others, perhaps strangling, weakened. New perceptions of one another, the opening up of clearer channels of communication, the release of latent positive forces within the family and its larger social network—these are additional goals.

Each session typically proceeds through several distinct phases. After some informal milling around, with intervenors scattered throughout the group, a number of encounter group excercises (holding hands, vigorously jumping up and down, screaming out in unison) are employed as warm-up exercises, knitting the group together into a network. Called **retribalization** by Speck and Attneave (1973), this experience is intended to begin to create or revive tribal-like bonds so that the network can sustain the process of seeking solutions to the current family crises. As they reach the point of perceiving themselves as a connected, functioning organic unit, they start to formulate, with the team's help, what needs to be done and how to go about doing it. Conflicting viewpoints become apparent, as the network becomes polarized (for example, between generations). Subgroups may form inner and outer circles, each in turn listening to the other and presenting their own positions (as, for instance, on the use of drugs). The point here is to increase tension, eliciting greater interpersonal involvement and tribal commitment. As the energy developed by polarization starts to become focused, each subgroup trying hard to change the other, the team moves in to mobilize the energy and emotion and channel them constructively. Tasks to be dealt with are introduced by the team conductor, aided by other team members and activists. It is common at this time for the network to become temporarily depressed, stymied by the difficulties they foresee in their problem solving. Finally a breakthrough is achieved by the network, as the assigned task is accomplished. Exhausted but elated, the team and network terminate the session, experiencing a natural recovery period between meetings. At the conclusion of all meetings, the group of people have likely formed a cohesive system as a result of their shared experiences, often (although not necessarily) keeping the network alive long after the formal sessions with the intervention team have ceased. Remaining a supportive, caring, tribal-like group, they may become their own future agents of needed change.

VIDEOPLAYBACK

More an adjunctive technique in family therapy than a full-fledged form of treatment, the use of immediate videoplayback during a family session provides an opportunity both to capture objective behavioral data and to examine (and reexamine) it on the spot (Alger, 1976a). The advent of videotape equipment has also opened new avenues for training with and studying the demonstrations of master therapists as well as sessions recorded by beginning family therapists for later playback during supervisory sessions. In the latter case, the "instant replay" of an interview can provide the trainee with immediate feedback information as well as being available for later scrutiny. The therapy event itself becomes retrievable; the therapist, now removed from the emotional intensity of the family session, can see how he presents himself to the family, what he missed or overlooked, what characteristic patterns of communication appear and reappear, what facial expressions belied what member's verbal comments, and so on (Berger, 1978). Other students, viewing the tape, can learn a variety of styles and profit from each other's mistakes. For the purposes of this chapter, however, we will concentrate on the use of videoplayback as a supplement to various approaches (for example, couples groups, family crisis therapy) in family therapy.

Videotape playback is ideally suited for the practice of family therapy. Having become technically feasible at the time when communication theory and general systems theory were directing clinical attention to transactional patterns between people, videoplayback permitted a look at the behavioral sequences and signalling of responses that go on within a family system. By allowing family members to view their behavior immediately after it takes place, a corrective maneuver is introduced. Put another way, videoplayback adds negative feedback into the system, calling for a change in the ongoing system's direction and promoting the development of equilibrium and stability (Alger, 1973).

Technically, videotape's great advance over filming a family session is in providing immediate playback without any time lost for film processing. In a teaching hospital, clinic, or university, audiovisual personnel are usually available for taping a session from behind a one-way mirror. Later, the tape can be studied by a class and/or supervisor or shown to the family involved. An even more immediate effect is achieved when the therapist (or the cotherapist) operates a camera equipped with a zoom lens, focusing on one person and then another during the session, or perhaps sets the camera up with a wide angle lens covering the entire group, therapist(s) included. In this way, the tape can be stopped, reversed, put into a freeze-frame or in slow motion, for everyone to see. Facial expressions, gestures, changes in body positions, covering of the face, raised eyebrows, a flushed face—these are all nonverbal signals, forms of communication whose meaning becomes clarified when captured by the camera. At certain times, it may be advantageous to have different family members operate the camera, in order to give each a fresh perspective on how the family operates. What the member chooses to focus on (for example, angry expressions) or avoid (for example, one other member may be excluded) may be clinically meaningful.

Alger (1976a) invites each family member to ask for an instant replay during a session whenever he or she wants to review or clarify what just took place. Typically, he reports, family members may ask for two or three playback interventions in the course of an hour. In some cases various families may request that the same sequence be replayed several times during a session, as different members react to their own perceptions and memories of what just took place. With more sophisticated equipment, involving a second camera, it is even possible to use a splitscreen replay technique. While the entire family is interacting on the television screen, a closeup of one member may be inserted in one corner of the screen, showing the details of that person's responses. In working with couples,[2] each may be seen, side by side on the screen, during a replay. A camera may even be brought into the home to tape what transpires for later playback.

Self-confrontation is an inescapable property of viewing oneself on screen. One may deny having an angry feeling, insisting that all he did was sit and listen, but the camera has caught his sneer. Another member's hurt feelings, although denied, are exposed. It is not possible to pretend a transaction never took place when confronted with evidence to the contrary. As a result, the effects of gaining self-awareness visually ("I'll never forget seeing that look on my face when . . .") may outlast the effect of verbal insights and interpretations. Through videoplayback, family members are likely to gain a new perspective of family functioning, seeing individual behavior as arising within a particular family context. As video recorders become more economical and reliable, they should become an invaluable tool for the majority of family therapists.

[2]Most marital therapists are accustomed to hearing one or both spouses say "I wish I'd had a tape recorder when we had that argument last night. Then you would see how you started it by looking for a fight." A videoplayback recaptures the action and its context for greater clarification of exactly what took place.

FAMILY SCULPTURE AND CHOREOGRAPHY

A novel and graphic technique for visually depicting a family's structure as seen through the eyes of one of the family's members, family sculpture utilizes space as a metaphor for understanding a family's relationships. Developed by Duhl, Kantor, and Duhl (1973) at the Boston Family Institute, the technique attempts to translate systems theory into physical form by portraying family relationships in space and time. A family sculpture is a nonverbal arrangement of people placed in various physical positions in space to represent their relationship to one another at a particular moment in time. While it is frequently extremely difficult to verbalize one's personal perception of how his or her family members deal with one another (how intimate or distant, how loving or indifferent), sculpting allows the person to reveal his or her private view of invisible but meaningful boundaries, alliances, subsystems, roles, and so on. When each member has offered his or her sculpture, the conflict is removed from the verbal arena to the action mode, and the entire family plus the therapist are in a better position quickly to understand each member's experiences and perceptions. In this manner, the way is left open for choosing new options—new actions—for changing relationships.

Sculpting may be called for by the family therapist at any point in the diagnostic or therapeutic process. Preferably at least three or four persons should be present, although at times mobile furniture may pinch-hit for an absent member. The request for a member to sculpture is often timed to cut through excessive verbalizations or when a member (often an adolescent) sits silently through a session or cannot easily express his or her thoughts verbally. According to Simon (1972), adolescents usually make excellent sculptors because of their awareness of family truths and their relish in manipulating their parents. Younger children, on the other hand, typically lack the comprehension of what is really taking place in the family, and their parents are often too anxious about the possible ensuing loss of dignity to participate fully themselves. Once the ice is broken by the first presentation, however, all are likely to want a turn at sculpting in order to present their points of view.

Basically, each member is requested to arrange the bodies of the entire family in space as he or she perceives their relationship to one another either at present or at a specific point in the past. Who is designed as domineering, meek and submissive, loving and touching, belligerent, benevolent, clinging, and so on, and how they relate to one another immediately becomes apparent for all to witness in this living tableau. The sculptor is invited to explain the creation, and a lively debate between members may follow. The adolescent boy who places his parents at opposite ends of the family group while he and his brothers and sisters are huddled together in the center conveys a great deal more about his views of the workings of the family system than he would probably be able to state in words. By the same token, his father's sculpture—placing himself apart from all others, including his wife—may reveal his sense of loneliness, isolation, and rejection by his family. The mother may present herself as a confidante of her daughter but left out by the males in the family, and so forth for all members present. Nonverbally, without emotional outbursts or intellectualizations, they have openly portrayed their various views of the family's difficulties. Their actions have spoken louder than could any words, often revealing to others for the first time what each had felt but never expressed before. As sculptures are repeated at various points during family therapy, all become aware of changing perceptions and therapeutic gain.

Family choreography (Papp, 1976) is an outgrowth of family sculpture, so named because the sculpture moves to show the shifting transactional patterns within the family (see Figure 8-2). Choreography is a method for actively intervening in the family, realigning relationships, creating new patterns, and changing the system. While fam-

FIGURE 8-2. In this simulation of a family choreography session, therapist Papp (rear) observes as a mother creates a tableau to illustrate her perception of her family's relationship to her. (Copyright 1978, by Newsweek, Inc.)

ily members seldom surprise each other by what they say—in most families the pattern of verbal exchange is all too predictable—they may be surprised by what they choreograph. Alliances, triangles, and shifting emotional currents are all projected by the family movement. Choreography may help a family to physically retrace old interactive patterns and create new ones. An entrenched vicious cycle within a family, dramatized through movement in the therapist's office, may be replayed with alternative ways of dealing with one another. Now experienced differently by the entire family, under the direction of the therapist, the newly enacted change may be made easier to recreate at home.

CONJOINT SEX THERAPY

Although not, strictly speaking, a form of family therapy, the successful treatment of sexual dysfunction may be so significant to family life overall, by correcting a disharmonious aspect of marriage, that in our opinion it deserves inclusion here. Probably the most promising therapeutic work has been developed at the Reproductive Biology Research Foundation in St. Louis under the direction of Masters and Johnson (1970). This is essentially a rapid treatment program that relies heavily on behavior-therapy techniques, and the procedures pioneered there have now been incorporated into numerous sex-therapy-clinic programs that are being offered throughout the United States. Two outstanding features of this program are its brevity (generally two weeks) and its proven high rate of success for certain types of sexual problems.

A basic assumption in the Masters and Johnson approach is that there is no such thing as an uninvolved partner in a relationship in which some form of sexual inadequacy exists. Consequently, husband and wife are always treated conjointly, to emphasize that any dysfunction is a marital-unit problem rather than one that belongs to only one partner. Each couple is seen by a team of cotherapists that consists of one man and one woman, preferably with one member coming from the biological sciences and one from the behavioral disciplines. The dual-sex team is designed to avoid potential misinterpretation by the therapist that is due to male or female bias, perhaps because Masters and Johnson believe that neither sex can ever fully understand the other's sexual experiences. The two-week program of daily sessions begins with an extensive sexual history-taking—involving not only chronological sexual experiences, but, more importantly, sexually oriented values, attitudes, feelings, expectations, and so on. Next, a medical history is taken and each partner is given a thorough physical examination. On the third day, the cotherapists and the marital partners meet to review the accrued clinical material and to begin to relate individual and marital histories to present sexual dysfunctions. During the next several days, the therapists concentrate on giving the couple instructions in "sensate focus"—that is, learning to touch and explore each other's bodies and learning what each other's sensate areas are, but without feeling any pressure for sexual performance or orgasm. Regular roundtable meetings that include both therapists and both marital partners during this period attempt to deal with either partner's discomforts, guilt feelings, or apprehensions. Procedures that are aimed at teaching both partners to work together on the specific sexual dysfunction occupy the remaining time.

According to Masters and Johnson, a primary reason for sexual dysfunction is that the participant(s) is critically watching (they refer to it as "spectatoring") his or her own sexual performance instead of abandoning himself or herself to the giving and receiving of erotic pleasure with a partner. In order to enjoy fully what is occurring, Masters and Johnson point out that it is necessary to suspend all such distracting thoughts or anxieties about being evaluated (or evaluating oneself) for sexual performance. Kaplan (1974) goes further, distinguishing a variety of immediate causes of sexual dysfunction in a couple attempting intercourse (sexual ignorance, fear of failure, demand for performance, excessive need to please one's partner, failure to communicate openly about sexual feelings and experiences). In addition, she points out that there may be various intrapsychic conflicts (for example, early sexual trauma, guilt and shame, repressed sexual thoughts and feelings) within one or both partners, hampering a satisfying sexual experience. Finally, Kaplan cites a third set of psychological determinants of sexual dysfunction, namely those arising from the relationship. Here she includes various forms of marital discord, lack of trust, power struggles between partners, and efforts to sabotage any pleasure from the experience. Any one or combination of these problems or conflicts may lead to distressing sexual symptoms (for example, impotence or premature ejaculation in a male, nonorgasmic [frigid] responses in a female) that threaten a marriage by heightening tensions and that may eventually lead to marriage dissolution.

Unlike Masters and Johnson, who require participating couples to go off together to St. Louis for two weeks of daily residential treatment, Kaplan treats couples conjointly on an outpatient basis once or twice per week. No time limit is placed on treatment; the program terminates when the couple achieve good sexual functioning (that is, when the presenting symptom is eliminated) and there are indications that the changes are more or less permanent. One therapist, rather than two as in Masters and Johnson's approach, treats the couple. In

Kaplan's case, she uses a combination of psychoanalytic and behavioral theories and techniques, assigns couples various sexual tasks (for example, taking turns stimulating or "pleasuring" each other's erotic areas, free of the demand for orgasm or coitus) to practice at home, and generally requires six to fifteen visits for successful treatment.

New techniques of sex therapy, often behavioral in nature (see LoPiccolo & LoPiccolo, 1978) continue to proliferate. Unlike most psychotherapeutic undertakings that have loose or vague criteria for achieving success (for example, patient is happier, more productive, feels more fulfilled), sex therapy is considered successful only if the presenting symptom in the marital unit is eliminated. Masters and Johnson have reported a remarkably high overall success rate despite their stringent criterion of success—no recurrence within five years. Their greatest success (97.8%) has come with treating premature ejaculation in men; for secondary impotence (losing the capacity to achieve or maintain an erection long enough to engage in intercourse) the success rate, while lower (73.7%), is nevertheless extraordinarily high compared to other therapeutic endeavors. Similarly in women, the comparable rate of 83.4% for primary orgasmic dysfunction (never having reached a climax) is very impressive. Kaplan reports similar results for rapidly relieving a wide variety of sexual dysfunctions. As she points out, however, while sex therapy seems to constitute a major advance in our understanding and treatment of a couple's sexual difficulties, it is no panacea for a marriage that has already failed.

SUMMARY

We have considered seven approaches or special techniques of family therapy. *Multiple Family Therapy*, originally developed from working with hospitalized schizophrenic patients and their families, is a form of group therapy in which several families meet regularly to share problems and help one another in the problem solving process. A variation of this technique is the marital couples group, which meets to discuss common marital problems and to help find solutions together. In *Multiple Impact Therapy*, a family in crisis, often because of the delinquent behavior of an adolescent member, is seen together over a two-day period for intensive interaction with a team of mental health professionals. Although essentially diagnostic, a number of therapeutic guidelines are introduced by the staff, who arrange for follow-up studies with the family before they depart in order to evaluate the extent of any therapeutic gains made. Another crisis-oriented approach, *Family Crisis Therapy*, is a time-limited and highly focused technique for mobilizing a family's coping skills to deal with a psychological emergency situation, thereby avoiding psychiatric hospitalization of a family member.

Conducted in the patient's home, *Social Network Intervention* (Network Therapy) brings together family, friends, neighbors, and significant others to aid in the patient's treatment and rehabilitation. The aim is to capitalize on the power of the assembled group to induce change in a dysfunctional family system. *Videoplayback* is an adjunctive therapeutic technique for allowing families to take a look at their own behavioral patterns by videorecording their family therapy session and immediately presenting them with what signals, messages, and transactions have just transpired. This negative feedback and self-confrontation facilitates change.

In *Family Sculpting*, various members are asked to portray in space and time how they see relationships within the family by arranging people in various physical positions vis-a-vis one another. An outgrowth of this nonverbal technique is family choreography, in which movement and interactive patterns within the family are physically recreated and thus become open to examination and possible change. *Conjoint Sex Therapy* is a rapid-treatment program, involving both marital partners, that aims at alleviating problems of sexual dysfunction in an effort to strengthen a marriage by correcting a disharmonious and thus a possibly destructive aspect of the relationship.

Part Four

TRAINING
AND EVALUATION

9

LEARNING, TEACHING, AND EVALUATING FAMILY THERAPY

We have noted a number of times in the previous chapters that preparing to become a family therapist calls for a discontinuous learning experience for those clinicians trained in one-to-one psychotherapy. One must learn to see all behavior, including the manifestation of symptoms in an individual, in its proper context, namely as a result of social or interpersonal sequences. The family system, rather than the symptomatic person, becomes the therapeutic unit for achieving change. The family therapist becomes a part of that system, not some outside healer as in many forms of individual treatment. The focus of therapy is on the present transactions within the family, rather than a description or recounting of the past. The goal is to change the family's interactive patterns, not simply to interpret or explain them.

When training a therapist to adopt a family focus, one frequently meets with resistance for several reasons: the therapist must stop seeing the identified patient as a victim to be supported; he or she must give up being the hub of interactions between family members; and he or she must give up the customary role of outsider and become a participant in the family social system, being careful to avoid entangling alliances. There is great risk that he or she may be drawn into the family members' ongoing relationships and, if not careful, may begin to adopt the family's myths about themselves (for example, jinxed, exploited, powerless) and their labels for individual family members (for example, stupid, selfish, unambitious) (Goldenberg, 1973b).

How best to train family therapists will concern us in the first section of this, the final chapter. Special problems and issues in family therapy will then be considered. In the last section, we will take up the findings of outcome research on the effectiveness of family therapy and make some closing comments on the future of family therapy.

BECOMING A FAMILY THERAPIST

A number of mental health and related disciplines—clinical psychology, psychiatry, psychiatric social work, psychiatric nursing, various forms of counseling, the human services—are apt to offer direct services to troubled or distressed families. In many cases, having previously learned therapeutic skills for working with individuals, practitioners in these disciplines may find themselves, after having agreed to gather a family group together, simply treating individual members separately but in a family context. As Haley (1970) has observed (see Table 9-1), many such therapists continue to perceive individual psychopathology as their central concern while acknowledging the context of family life in which such psychopathology developed. Others may find it easier to shift their perspective to a larger canvas, thus viewing individual intrapsychic conflicts to be secondary to improving overall family functioning. In either case, as Skynner (1976) reminds us, the passive, neutral, nonjudgmental, uninvolved position developed with so much care in conventional individual psychotherapy has to be overcome. Family therapists must become involved in the family's interpersonal processes (without losing balance or independence), flexibly supporting and nurturing at one point and challenging and demanding at another, keeping in mind (but not overidentifying with) members of different ages, moving swiftly in and out of emotional involvements, and never losing track of family interactions and transaction patterns.

While a considerable body of data exists concerning family life, we have seen that there is as yet neither a single theory of family process or set of intervention techniques for helping distressed families. Learning family therapy requires a theoretical understanding (personality development; family concepts, including cross-cultural studies; group dynamics; systems theory; and so on) and, probably more important, firsthand contact with family units for which the trainee takes responsibility. Since therapy is such a personal encounter, the trainee can learn to do it best by doing it, preferably under supervision. Each must find his or her style of interacting with families and his or her orientation to what makes for successful therapy. Most authorities would probably agree with Mendelsohn and Ferber's (1972) assessment that training is best done in small groups (five to fifteen) of trainees who meet regularly with a supervisor or two over a prolonged period of time, such as a year. Working therapeutically with families within a framework of **didactic** and supervisory experiences seems to represent the ideal learning climate.

TABLE 9-1. A Comparison between Individual-Oriented and Family-Oriented Family Therapy

Individual-Oriented	*Family-Oriented*
1. Family therapy is one of many methods of treatment.	1. Family therapy is a new orientation to viewing human problems.
2. The individual's psychopathology is the focus of study and treatment; the family is seen as a stress factor.	2. The disordered family system needs some family member to express its psychopathology.
3. The identified patient is the victim of family strife.	3. The identified patient contributes to and is an essential part of family strife.
4. The family is a collection of individuals behaving on the basis of past experiences with each other.	4. The present situation is the major causal factor, since current problems must be currently reinforced if they continue to exist.
5. Diagnosis and evaluation of the family problem should precede intervention.	5. Immediate action-oriented intervention takes place at the first session, which is usually a time of family crisis, when the family is ripe for change.
6. The therapist is an observer evaluating the family's problems.	6. The therapist is a part of the context of treatment; his or her active participation affects the family system.
7. The therapist brings out clients' feelings and attitudes toward each other; he or she uses interpretation to show them what they are expressing.	7. The therapist uses fewer interpretations; he or she is interested in enhancing positive aspects of the relationships.
8. The therapist talks to one person at a time; family members talk largely to him rather than to each other.	8. Family members talk to each other, not the therapist; all members are urged to participate.
9. The therapist takes sides in family conflict, supporting one member (for example, a child, a schizophrenic).	9. The therapist avoids being caught up in factional struggles in the family.
10. Family therapy is a technique for gathering additional information about individuals in the family.	10. Individual psychological problems are social problems involving the total ecological system, including the social institutions in which the family is embedded.

Adapted from "Family Therapy," by J. Haley, *International Journal of Psychiatry*, 1970, *9*, 233–242. Reprinted by permission.

What are the learning objectives of a family therapy training program? Goals range from an emphasis on the trainee's personal growth and development to programs that focus primarily on acquiring skills and competencies (Liddle & Halpin, 1978). As an example of the former, Constantine (1976) has described the training offered members of different mental health professions at Boston State Hospital, where supervisors strive to "create an environment conducive to growth and learning" (p. 373). The two-year curriculum in this combined cognitive and experientially oriented program is designed to gradually prepare the trainee to work with families, with nonpathological families as the major focus.

At the other extreme, Cleghorn and Levin (1973), more behavioral in outlook, set goals of training that are more strictly cognitively based. They attempt to teach trainees specific skills and particular ways of intervening in a dysfunctional family system. They distinguish three sets of learning objectives: perceptual, conceptual, and executive. Table 9-2 offers their checklist of whether the trainee has de-

TABLE 9-2. Checklist of Basic Objectives in Training Family Therapists

Perceptual and Conceptual	*Executive Skills*
1. Recognize and describe interactions and transactions.	1. Develop collaborative working relationship with family.
2. Describe a family systematically; include assessment of current problem.	2. Establish therapeutic contract.
	3. Stimulate transactions.
3. Recognize effect of family group on oneself.	4. Clarify communications.
	5. Help family members label effects of interactions.
4. Recognize and describe the experience of being taken into the family system.	6. Extricate oneself from the family system.
5. Recognize one's idiosyncratic reactions to family members.	7. Focus on a problem.

From "Training Family Therapists by Setting Learning Objectives," by J. M. Cleghorn and S. Levin, *American Journal of Orthopsychiatry*, 1973, 43 (3), 439–446. Copyright © 1973 by the American Orthopsychiatric Association, Inc. Reproduced by permission.

veloped the basic observational or *perceptual skills* (recognizing interactions and their meaning and effect on the family members and the family system), *conceptual skills* (formulating the family's problems in systems terms), and therapeutic or *executive skills* (extracting and altering the family's sequences of transactions) to be potentially effective with ordinarily functional families who have been exposed to unusual (and presumably temporary) stress. Having developed these basic competencies, the trainee should be able to deal with families exposed to situational problems (for example, shared grief over a death of a family member), helping to mobilize the family's natural reparative devices in working toward a solution. Essentially, the therapist's role here is in facilitating constructive problem-solving communication. A great deal more training is required before the therapist can deal successfully with families with chronic fixed, rigid, and unproductive problem-solving transactional patterns. As Table 9-3 suggests,

TABLE 9-3. Checklist of Advanced Objectives in Training Family Therapists

Perceptual and Conceptual	*Executive Skills*
Regarding the Family	1. Redefine the therapeutic contract periodically.
1. Conceive of symptomatic behaviors as a function of the family system.	2. Demonstrate relationship between transactions and the symptomatic problem.
2. Assess family's capacity to change.	3. Be a facilitator of change, not a member of the group.
3. Recognize that change in a family is more threatening than recognition of a problem.	4. Develop a style of interviewing consistent with one's personality.
4. Define key concepts operationally.	5. Take control of maladaptive transactions by:
Regarding Himself	a. Stopping a sequence and labeling the process.
1. Deal with feelings about being a change agent, not just a helper.	b. Making confrontations in the context of support.
2. Become aware of how one's personal characteristics influence one's becoming a family therapist.	6. Work out new adaptive behaviors and rewards for them.
3. Assess the effectiveness of one's interventions and explore alternatives.	7. Relinquish control of the family when adaptive patterns occur.
4. Articulate rewards to be gained by family members making specific changes.	

From "Training Family Therapists by Setting Learning Objectives," by J. M. Cleghorn and S. Levin, *American Journal of Orthopsychiatry*, 1973, 43 (3), 439–446. Copyright © 1973 by the American Orthopsychiatric Association, Inc. Reproduced by permission.

being an agent of change requires different skills than being a helper to distressed families. Here the trainee must learn to catalyze interactions, understand and label relationship messages, and confront family members with what they are doing to each other. The family must be challenged to find new solutions, to utilize its strength as a family in order to take the responsibility for change in its members. Finally, the advanced therapist must be able to judge the effectiveness of his or her interventions and to alter the approach whenever necessary to aid the family to work together more efficiently and with less distress.

TRAINING AIDS

While the following pedagogic techniques in training family therapists are discussed separately, the reader should be aware that several almost certainly go on simultaneously in any training program. Trainees must do more than take a course in family therapy; as in learning any skill (typing, roller skating, driving a car, or lovemaking) practice and firsthand experience are necessary. Reading about families and family therapy, observing teachers demonstrate work with families, seeing films and videotapes of eminent family therapists at work all add to abstract knowledge, but in the last analysis the trainee learns experientially—by treating families.

Didactic Course Work

Lectures, group discussion, demonstrations, assigned readings, and role-playing are included here. Typically, such courses, as for example at the Albert Einstein College of Medicine in New York City (Sander & Beels, 1970), examine available theories and the existing scientific evidence for a variety of clinical intervention techniques. Often such courses are team taught by two supervisors; in this way, they may share the lead in discussion groups and one may comment to the trainees on what is taking place as the other demonstrates behind a one-way mirror with a real or simulated family. In some cases, formal course work follows the actual experience of working with families, in order to avoid premature conceptualizations by trainees before they have had firsthand contact conducting family therapy sessions. In this way, they may be in a better position to integrate family therapy concepts into their understanding of family process (Shapiro, 1975). More often, perhaps, some initial lectures, assigned readings, and demonstrations precede permitting trainees to work with families; this is done so that the student will be better prepared and thus less likely to be overwhelmed by the amount and richness of clinical material gathered from the family interview. Following these initial didactic presentations, trainees begin their clinical work involving evaluation and ongoing treatment while continuing to attend the seminar (Constantine, 1976).

Seminars may be conducted in an informal way, sharing experiences, or in a highly structured fashion. Bodin (1969a) has offered a useful training guide to the literature in family therapy though the 1960s, and more recent books of readings in family therapy (for example, Erickson & Hogan, 1972; Guerin, 1976), as well as recent issues of such journals as *Family Process, Family Therapy, Family Coordinator, Jour-*

nal of Marriage and the Family, Journal of Family Counseling, Journal of Sex and Marital Therapy, International Journal of Family Therapy, or the *Journal of Marital and Family Therapy* (formerly the *Journal of Marriage and Family Counseling*), provide more up to date references. In addition, a number of authorities in the field, such as Minuchin (1974a) and Bowen (1978), have presented their work in book form. Finally, it is often a worthwhile learning experience to read verbatim accounts of family therapy sessions (for example, Haley & Hoffman, 1967; Papp, 1977), following step-by-step what took place as master therapists put some of their theoretical writings into practice.

Videotapes

Clearly one of the greatest boons to teaching family therapy, the advent of videotape has opened new avenues of development in therapy (see Chapter 8), training, and research. Taping by supervisors of initial family sessions may be done prior to particular courses, for presentation to students at a later date. In this way, students have a basis for noting changes in family interactive patterns as they watch "live" demonstrations of subsequent sessions with the same family (Bodin, 1969b). Tape libraries of family sessions from initial interview to termination and follow-up can be developed and will be particularly valuable for students to view at their leisure or when confronted with a particular set of technical problems or therapeutic impasses. The student may watch his or her own progressive proficiency by comparing tapes made early and late in training.

Postsession viewing ("instant replay") of a family session becomes possible by capturing the interview on videotape. Instead of reporting verbally what took place to the supervisor and/or class (with its inherent risk of unreliable memories, defensiveness, distortions, impressionistic descriptions, and fear of exposing mistakes), the trainee's tape is played. Subtle nuances, perhaps not seen during the session, may become more obvious while being viewed. The interplay of verbal and nonverbal messages and interactions may suddenly become clearer. In all cases, the trainee confronts his or her own behavior with a family, and the other viewers provide additional corrective feedback information. The tape can be played and replayed, over and over again, preserved and retrieved for further study and analysis (Berger, 1978). Trainees learn from each other's errors as well as successful procedures.

Clinical research has benefited greatly from videotaping family therapy sessions. With family interaction no longer real only the moment it occurred, then immediately and irretrievably lost, videotaping

FIGURE 9-1. Videotaping family therapy sessions preserves these events for research study. This psychologist is rating certain family interactive patterns along previously determined empirical categories in an effort to clarify what distinguishes the functioning levels of different families. (Photo © by Bruce W. Talamon/People Magazine.)

allows researchers (see Figure 9-1) to examine and score family interactive patterns. Out of the clinical complexity that treatment of a family reveals, meaningful variables may be extracted and subjected to experimental research (Framo, 1972). For example, the research on optimal family functioning (Lewis, Beavers, Gossett, & Phillips, 1976) and on moderately and severely dysfunctional families (Beavers, 1977), reported in Chapter 2, both based their conclusions on data obtained by videotape. In both cases, judges trained to measure various systems variables rated families (see, for example, Figure 2-5) after observing them perform a variety of assigned tasks as a group. These judgments helped determine the differences in interactive patterns between families at various levels of functioning.

Marathons

A **marathon** is an intensive, uninterrupted group-therapy experience, sometimes extending over several days, that focuses on the ongoing process of encounter among group members. Often used as a therapeutic device, in order to intensify and accelerate a therapeutic experience by building up group pressure over time, the technique has been adapted by Goldenberg, Stier, and Preston (1975) as a family therapy teaching device.

As an extension of their group supervision seminar on family therapy at the UCLA Neuropsychiatric Institute, these clinicians reasoned that another dimension might be added to the learning experience if they, together with their ten trainees and their client families, participated in one extended group therapy session. The students were all advanced trainees who had taken part in the seminar over a year's time. Through viewing each other's videotaped sessions over that extended period, they were familiar with each other's client families. The six-hour, multiple-family marathon was led by the supervisors, who hoped to provide a useful training experience through their modeling behavior. No attempt was made during the marathon to identify separate families; the various children and adults (supervisors, trainees, parents) intermingled freely. Various role-playing, psychodrama, and encounter group techniques took place throughout the session. A comparison of student responses to a premarathon and postmarathon questionnaire revealed that most perceived the experience as a valuable training aid. Most changed their views of the family with whom they had worked previously (for example, "I now recognize that they have the capacity to listen and understand another's viewpoint"). All ten trainees indicated a better and more self-confident self-image as a family therapist following the marathon session. Several acknowledged that through certain self-revelations they personally had discovered new aspects of themselves.

Live Supervision

An effective teaching program in family therapy must meld relevant theory with profitable practical experience. The trainee must be given an opportunity to gain firsthand contact with families (and an ever wider variety of families as his or her clinical skills and competencies develop) as well as exposure to a broad range of family therapy techniques. However, clinical experience is of limited value without careful, proper supervision, especially during the early stages of training. Such supervision, by highly competent and experienced family therapists who also have teaching skills, may take a number of forms: reviewing videotapes of trainee sessions with families, either in a trainee/supervisor conference or in a small group session with several trainees and a supervisor (Stier & Goldenberg, 1975); **cotherapy,** in which a supervisor and a trainee together work with a family (Skynner, 1976); observing trainee's work through a one-way mirror (Haley,

1976); continuous case conferences during which a trainee will present his or her client family for several class sessions; group marathons, as described in the preceding section; and live or "on the spot" supervision, in which the supervisor stays in direct communication with the trainee during a session (Glick & Kessler, 1974).

Live supervision (Montalvo, 1973) introduces a relatively new concept to the supervisory process, namely that someone actively guides the therapist while at work by providing corrective feedback to what the therapist is doing. The person supervising watches the session behind a one-way mirror, with or without a group or trainees, and intrudes on the session to offer suggestions to the therapist at the very moment that the action is taking place, in order to help the trainee get disentangled from recurring, nonproductive sequences with the family and recover control and direction of the session. The supervisor and supervisee agree beforehand that the former may feel free to call the latter out of the therapy room or the latter may leave the session for consultation if he or she so wishes. (This technique is frequently employed by Minuchin[1] and others, such as Montalvo, at the Philadelphia Child Guidance Clinic.) Both must feel comfortable with the procedure; the trainee must accept the supervisor's right to intervene if the latter believes a disservice will be done to the family if what is occurring continues, and the supervisor must accept the trainee's right to question or challenge the suggestion and ignore it as he or she sees fit. In a sense, the supervisor, as a coach on the sidelines, introduces feedback into the new ongoing system, which now is composed of the student therapist and the family.

A basic assumption in live supervision is that any family can direct the therapist away from his or her function as a change agent, maneuvering the therapist into behaving with the family in ways that reinforce the very patterns that brought them to family therapy. The more experienced supervisor, not caught up in the action, may be able to help the supervisee correct such missteps before they go too far, rather than waiting to repair the damage at a later session. It is usually arranged before the session that the supervisor will not interfere unless it is considered essential to do so; disagreement regarding a particular theory or therapeutic approach is not sufficient grounds for the intrusion. Another important rule is that the trainee is in charge of the family session, so that the supervisor's suggestion may be treated only as a suggestion and not a directive that must be followed.

Perhaps even more common than walking in or out of a session is the supervisory technique of communicating with the trainee by

---

[1]Minuchin frequently goes one step further, entering the therapy room to act as a consultant to the therapist-trainee; he may or may not stay for the remainder of the session with the family (Malcolm, 1978). His rationale is similar to that used in his structural therapy, namely that change occurs through a reshaping or reframing experience.

telephone or earphone (a "bug" in the therapist's ear). As practiced at the Family Therapy Institute in Washington, D.C. (Haley, 1976) and the Mental Research Institute in Palo Alto (Watzlawick, Weakland, & Fisch, 1974), the supervisor, again watching behind a one-way mirror, may call the trainee during a session for a brief conversation. Haley cautions against the overuse of this technique, contending that the supervisor should adopt a "call with reluctance" philosophy, use the telephone (so the therapist is not drawn into two conversations at once) rather than the "bug," and offer only one or two very specific suggestions before hanging up the phone.

The advantages in live supervision lie in the timeliness of supervisor questions or suggestions, on-the-spot relevance, and the reduction of possible distortions by the trainee who, in the past, reported later to the supervisor on what had taken place during the session. With live supervision, the therapist/trainee can make corrections as he or she goes along. Probably the major disadvantage is the added stress felt by the student being observed. In addition, the student therapist may become too dependent on supervisory interventions, the intrusions may be disruptive to the therapeutic process, and they may interfere with the therapist's evolvement of his or her own style (Liddle & Halpin, 1978). Some sense of confidentiality may be jeopardized in this technique if the family knows (as they must be told) that they are being observed. Finally, as Whitaker (1976), a foe of live supervision, notes, this technique tends to make the supervisee less self-confident and more reliant on following a technical method.

Despite these objections, authorities such as Haley (1976) consider this technique the most effective form of supervision. He notes that in the past, all that was revealed about a session was what the therapist chose to reveal, relying on notes taken during or immediately following a therapeutic session. With the introduction of audiotapes, 25 years ago or so, the supervisor could at least learn what was actually said. Videotapes revealed both words and movement, but still did not provide guidance at the time the student most needed it—in the act of interviewing. Live supervision protects the families from incompetence while teaching inexperienced therapists how to do therapy at the very moment they need to know.

Films

Films showing master therapists at work with real patients came into general use in the 1950s, as the taboos against revealing the privacy of the therapeutic relationship began to recede. In the years since, a number of films on a variety of techniques have been distributed. Gladfelter (1972) counted 62 films available in the area of group and family therapy alone, and since his compilation the list has undoubt-edly doubled at least. Together with videotapes of real therapy ses-sions, films now play a significant part in training family therapists.

Films give the viewer an awareness of the actual processes by which therapists and patients communicate. In a well made film, the trainee feels a part of the interactions taking place. Family therapy films in particular rely on cinema verité techniques, entering into the multiple transactions going on simultaneously within a family. There the verbal—and especially the nonverbal—elements of family commu-nication become more evident. In one classic set of eight films, the Hillcrest Family Series (available through the Psychological Cinema Register at Pennsylvania State University), Ackerman, Whitaker, Jack-son, and Bowen conduct independent assessment interviews with the same family and then comment, on separate films, about their views of the dynamics of the family situation with a therapist who has been working with the family. Satir illustrates her therapeutic techniques with a simulated family in a film entitled *Target Five*, in which four forms of manipulation within a family are considered (see pages 117–118) and then the family is seen engaging in "actualizing" behavior together. This film is available from Psychological Films in Santa Ana, California. Kempler demonstrates, in a series of films available from the Kempler Institute in Newport Beach, California, his experiential form of family therapy showing entire sessions with a variety of real families and kinds of family problems.

Films and videotapes can now be obtained from several institu-tions in addition to those listed above. The Ackerman Institute for Family Therapy in New York, the Boston Family Institute, the Mental Research Institute in Palo Alto, the Philadelphia Child Guidance Cen-ter, as well as the Eastern Pennsylvania Psychiatric Institute, also in Philadelphia, are just some of the more well-known places that have established film libraries, where these materials may be purchased or rented. Most insist that their films and tapes be shown only to restrict-ed audiences made up of students or professionals in the field of fam-ily therapy.

Looking at Your Own Family

Just as individual psychotherapy or psychoanalysis was consid-ered highly desirable or even mandatory for therapists in training 25 years ago, so Bowen (1975) has suggested family therapy for his stu-dents and their spouses since the early 1960s. Similar in nature to guiding family members in therapy through "family voyages" in or-der to differentiate themselves from their families of origin, Bowen, serving as "coach," expects his trainees to make similar journeys in an effort to free themselves of remaining unresolved conflicts from their families.

As we noted in Chapter 7, Bowen believes personal maturation occurs as the individual differentiates himself or herself from the "undifferentiated family ego mass" while remaining in contact with one's own family. In an unsigned statement ("Towards," 1972) attributed to Bowen, the author openly and in detail describes his personal struggle to achieve a differentiation of self from his family of origin. Without achieving this, Bowen argues that family therapists may unknowingly be triangled into family conflicts within their client families, much as they were as children in their own family, perhaps overidentifying with one family member or currently projecting onto others their own unresolved difficulties from earlier in life. In general, the therapist is in danger of falling prey to the client family's effort to resist change and retain homeostasis. Family therapists need to get in touch with and be free of their own "internalized" family, so that unfinished business from the past does not intrude on current dealings with client families.

Guerin and Fogarty (1972), both former students of Bowen, now supervising and training family therapists, openly discuss with students their experiences in current relationships with their own families. Their effort to achieve their own differentiation is meant to serve as a model for trainees to study their own families and to be equally self-disclosing in the supervisory relationship. Fogarty in particular sees no difference between treatment, teaching, living in one's own family, or one's professional life; triangles, fusions, distances, and so on occur in each, and to understand them in one's own family is to learn best what these concepts really mean in client families.

COTHERAPY: THE USE OF THERAPEUTIC TEAMWORK

Originally created in order to include a trainee in a therapeutic session for teaching purposes, cotherapy—the simultaneous involvement of two therapists in the treatment setting—has been employed successfully in working with individuals, groups, and families (Rubinstein & Weiner, 1967). Whitaker (1967), for example, routinely used a cotherapist in working with individual schizophrenic patients long before doing so with families; today he is perhaps the leading exponent of using a therapeutic team for training family therapists as well as for family treatment.

Cotherapy has some obvious training advantages. The trainee has an opportunity to learn a distinctive approach at close range and to see an expert model in action, without having the full or even the major responsibility for the family. The trainee has the added benefit of seeing the supervisor as a real person who makes mistakes at times, doesn't always understand all that is happening, and isn't always loving—all very reassuring to a beginning family therapist who has felt exactly the same way at times about himself or herself! The supervisor as cotherapist can provide the supervisee with an opportunity to try creative interventions with the family, assured of skillful support and rescue when trouble arises, as it inevitably does. Family therapy is taught as a personal experience in this way. The *process* is kept in focus, rather than discussions of abstract theoretical issues, as in much supervision (Napier & Whitaker, 1972).

As a training device, cotherapy is not without its pitfalls, both real and potential. The trainee may become too identified with the supervisor, especially if the latter's style is colorful and dramatic, so that he or she merely mimics without developing a style more personally authentic and consistent with his or her own personality. Overdependency may also become a problem. As Haley (1976), a critic of cotherapy, points out, cotherapy with a more experienced person may simply teach the student to sit back and not take responsibility for the case, as he or she must ultimately learn to do. Haley prefers live supervision behind a one-way mirror, so that the trainee can receive immediate assistance whenever needed. He argues that cotherapy is set up to support uncertain therapists and not to aid families.

Mutual support is indeed a reason often advanced by family therapists who prefer working as a team. Whitaker, for example (Napier & Whitaker, 1972), contends that knowing a cotherapist is there allows him to become involved with a family in a way and at a level he would not dare if he worked alone. Because he equates being a therapist with the pursuit of personal growth, he may expose a great deal about his own fantasies and free associations to the family, knowing his cotherapist remains a backup person, tied to reality and ready to step in if that should become necessary. That is, as one therapist becomes emotionally involved with the family, the other may wait silently, observing, less involved and more objective than the more active teammate (Napier & Whitaker, 1978). Here the cotherapist acts as reality tester, making it possible for the therapist to express himself freely (and sometimes loosely), rather than remaining silently preoccupied with his own inner thoughts, knowing the cotherapist will provide corrective feedback, without fear of causing chaos in the family. Cotherapists may also support each other by remaining calm in the midst of intense family anxiety. As Rubenstein and Weiner (1967) note, some families have had much experience in arousing anxieties in

FIGURE 9-2. Carl A. Whitaker, M.D. (Photo courtesy of Carl A. Whitaker.)

other people and may find a new situation in which a team of therapists is not easily provoked to be a very relieving experience.

The nature of the relationship between therapists has a powerful impact on the family they are treating. If they like, trust, respect, and remain loyal to each other and if their personalities complement each other, they may serve as models for effective and mutually satisfying relationships (Boszormenyi-Nagy & Spark, 1973). Ideally, a male/female team may also serve symbolically, as gender role models or sometimes as parents, with a highly visible relationship for all family members to see. The way the cotherapists *live* their relationship—degrading and undercutting each other or supporting and allowing freedom for one another—teaches the family far more about interpersonal relations than what the therapists may *say* about family relationships. As in a good marriage, the cotherapists need to have a basically loving involvement with each other in which both struggle actively to grow; if such a relationship is present, they may feel unafraid to fight in front of the family. An intense fight, according to Napier and Whitaker (1972), can be enormously beneficial for the family, in that it

FIGURE 9-3. In this family therapy scene, cotherapists work together with a husband and wife who sought help because of their frequent quarrels over disciplining their 6-year-old hyperactive daughter.

teaches them how to fight and to recognize that any two people are likely to have problems with each other, no matter how close or caring. The alternative to fighting—pretending pseudomutuality—is dishonest and transparent, tempting the family to act out the therapists' unexpressed aggression. Here the family may attempt to split the cotherapy team, who, like effective parents, must not permit this to happen. On the other hand, if incessant competition between therapists characterizes their relationship, and each wants consistently to be dominant and win favor from the family, such splitting will likely occur and family therapy will be ineffective.

Many therapists, working alone, may be overwhelmed or "swallowed up" by the family system, seduced or otherwise manipulated by family resistance into maintaining the family status quo. Two therapists working together may keep a check on each other, meeting after or between sessions to discuss their independent perspectives on what is transpiring. Equally important, the two can confront each others' manipulativeness and deception (Holt & Greiner, 1976). Cotherapy, in one sense, keeps both honestly practicing what they intellectually espouse. However, a practical drawback in many cases is the increased expense to the client family and the inefficient use of professional time.

THE EFFECTIVENESS OF FAMILY THERAPY

The Question of Psychotherapy Research

Ultimately, all issues in psychotherapy come down to the answer to one simple question: "Does it help?" Outcome research in family therapy must address itself to the same sets of problems that have hindered such research in individual psychotherapy, in addition to the further complication introduced by attempting to gauge and measure the various interactions and changes taking place within the family group. To be meaningful, such research must do more than investigate general therapeutic efficacy; it must consider the conditions that make for the greatest effectiveness, with which types of families having which kinds of problems and functioning at which level, with which therapeutic techniques, which goals, and so on. The question posed at the beginning of this paragraph—Does psychotherapy help?—cannot be answered by a simple yes or no response. It is too vague as stated and too limiting (for example, help compared to what? No formal treatment, individual psychotherapy, another form of family therapy?) to provide a useful answer. In addition, the question presumes psychotherapy to be a unitary phenomenon, which it is not; various forms are practiced and are all subsumed under a general psychotherapy rubric.

Another stumbling block in evaluating the outcome of psychotherapy arises from the lack of agreement on what represents acceptable evidence of success. Strupp (1971) draws a provocative analogy between psychotherapy and education in attempting to answer the question: "Does a college education help?" The effectiveness of such an education depends largely on what criterion is used to judge success (the graduate is a better person or a happier person than he or she might otherwise be, is better able to get a higher paying job or a more fulfilling job, and so forth). Strupp's point is that different educators use different criteria to evaluate success in their work, and so do different therapists. Some family therapists have the specific goal of eliminating symptoms, others of more generally improving communication. Some are satisfied if they help the family achieve behavior changes, while others insist that the whole family system must change. The favorableness of clinical outcomes reported in the literature may satisfy some therapists but still miss the mark as far as other therapists are concerned.

For many years it was argued that psychotherapy is too complex—and family therapy even more so—for research. Many clinicians felt each therapeutic experience with a patient was a unique psychosocial event, not open to scientific study or measurement. Others were concerned that some of the requirements of research, such as observations by judges, ratings, audio and videotapes, pre- and posttherapy testing, might endanger the intimate and private therapeutic process. In recent years, such barriers to research have slowly disappeared while the confidentiality of the therapeutic encounter has been maintained. As we have indicated, family therapists have been in the forefront of publicly demonstrating their techniques with real families, with no apparent detrimental effects as a result of the exposure.

Family Therapy Outcome Studies

Unfortunately, the scientific evidence for the efficacy of family therapy has not kept pace with the surge of interest in its use. A number of outcome studies have been reported, but by and large they have been fraught with enough methodological problems (for example, inappropriate experimental design, only certain kinds of families included, unreliable or invalid or nonexistent objective measures of change, no follow-up assessments) to make it risky to draw any conclusions about the overall effectiveness of family therapy (Wellisch, Vincent, & Ro-Trock, 1976).

In an effort to pin down what results from well-designed studies are available, Wells and his colleagues critically reviewed the available literature on the effectiveness of family therapy. A comparison of their early search (Wells, Dilkes, & Trevelli, 1972) and their more recent one (Wells & Dezen, 1978) reveals a steady improvement in both the quality and quantity of such research in recent years. In their earlier review (Wells, et al., 1972) of outcome studies published between 1950–1970, the authors located 18 studies that met their minimal search criteria (three or more families were included and outcome measures were explicitly stated). Of these, only two were adequately designed for research purposes. Most of the others lacked a "no treatment" control group against which to compare changes in the experimental group[2] that was undergoing family therapy. Others relied either on the therapist evaluating his or her own work, rather than an independent judge, or on the family members' subjective self-reports at termination. Most studies neglected testing patient pre- and posttherapy or in carrying out adequate follow-up measurements after therapy had terminated. Only the studies carried out at the Family Treatment Unit at the Colorado Psychiatric Hospital by Langsley and his associates on

---

[2]It is only fair to point out here that most of these studies were meant to exemplify a particular treatment approach rather than being specifically designed as research projects. Under such circumstances, it is not surprising that a control group is missing. However, there is the danger that once a method has begun to be practiced and the results published, readers may assume it to be valid and the need for careful and systematic scrutiny of its effectiveness will recede (Wells & Dezen, 1978).

the success of family crisis therapy in avoiding hospitalization were considered adequate in research design.

As investigators have set about more carefully designing their studies in recent years, more encouraging results have begun to emerge. Using the same minimal criteria as in the previous search, Wells and Dezen (1978) located three types of studies that attempt to answer important questions regarding family therapy outcome: single-group studies, comparison studies between a particular treatment method of family therapy and no formal treatment, and comparisons between alternative approaches with a particular client or problem population.

Single-group studies, although flawed because of the absence of a comparable control group, attempt to examine the effects of a particular treatment method on a particular client population ("Does treatment X produce measurable positive changes in population Y?"). The work of Minuchin and associates (1978) on the effectiveness of structural family therapy with psychosomatic families is relevant here (see Chapter 3). Basing their evaluation on 50 adolescent anoretics seen for therapy together with their families for an average of six months, these researchers assessed outcomes in two areas: medical (remission of anoretic symptoms) and psychosocial functioning (adjustment ratings at home, school, or work, and involvement with peers). Follow-up assessments, from one and a half to seven years later, were also carried out. Eighty-six percent of the cases were judged to have recovered from both the anorexia and its psychosocial components (see Table 9-4), a figure that compares very favorably indeed with other previously reported individual efforts to treat this seemingly intractable disorder. These highly positive gains persisted at subsequent follow-up evaluations. Such positive results give considerable credibility to Minuchin's family therapy approach, although the lack of a control group limits any further conclusions regarding its advantages over other methods or techniques of treatment.

Is there research evidence that a particular form of family therapy produces greater measurable positive changes with a particular client population than if that group received no formal treatment? In such studies, families must be assigned randomly to treatment or no treatment, measurements must be made before and after treatment, and a specific form of family therapy must be given the families in the experimental group. Wells and Dezen (1978) located nine such studies in the literature. However, only five were judged by them to have at least adequate methodology in their design, by meeting the above criteria. Of these, the series of studies by Bernard Guerney on filial therapy (training parents to function as play therapists with their young children) appears to be especially noteworthy in demonstrating a tech-

TABLE 9-4. Medical and Psychosocial Assessment of 50 Anoretic Patients following Family Therapy

Rating	Characteristics	Number of cases	Percentage of total
	Medical assessment		
Recovered	Eating patterns normal, body weight stabilized within normal limits for height and age	43	86
Fair	Weight gain but continuing effects of illness (borderline weight, obesity, occasional vomiting)	2	4
Unimproved	Little or no change	3	6
Relapsed	Reappearance of anorexia symptoms after apparently successful treatment	2	4
	Psychological assessment		
Good	Satisfactory adjustment in family, school or work, and social and peer relationships	43	86
Fair	Adjustment in one or another of these areas unsatisfactory	2	4
Unimproved	Inability to function even at borderline levels; disturbances of behavior, thought, and affect	3	6
Relapsed	Reappearance of anorexia symptoms after apparently successful treatment	2	4

nique superior to no treatment with the parents and children of moderately disturbed families (Guerney, 1976).

Finally, there are the studies that compare two forms of treatment in order to determine which produces the greater measurable positive change with a specific population. Once again, the random assignment to one group or the other is essential to the design. Wellisch and associates (1976) compared the effectiveness of short-term family therapy versus short-term individual therapy with 28 hospitalized adolescents and their parents in a well-designed study in which pre-, post-, and follow-up repeated objective assessment and observational measures by independent judges were employed with families randomly assigned to the experimental family therapy condition or to the control individual therapy condition. To eliminate the potential confounding effect of a particular therapist using a particular technique, two therapy teams were used, each responsible for an equal number of cases in both therapy conditions. Eight sessions of either family therapy or individual therapy with the adolescent made up the program.

Results indicated that family therapy with inpatient adolescents was superior in terms of aiding community adaptation and reducing recidivism (rehospitalization) rates. Compared to those adolescents treated individually, those in family therapy returned to functioning (school or work) more rapidly and remained functional throughout the ordinarily stressful adjustment period immediately following hospital discharge. The authors suggest that without intervention into a pathological family system, it might be expected that the discharged patient would return to the family where the previous level of dysfunction would be quickly reinduced, leading to possible rehospitalization; in the case of those adolescents receiving individual treatment but no family therapy, 43% did return to the hospital within three months. A three-month follow-up of the 14 family therapy patients found none had to be rehospitalized.

The studies reported in this section add credibility and legitimacy to intervention by family therapy. Although the data remain scanty, there is now considerable evidence of efforts—although still far from universal among the leading family therapists—to test out techniques through research. In contrast to the paucity of projects judged to meet even minimal standards of design adequacy in an earlier survey, Wells and Dezen (1978) found 20 such studies of nonbehavioral family therapy. To these must be added the increased involvement in the field of behaviorists and their generally careful objective measures of attitude and behavior changes within a family. Well-designed and carefully executed family therapy outcome studies should go a long way toward adding, or withholding, scientific support for the current techniques that have evolved out of clinical experience. In a new and expanding field such as family therapy, such supporting evidence is essential in encouraging the expansion of effective therapeutic services and discouraging the use of techniques that have no positive or even adverse effects. Both the consumers and practitioners of family therapy stand to benefit as our knowledge of effective family therapy methods for particular populations increases. The real question regarding future research, as Fox (1976) reminds us, is not whether family therapy "works" but rather which kind of therapy carried out by which therapist is likely to lead to what specific result in specified types of families.

THE FUTURE OF FAMILY THERAPY

Whither family therapy? No longer the radical departure it represented three decades ago, where is it now and where is it headed? Today, many therapists still continue to see most of their patients in individual treatment, but accept the appropriateness of the family approach for others. Some therapists, increasing in number, now think in nonlinear or systems terms; for them, the behavior and personality characteristics of an individual, and any symptoms he or she may develop, are best understood in the context of the person's family life. The latter group emphasizes that the transactions between family members govern each person's range of experiences and of behavior patterns. As we have attempted to make clear throughout this book, it is the family system—the interdependent parts within the family context—that becomes the focus of interventions.

Family therapy appears to us to be the appropriate method of intervention for our times. Although many of the examples we have offered suggest either intact families or those striving to reunite, we recognize and have noted in Chapter 1 that family life today is in transition. High divorce rates, working wives, smaller families, single-parent households, blended families, and other situations all confront us with new forms of family life, new sets of problems, realignments in relationships, and the necessity to devise new therapeutic methods for effective intervention. As Bell (1975) forecasts:

> The picture postcard representation of the family as healthy, young parents of three lively children, petting the family dog, joyously indulging in a life that is more leisure than work, setting out on Sunday morning hand in hand for church, conscientiously attending the meetings of the PTA, happily visited by grandmother and grandfather, will be consigned to some kind of antique family album [p. 277].

Such an idealization of a family never adequately represented how members dealt with each other behind the socially acceptable facade. Now the variety of family patterns is more out in the open.

What can we say of family therapy's future? A number of serious deficiencies still exist:

1. *The field requires a broader set of theoretical conceptions.* We still lack an overall body of theory of family dysfunction, although pioneers such as Bowen (1978) have made efforts in this direction. As a consequence, no widely prevailing theory of family therapy exists, and this holds back an orderly development of the field. One promising effort is Auerswald's (1972) broad proposal of an ecological approach, in which the family system and its interface with other systems becomes the focus of attention. The family as a whole interacts within its subsystems and is itself a part of a larger societal system. The ecological perspective focuses on the communications within and between systems, not one or the other. More holistic in outlook, it offers broader understanding of the family in its interplay with the outside environment, minimizing the dangers of excessive selectivity in

the collection of data and greater awareness of all factors interacting within the larger context. Extending the family systems concept, Auerswald proposes that we take into consideration the wide spectrum of systems that impinge on the individual.

2. *More attention should be paid to cultural influences on family functioning.* There are significant subcultural and ethnic variations in families within our own society, to say nothing of transcultural differences. Yet, as Cohen (1974) observes, many practitioners avoid ethnicity, race, subcultural identity, and bilingualism in their diagnostic or therapeutic efforts. Perhaps they lean over backwards not to show prejudice or discriminate in the clinical setting, but the overall effect is to ignore a potentially rich source of data regarding individual and family functioning. Black ghetto families, rural farm families, refugee Vietnamese families, and upper middle-class suburban families are hardly alike; each has a different background, separate sets of current stresses and pressures, varied sets of values and attitudes, differential role assignments to family members, and so on. To treat them all in a homogenized fashion is to deny the realities of their lives and to be of limited effectiveness.

3. *Family therapy programs need to be extended to new settings.* During the period of time that the field of family therapy has taken shape, there has been a dramatic change in our thinking regarding how best to deliver mental health services (Goldenberg, 1977). As community-based programs (for example, aftercare services, emergency services, day treatment programs) have developed, however, family therapy efforts have not kept pace. Grounded in the traditions of personal health services, family therapy has remained primarily a method of treatment in private offices and outpatient clinics (Bell, 1975). A number of influential clinicians, such as Spiegel (1974), urge that some form of family treatment play an important part in community health and the efforts now underway to develop comprehensive systems of care. By its very nature, the family will have a central role in linking up various health and human service delivery systems. Family therapy needs to be extended to various social agencies, mental hospital inpatient and outpatient (for example, psychosomatic) services, general hospitals, rehabilitation programs, and other programs that together comprise a community's comprehensive mental health services.

4. *Family therapy theories and techniques must be evaluated more systematically.* Generally speaking, research has been slim indeed in family therapy. We need to know a great deal more about what factors make for better family functioning. We reported a start in that direction in Chapter 2. In planning preventive programs, the family is the logical and most strategically located social unit toward which services should be oriented (Bolman, 1972). Once again a comprehensive the-

ory, supported by adequately designed research, is necessary if the systematic study of how best to prevent family problems is to become a reality. As we have seen earlier in this chapter, research on therapeutic effectiveness—which kind of family therapy for which kind of family—is imperative before the field can progress much further. Family therapy outcomes need to be scrutinized more closely, to see if specific measurable treatment goals were attained, exceeded, or failed for a particular family (Woodward, Santa-Barbara, Levin, & Epstein, 1978).

During the 1980s we anticipate the following developments: (1) *greater use of crisis-focused family therapy in a variety of clinical settings.* As an illustration, Cohen, Goldenberg, and Goldenberg (1977) have described a program on the oncology (cancer) ward of a university general hospital in which bone marrow recipients and donors were all helped to develop more adaptive coping strategies while learning to deal realistically, but hopefully, with the life-threatening illness in a family member; (2) *brief, inpatient treatment of whole families in a psychiatric hospital.* Intensive treatment with the entire family, with the family remaining hospitalized together for a short period, or simply receiving family therapy together with a hospitalized member (Wellisch, et al., 1976); (3) *training parents to function as therapists or change agents for their children),* as in filial therapy (Guerney, 1976). The Parent-Adolescent Relationship Development (PARD) program developed by Guerney and his associates (Guerney, 1977) represents a structured attempt to train families to improve communication and enhance parent/adolescent relationships; *(4) social network intervention on a regular basis.* The retribalization phenomenon described by Speck and Attneave (1973) might be utilized for reviving bonds within extended families, work groups, teacher/student groups, and so on; (5) *reorganization of child guidance clinic services in order to emphasize family therapy services.* As in the Philadelphia Child Guidance Clinic organized by Minuchin (1974a) and in a number of similar institutions in the United States and Canada, an attempt is being made to offer services to families as a whole rather than to children and parents separately. This trend is becoming more common and should increase in frequency over the next decade; (6) *reorganization of clinical training programs to include family therapy.* Heretofore, it has been common for trainees to work in adult or children's services, perhaps rotating from one to the other. We anticipate some future programs where training will be offered in working therapeutically with the entire family unit. If no natural family is present (for example, with college students), then therapy might be offered to that person's substitute families (friends, roommates). Of all programs to train clinicians, family therapy lends itself best to interdisciplinary training and teamwork.

The next decade promises considerable changes in the form and organization of family systems. Bold and resourceful therapeutic programs, based on solid research findings and a comprehensive theory of family functioning, must develop to meet the challenge of the 1980s. New ways of training, new populations to serve, new settings for clinical activities, new and better family therapy techniques—these are our expectations for the future. We can hardly wait!

SUMMARY

Becoming a family therapist is often a discontinuous learning experience for clinicians trained in understanding individual functioning and offering individual psychotherapy. Acquiring the necessary theoretical understanding of family relationships, having firsthand therapeutic experience with real families, and receiving careful supervision are all indispensable to a family therapist's training. Training aids include: didactic course work (lectures, demonstrations, assigned readings); the use of videotapes for postsession viewing by the trainee and his or her supervisor and/or classmates; multiple family time-extended marathon sessions composed of trainees, their client families, and supervisors; live supervision through active guidance by a supervisor who watches the session behind a one-way mirror and offers corrective feedback, sometimes by telephone or calling the trainee out of the therapy room; films of master therapists conducting actual sessions with families; and looking at the trainee's own family of origin in an effort to free the trainee of remaining unresolved family conflicts from the past.

Cotherapy, simultaneously involving two therapists with a single family, may be used for training purposes, as when a supervisor and supervisee work together. The technique is sometimes used in practice by family therapists, such as Whitaker, who prefers the mutual support, teamwork, and the opportunity to freely pursue unexplored areas with a family while knowing the other therapist remains in a backup position, tied to reality. Other family therapists, such as Haley, find cotherapy more useful to the therapist's sense of security than to the family, and argue that it is expensive and an inefficient use of professional time.

Outcome research in family therapy has been lacking in the past, either because of poor research methodology or because the early emphasis was on exploring new techniques and not evaluating them scientifically. More recently, better designed research studies have begun to appear. Single-group studies, studies comparing family treatment/

no treatment with a particular client population, and those comparing two forms of treatment with a specific population are the typical types of outcome research in family therapy. Favorable results in each, although limited by the small number of such reports and the specific populations to which they apply, add credibility to intervention by family therapy.

The future of family therapy appears bright and the technique appropriate for our times. Several improvements are needed: broader theories, more attention to cultural factors, applicability to new settings, and a more systematic set of procedures for evaluating existing theories and therapeutic techniques. During the 1980s, it is anticipated that new ways of training will develop, new populations will be served, and new family therapy techniques will emerge and will be offered in new clinical settings.

GLOSSARY

acting out: The overt manifestation of feelings and impulses through behavioral acts rather than through verbalizations.

acute: Of rapid onset and short duration.

affect: The state of emotion, feeling, or mood that accompanies a thought.

ambivalence: The coexistence of two opposing emotions or attitudes within an individual toward the same person, object, or goal.

anorexia nervosa: Prolonged, severe diminution of appetite, particularly in adolescent females, to the point of becoming life-threatening.

anxiety: A generalized feeling of apprehension or dread without awareness or recognition of a specific danger.

autonomy: Differentiation from others, allowing for self-direction and self-regulation.

behavior therapy: A group of therapeutic techniques based on learning principles that are aimed at altering maladaptive behavior without inquiring into its dynamic or historic causes.

biopsychosocial therapy: A broadly based family therapeutic approach, identifed with Ackerman, utilizing principles from biology, psychoanalysis, social psychology, and child psychiatry.

blank screen: In psychoanalytic therapy, the passive, neutral, unrevealing behavior of the analyst, onto which the patient may project his or her own fantasies.

blended family: A reconstituted family formed by the marriage of divorced persons, establishing stepparent relationships as children from previous families merge into a new family unit.

boundaries: Delineations between parts of a system or between systems.

centrifugal: Tending to move outward or away from a center.

centripetal: Tending to move toward the center.

choreography: The charting of shifting transactional patterns within a family through a succession of sculpting experiences.

classification: A systematic ordering of data.

closed system: A system with impermeable boundaries, operating without interactions outside the system, and thus prone to increasing disorder.

coalition: An alliance of factions for some specific purpose.

cohabitation: A more or less permanent, but not legally binding, living arrangement shared between two unmarried persons of the opposite sex.

common-law marriage: A cohabiting man and woman presenting themselves as married although they have not gone through a formal legal wedding ceremony.

community mental health: An approach that sees psychological dysfunction in any individual as a community responsibility that must be treated quickly within the community or prevented whenever possible.

complementarity: According to Ackerman, the degree of harmony in the meshing of social roles in a family system.

complementary relationship: A pattern of communication between people characterized by inequality and the maximization of differences (for example, dominant/submissive).

conductor: A type of family therapist who is active, aggressive, colorful, and typically becomes the center of the family's star-shaped verbal communication pattern.

conjoint: A single therapist working with family members simultaneously and together.

contingency: A close relationship between two events, one of which regularly follows the other and is assumed to be caused by it.

contingency contracting: An agreement, by two or more family members, specifying the circumstances under which who is to do what for whom, so that they may exchange positively rewarding behaviors in one another.

cotherapy: The simultaneous involvement of two therapists in working with an individual, group, or family.

control group: A group that, for the purposes of an experiment, is matched to an experimental group on most relevant variables but is not subjected to the independent variable under study.

crisis intervention: Brief, direct therapy focused on the here and now in response to an immediate psychological emergency situation.

defense mechanism: In psychoanalytic theory, the process, which is usually an unconscious one, whereby the ego protects the individual from conscious awareness of threatening and therefore anxiety-producing thoughts, feelings, and impulses.

delinquent: A minor who engages in illegal or antisocial behavior.

developmental tasks: Problems to be overcome and conflicts mastered at various stages of the life cycle, enabling movement on to the next stage of development.

diagnosis: The identification and classification of a specific disorder or abnormality.

didactic: Used for teaching purposes.

disengagement: Family interaction in which members are isolated and unrelated to each other, each functioning separately and autonomously.

double-bind messages: A set of contradictory messages from the same person to which an individual must respond, although his or her failure to please is inevitable whatever response is made.

dual-career marriage: A marriage in which both husband and wife work at paid jobs outside of the home.

dyad: A liaison, temporary or permanent, between two people.

dysfunctional: Abnormal or impaired in functioning.

ego: In psychoanalytic theory, the mediator between the demands of the instinctual drives (id) and the social prohibitions (superego); thus, it is the rational problem-solving aspect of the personality.

emotional divorce: According to Bowen, marked emotional distance between parents, both of whom are equally immature, although one may accentuate the immaturity and the other deny it by appearing overadequate.

enmeshment: An extreme form of proximity and intensity in family interactions in which members are overconcerned and overinvolved in each other's life.

entropy: The tendency of a system to go into disorder, that is, to reach a disorganized and undifferentiated state.

equifinality: The ability of a system to reach the same final state from different initial conditions and in different ways.

etiology: The cause or causes of a disorder.

experiential therapy: The therapeutic approach in which the therapist reveals himself or herself as a full and real person and uses that self in interacting with a family.

extended family: An enlarged and complex family unit in which a married couple and their children plus relatives of other generations (for example, grandparents, uncles, aunts) make up the family structure, all living together or in proximity to one another.

facilitator: A group leader whose major function is to stimulate and encourage open communication among group members.

family crisis therapy: A crisis-intervention orientation to family therapy, in which the family as a system is helped to restore its previous level of functioning; in some cases, with schizophrenics, hospitalization can be avoided.

family group therapy: Bell's approach to family therapy, applying the social psychological theories of small group behavior to a family.

family systems therapy: A therapeutic approach, identified with

Bowen, designed to help the family to modify its customary triangular emotional system.

fantasy: Gratification of wishes by conscious daydreaming and imagining.

feedback: Returned information about the consequences of an event.

feedback loop: A circle of responses, in which there is a return flow of information in a system.

fusion: In Bowen's theory, a lack of differentiation between the intellect and emotionality, so that the former exists as an appendage of the latter.

general systems theory: The study of the relationship of interactional parts in context, emphasizing their unity and organizational hierarchy.

generational boundaries: The natural (psychological) distance (differences) between members of separate generations.

gestalt therapy: A phenomenological therapy created by Fritz Perls that emphasizes awareness of the moment, the here and now.

group therapy: A form of psychotherapy in which several persons are treated simultaneously by a therapist and are helped therapeutically through their interaction with one another.

hierarchy: Within a system, an arranged order of parts within the whole.

homeostasis: The self-maintenance of a system in balance or equilibrium.

human potential movement: Movement concerned with expanded sensory awareness, enrichment of life experiences, and fulfillment of the potential for creativity and joy within each individual.

humanistic: The life-affirming viewpoint that emphasizes each person's uniqueness and worth, as well as his or her potential for continued personal growth and fulfillment.

id: In psychoanalytic theory, the part of the personality, present from birth, that is composed of primitive, instinctual strivings.

identified patient: The family member with the presenting symptoms; thus, the person who initially seeks treatment.

index patient: See **identified patient**.

information processing: The gathering, distilling, storing, and retrieving of information; the flow of information through a system, as in a computer program.

insight: Self-awareness, especially regarding one's own motivation and behavior.

interlocking pathology: According to Ackerman, several disabilities within the same family that are dependent on each other for either expression or control.

interpersonal: Transactions, verbal and otherwise, between two or more persons.

intrapsychic: Within the mind or psyche; this term is used especially in relation to conflicting forces.

life cycle: The career or history of an individual or group (for example, a family) from its beginning to its termination.

live supervision: The active guidance of a therapist while at work by an observing person behind a one-way mirror who offers suggestions by telephone, earphone, or by calling the therapist out of the consultation room.

longitudinal study: A research approach in which people's behavior is systematically studied over an extended period of time.

marathon: An intensive, uninterrupted group experience, generally extending over several days, that is focused on the ongoing process of encounter among group members.

marital schism: According to Lidz, a marital situation characterized by disharmony, self-preoccupation, the undermining of the spouse, and frequent threats of divorce by one or both partners.

marital skew: According to Lidz, a situation in which a marriage is maintained at the expense of the distortion of reality.

medical model: A set of assumptions underlying the view that abnormal behavior patterns are analogous to physical diseases.

mental illness: A mental, psychological, or behavioral disorder that is usually severe, as in psychosis; this term is particularly favored by proponents of the medical model in abnormal psychology.

metacommunication: A communication at a second level that structures and adds meaning to what is said at the first or surface level (for example, a communication, such as a nonverbal nod, wink, or smile, that qualifies a verbal message).

modeling: A form of learning that is based on the imitation of behavior that is observed in others; it is especially common in young children.

multiple-family therapy: A form of psychotherapy in which the members of several families are seen together as a group.

multiple-impact therapy: A form of psychotherapy in which the members of a single family are seen all together or in various combinations over a two-day period for intensive interaction with a team of professionals.

multiple marital couple therapy: A variation of multiple family therapy in which the therapy group is composed of sets of husbands and wives.

mystification: A masking effect, used by one or more persons who are interacting, in order to obscure the real nature of their conflicts and maintain the status quo.

network therapy: A form of group therapy carried out in the home of a patient, typically a schizophrenic, in which family, friends, neighbors, and others all aid in his or her treatment and rehabilitation.

neuroses: Mild to moderate functional disorders marked by subjective feelings of anxiety as well as by inadequate coping devices that are used as defenses against the anxiety.

nuclear family: A family composed of a husband, wife, and their offspring, living together as a unit.

obsession: A persistent, unwanted, repetitive idea that is intrusive and disturbing to an individual's normal thinking.

Oedipus complex: In psychoanalytic theory, the unconscious desire of a boy during the phallic stage for sexual relations with his mother, while at the same time he fears castration by his father because of his rivalry.

open system: A system with more or less permeable boundaries, allowing interaction between component parts or subsystems, and thus likely to function in an orderly manner.

operant conditioning: A form of learning in which correct or desired responses are rewarded or reinforced, thus increasing the probability that these responses will recur.

operant-interpersonal therapy: An approach in marriage counseling, advocated by Stuart, based on operant conditioning theory, particularly the exchange between partners of positive reinforcements.

paradigm: A set of assumptions, delimiting the area to be investigated scientifically and specifying the methods to be used to collect and interpret the forthcoming data.

paradoxical intervention: A clinical intervention technique whereby a therapist gives a patient or family a directive he or she wants resisted; the resulting change takes place as a result of defying the therapist.

parentification: The taking on of the nurturing, teaching role of a parent by a child, temporarily or permanently.

pathogenic: Pathology-producing.

pathological: Concerned with disease or dysfunction.

phobia: An intense, irrational fear of a harmless object or situation that the individual seeks to avoid.

positive reinforcement: An affirmative response (that is, reward) to an action, intended to increase the probability of the recurrence of that action.

prognosis: A prediction or forecast about the outcome of a disorder, including an indication of its probable duration and course.

pseudomutuality: A relationship among family members that gives the appearance of being open and with mutual understanding, but in fact is not.

psychoanalysis: A comprehensive theory of personality development and a set of therapeutic techniques developed by Sigmund Freud.

psychodrama: A form of group therapy in which patients role-play themselves or others in their lives in order to achieve catharsis or resolve conflicts and gain greater spontaneity.

psychodynamics: The interplay of opposing forces within a person as the basis for understanding human motivation.

psychonosis: According to Howells, a form of psychopathology, occurring in varying degrees, in which there is a disruption of psychological functioning.

psychopath: A psychological disorder in which an individual manifests unreliable behavior, egocentricity, impulsiveness, and irresponsibility without remorse or shame.

psychosomatic: A physical disorder of the body caused or aggravated by chronic emotional stress, usually involving a single organ system under autonomic nervous system innervation.

reactor: A type of family therapist who is subtle and indirect, observing and clarifying the family group process, rather than an active, aggressive, or colorful group leader.

reframing: Verbal relabeling in order to make seemingly dysfunctional behavior be designated as reasonable and understandable, so that the behavior can be reacted to differently.

regression: An unconscious defense mechanism in which an individual exhibits behavior that is more appropriate to an earlier developmental level.

resistance: In psychoanalytic therapy, a person's reluctance to bring threatening unconscious material that has previously been repressed into conscious awareness.

retribalization: In network therapy, the effort to create or strengthen tribal-like bonds between the members, facilitating the group's ability to seek solutions to the family crisis.

role: An expected behavior pattern, socially defined, that accompanies a social position, as in a family.

role overload: Stress in a family as a result of members (for example, husband and wife) attempting to fulfill a greater variety of roles than their energies or available time will permit.

"rubber fence": According to Wynne, a family boundary that is unstable but so flexible that it stretches to include whatever it considers complementary to its structure or contracts to extrude whatever it considers alien.

scapegoating: The assigning of a "bad" or "guilty" label onto a family member, who is held responsible by all for family dysfunction.

schizophrenogenic mother: A cold, domineering, possessive but rejecting mother as described by Fromm-Reichmann, believed by her to be a causative factor in the offspring's schizophrenia.

schizophrenia: A major form of functional psychosis that is marked by severe disturbances in thinking, restricted affect, delusions, hallucinations, and a withdrawal from reality.

sculpting: A nonverbal arranging by a family member of his or her entire family placed in various physical positions in space; the purpose is to represent a view of their relationship to one another through the tableau.

sensitivity training group: A type of encounter group designed to provide an intensive interactional experience in order for the participants to gain greater self-understanding and personal growth.

sex therapy: A brief treatment program, relying heavily on behavior-therapy techniques, that is aimed at alleviating problems of sexual dysfunction, such as impotence or premature ejaculation in men and nonorgasmic response in women.

shaping: A form of behavior therapy, based on operant-conditioning principles, in which successive approximations of desired behavior are reinforced until the desired behavior is achieved.

sibling rivalry: Competition between two or more children in the same family to achieve recognition or ascendency.

single-parent households: Households with children led by one parent, male or female, due to divorce or death or desertion by a spouse, or because of never having married.

social learning theory: The view that a person's behavior is best understood when the social conditions under which he or she learned that behavior are understood.

social network intervention: See network therapy.

stress: A traumatic circumstance that strains an individual's or family's ordinary coping abilities.

structural family therapy: A family therapy approach, identified with Minuchin, directed at changing the family organization or structure in order to alter behavior patterns in its members; the therapist changes the system by actively participating in its interpersonal transactions.

subsystem: An organized unit within an overall system; every system contains within it a number of such coexisting component parts.

superego: In psychoanalytic theory, the internalized moral and ethical values of one's parents and of society in general; thus, one's conscience.

symbiosis: The close association or interdependence of two persons, the union being advantageous to both and to the maintenance of the family system.

symmetrical relationship: A pattern of communication between people characterized by equality and the minimization of difference.

symptom: A medical term for an observed physical, emotional, or behavioral sign of a disorder or disease.

system: A set of units and the interrelationships between those units.

three-generation hypothesis: According to Bowen's theory, the notion that schizophrenia as a process requires at least three generations to develop.

token economy: A behavior-therapy system, based on the principles of operant conditioning, in which institutionalized patients are given rewards (such as poker chips) for socially constructive behavior; the rewards are later exchangeable for special privileges not available to other patients.

tranquilizer: An anti-anxiety drug that is used to decrease tension and agitation without causing drowsiness.

trauma: Severe stress of a physical or psychological nature.

triadic-based therapy: A family therapy approach advocated by Zuk in which the therapist, as a third person, acts as go-between in working with a couple in order to disrupt their chronic pattern of relating to one another.

triangle: According to Bowen, the tendency of a two-person emotional system, under stress, to recruit a third person into an expanded system in order to lower the intensity and anxiety and to gain stability.

triangulation: The act of involving an outsider when two persons are in tension situations; according to Bowen, a family's emotional system is composed of a series of interlocking triangles.

typecasting: Ascribing or assigning a stereotypical role to someone.

unconscious: In psychoanalytic theory, that part of his or her own personality about which the individual lacks awareness.

undifferentiated family ego mass: Bowen's term for the intense interdependency (symbiosis) in a family; an individual sense of self fails to develop in members because of the existing fusion or emotional oneness.

videoplayback: The videotape recording and replaying of a family therapy session for therapeutic or training purposes.

vulnerability: A particular susceptibility to a specific type or form of stress.

REFERENCES

Ackerman, N. W. Interlocking pathology in family relationships. In S. Rado & G. Daniels (Eds.), *Changing concepts of psychoanalytic medicine.* New York: Grune & Stratton, 1956.

Ackerman, N. W. *The psychodynamics of family life.* New York: Basic Books, 1958.

Ackerman, N. W. *Treating the troubled family.* New York: Basic Books, 1966.

Ackerman, N. W. Family psychotherapy and psychoanalysis: The implications of difference. In N. W. Ackerman (Ed.), *Family process.* New York: Basic Books, 1970. (a)

Ackerman, N. W. (Ed.). *Family therapy in transition.* New York: Little, Brown, 1970. (b)

Ackerman, N. W., & Behrens, M. L. Family diagnosis and clinical process. In S. Arieti & G. Caplan (Eds.), *American handbook of psychiatry II. Child and adolescent psychiatry, sociocultural and community psychiatry* (2nd ed.). New York: Basic Books, 1974.

Alger, I. Audio-visual techniques in family therapy. In D. A. Bloch (Ed.), *Techniques of family psychotherapy: A primer.* New York: Grune & Stratton, 1973.

Alger, I. Integrating immediate video playback in family therapy. In P. J. Guerin, Jr. (Ed.), *Family therapy: Theory and practice.* New York: Gardner Press, 1976. (a)

Alger, I. Multiple couple therapy. In P. J. Guerin, Jr. (Ed.), *Family Therapy: Theory and practice.* New York: Gardner Press, 1976. (b)

Ard, B. N., Jr., & Ard, C. C. (Eds.). *Handbook of marriage counseling* (2nd ed.). Palo Alto, Calif.: Science & Behavior Books, 1977.

Arnold, J. E., Levine, A. G., & Patterson, G. R. Changes in sibling behavior following family intervention. *Journal of Consulting and Clinical Psychology,* 1975, *43,* 683–688.

Auerswald, E. H. Interdisciplinary versus ecological approach. In C. J. Sager & H. S. Kaplan (Eds.), *Progress in group and family therapy.* New York: Brunner/Mazel, 1972.

Back, K. W. Intervention techniques: Small groups. In M. R. Rosenzweig & L. W. Porter (Eds.), *Annual review of psychology* (Vol. 25). Palo Alto, Calif.: Annual Reviews, 1974.

Bandler, R., Grinder, J., & Satir, V. *Changing with families.* Palo Alto, Calif.: Science & Behavior Books, 1976.

Bateson, G. *Naven* (2nd ed.). Stanford, Calif.: Stanford University Press, 1958.

Bateson, G. *Steps to an ecology of mind.* New York: Ballantine, 1972.

Bateson, G., Jackson, D., Haley, J., & Weakland, J. Towards a theory of schizophrenia. *Behavioral Science,* 1956, *1,* 251–264.

Beavers, W. R. *Psychotherapy and growth: Family systems perspective.* New York: Brunner/Mazel, 1977.

Beck, D. F., & Jones, M. A. *Progress on family problems.* New York: Family Service Association of America, 1973.

Beels, C., & Ferber, A. Family therapy: A view. *Family Process,* 1969, *8,* 280–332.

Bell, J. E. *Family group therapy* (Public Health Monograph No. 64). Washington, D.C.: U.S. Government Printing Office, 1961.

Bell, J. E. *Family therapy.* New York: Jason Aronson, 1975.

Bell, J. E. A theoretical framework for family group therapy. In P. J. Guerin, Jr. (Ed.), *Family therapy: Theory and practice.* New York: Gardner Press, 1976.

Berger, M. M. (Ed.). *Videotape techniques in psychiatric training and treatment* (Rev. ed.). New York: Brunner/Mazel, 1978.

Berkowitz, B. P., & Graziano, A. M. Training parents as behavior therapists: A review. *Behavior Research and Therapy,* 1972, *10,* 297–317.

Bertalanffy, L. von. *General systems theory: Foundation, development, applications.* New York: Brazillier, 1968.

Bion, W. R. *Experiences in groups.* New York: Basic Books, 1961.

Blechman, E. A. The family contract game: A tool to teach interpersonal problem solving. *Family Coordinator,* 1974, *23,* 269–281.

Bloch, D. A. The family of the psychiatric patient. In S. Arieti (Ed.), *American handbook of psychiatry I: The foundations of psychiatry.* New York: Basic Books, 1974.

Bloch, D. A., & LaPerriere, K. Techniques of family therapy: A conceptual frame. In D. A. Bloch (Ed.), *Techniques of family psychotherapy: A primer.* New York: Grune & Stratton, 1973.

Bodin, A. M. Family therapy training literature: A brief guide. *Family Process,* 1969, *8,* 729–779. (a)

Bodin, A. M. Videotape in training family therapists. *The Journal of Nervous and Mental Disease,* 1969, *148,* 251–261. (b)

Bolman, W. M. Preventive psychiatry for the family: Theory, approaches, and the programs. In G. D. Erickson & T. P. Hogan (Eds.), *Family therapy: An introduction to theory and technique.* Monterey, Calif.: Brooks/Cole, 1972.

Boszormenyi-Nagy, I., & Framo, J. L. *Intensive family therapy: Theoretical and practical aspects.* New York: Harper & Row, 1965.

Boszormenyi-Nagy, I., & Spark, G. M. *Invisible loyalties: Reciprocity in intergenerational family therapy.* New York: Harper & Row, 1973.

Bowen, M. A family concept of schizophrenia. In D. D. Jackson (Ed.), *The etiology of schizophrenia.* New York: Basic Books, 1960.

Bowen, M. The use of family theory in clinical practice. *Comprehensive Psychiatry*, 1966, *7*, 345–374.

Bowen, M. Family therapy after twenty years. In S. Arieti, D. X. Freeman, & J. E. Dyrud (Eds.), *American handbook of psychiatry V: Treatment* (2nd ed.). New York: Basic Books, 1975.

Bowen, M. Theory in the practice of psychotherapy. In P. J. Guerin, Jr. (Ed.), *Family therapy: Theory and practice.* New York: Gardner Press, 1976.

Bowen, M. *Family therapy in clinical practice.* New York: Jason Aronson, 1978.

Brody, E. M. Aging and family personality: A developmental view. *Family Process*, 1974, *13*, 23–38.

Cleghorn, J. M., & Levin, S. Training family therapists by setting learning objectives. *American Journal of Orthopsychiatry*, 1973, *43*, 439–446.

Cohen, M., Goldenberg, I. T., & Goldenberg, H. Treating families of bone marrow recipients and donors. *Journal of Marriage and Family Counseling*, 1977, *3*, 45–51.

Cohen, R. E. Borderline conditions: A transcultural perspective. *Psychiatric Annals*, 1974, *4*, 7–20.

Constantine, L. Designed experience: A multiple, goal-directed training program in family therapy. *Family Process*, 1976, *15*, 373–387.

Cooper, D. *The death of the family.* New York: Vintage, 1970.

Cooper, S. Treatment of parents. In S. Arieti & G. Caplan (Eds.), *American handbook of psychiatry II. Child and adolescent psychiatry, sociocultural and community psychiatry* (2nd ed.). New York: Basic Books, 1974.

Cromwell, R. E., Olson, D. H. L., & Fournier, D. G. Diagnosis and evaluation in marital and family counseling. In D. H. L. Olson (Ed.), *Treating relationships.* Lake Mills, Iowa: Graphic, 1976.

D'Andrade, R. G. Sex differences and cultural institutions. In R. A. LeVine (Ed.), *Culture and personality: Contemporary readings.* Chicago: Aldine, 1974.

Doyle, A. M., & Dorlac, C. Treating chronic crisis bearers and their families. *Journal of Marriage and Family Counseling*, 1978, *4* (3), 37–42.

Duhl, F. J., Kantor, D., & Duhl, B. S. Learning, space, and action in family therapy: A primer of sculpture. In D. A. Bloch (Ed.), *Techniques of family psychotherapy: A primer.* New York: Grune Stratton, 1973.

Duvall, E. M. *Marriage and family development* (5th ed.). New York: Lippincott, 1977.

Erickson, G. D., & Hogan, T. P. *Family therapy: An introduction to theory and technique.* Monterey, Calif.: Brooks/Cole, 1972.

Ferber, A., & Ranz, J. How to succeed in family therapy: Set reachable goals—give workable tasks. In C. J. Sager & H. S. Kaplan (Eds.), *Progress in group and family therapy.* New York: Brunner/Mazel, 1972.

Ferreira, A. J. Family myths. *Psychiatric Research Reports* (No. 20), 1966, 86–87.

Fisher, L. Dimensions of family assessment: A critical review. *Journal of Marriage and Family Counseling*, 1976, *2* (4), 367–382.

Fleck, S. An approach to family pathology. In G. D. Erickson & T. P. Hogan (Eds.), *Family therapy: An introduction to theory and technique.* Monterey, Calif.: Brooks/Cole, 1972.

Fleck, S. A general systems approach to severe family pathology. *American Journal of Psychiatry*, 1976, *133*, 669–673.

Foley, V. D. *An introduction to family therapy.* New York: Grune & Stratton, 1974.

Fox, R. E. Family therapy. In I. B. Weiner (Ed.), *Clinical methods in psychology.* New York: Wiley, 1976.

Framo, J. L. Rationale and techniques of intensive family therapy. In I. Boszormenyi-Nagy & J. L. Framo (Eds.), *Intensive family therapy: Theoretical and practical aspects*. New York: Harper & Row, 1965.

Framo, J. L. Symptoms from a family transactional viewpoint. In N. W. Ackerman, J. Lieb, & J. Pierce (Eds.), *Family therapy in transition*. New York: Little, Brown, 1970.

Framo, J. L. (Ed.), *Family interaction: A dialogue between family researchers and family therapists*. New York: Springer, 1972.

Framo, J. L. Marriage therapy in a couples group. In D. A. Bloch (Ed.), *Techniques of family psychotherapy: A primer*. New York: Grune & Stratton, 1973.

Framo, J. L. Personal reflections of a family therapist. *Journal of Marriage and Family Counseling*, 1975, *1*, 1–22.

Framo, J. L. Chronicle of a struggle to establish a family unit within a community mental health center. In P. J. Guerin, Jr. (Ed.), *Family therapy: Theory and practice*. New York: Gardner Press, 1976.

Franklin, P., & Prosky, P. A standard initial interview. In D. A. Bloch (Ed.), *Techniques of family psychotherapy: A primer*. New York: Grune & Stratton, 1973.

Freud, S. Analysis of a phobia in a five-year-old boy (1909). *The standard edition of the complete psychological works of Sigmund Freud* (Vol. 10). London: Hogarth Press, 1955.

Fromm-Reichmann, F. Notes on the development of treatment of schizophrenics by psychoanalytic psychotherapy. *Psychiatry*, 1948, *11*, 263–273.

Gazda, G. M. Group psychotherapy and group counseling: Definitions and heritage. In G. M. Gazda (Ed.), *Basic approaches to group psychotherapy and group counseling* (2nd ed.). Springfield, Ill.: Charles C Thomas, 1975.

Gladfelter, J. Films on group and family psychotherapy. In C. J. Sager and H. S. Kaplan (Eds.), *Progress in group and family therapy*. New York: Brunner/Mazel, 1972.

Glick, I. D., & Kessler, D. R. *Marital and family therapy*. New York: Grune & Stratton, 1974.

Glick, P. C. Living arrangements of children and young adults. *Journal of Comparative Family Studies*, 1976, *7*, 321–323.

Glick, P. C. Updating the life cycle of the family. *Journal of Marriage and the Family*, 1977, *39*, 5–13.

Goldenberg, H. *Contemporary clinical psychology*. Monterey, Calif.: Brooks/Cole, 1973. (a)

Goldenberg, H. *Is training family therapists different from clinical training in general?* Paper presented at the American Psychological Association annual meeting, Montreal, Canada, 1973. (b)

Goldenberg, H. *Abnormal psychology: A social/community approach*. Monterey, Calif.: Brooks/Cole, 1977.

Goldenberg, I., & Goldenberg, H. A family approach to psychological services. *American Journal of Psychoanalysis*, 1975, *35*, 317–328.

Goldenberg, I., & Goldenberg, H. *Treating a family following an adolescent member's suicide*. Paper and videotape presented at the International Congress on Suicide Prevention and Crisis Intervention, Helsinki, Finland, June 1977.

Goldenberg, I., Stier, S., & Preston, T. A. The use of multiple family marathon as a teaching device. *Journal of Marriage and Family Counseling*, 1975, *1*, 343–349.

Goldstein, M., & Rodnick, E. The family's contribution to the etiology of schizophrenia: Current status. *Schizophrenia Bulletin*, 1975, *14*, 263–273.

Greenberg, I. A. (Ed.). *Psychodrama: Theory and therapy.* New York: Behavioral Publications, 1974.

Grotjahn, M. *Psychoanalysis and the family neurosis.* New York: Norton, 1960.

Group for the Advancement of Psychiatry. *The field of family therapy* (Report No. 78). New York: Group for the Advancement of Psychiatry, 1970.

Guerin, P. J., Jr. Family therapy: The first twenty-five years. In P. J. Guerin, Jr. (Ed.), *Family therapy: theory and practice.* New York: Gardner Press, 1976.

Guerin, P. J., Jr. & Fogarty, T. Study your own family. In A. Ferber, M. Mendelsohn, & A. Napier (Eds.), *The book of family therapy.* New York: Science House, 1972.

Guerney, B. G., Jr. *Relationship enhancement: Skill-training programs for therapy, problem prevention, and enrichment.* San Francisco: Jossey-Bass, 1977.

Guerney, L. F. Filial therapy program. In D. H. L. Olson (Ed.), *Treating relationships.* Lake Mills, Iowa: Graphic, 1976.

Gurin, G., Veroff, J., & Feld, S. *Americans view their mental health.* New York: Basic Books, 1960.

Haley, J. *Strategies of psychotherapy.* New York: Grune & Stratton, 1963.

Haley, J. Family therapy. *International Journal of Psychiatry,* 1970, *9,* 233–242.

Haley, J. Approaches to family therapy. In J. Haley (Ed.), *Changing families: A family therapy reader.* New York: Grune & Stratton, 1971. (a)

Haley, J. Family therapy: A radical change. In J. Haley (Ed.), *Changing families: A family therapy reader.* New York: Grune & Stratton, 1971. (b)

Haley, J. (Ed.). *Changing families: A family therapy reader.* New York: Grune & Stratton, 1971. (c)

Haley, J. *Uncommon therapy: The psychiatric techniques of Milton H. Erickson, M.D.* New York: Norton, 1973.

Haley, J. *Problem-solving therapy.* San Francisco: Jossey-Bass, 1976.

Haley, J., & Hoffman, L. *Techniques of family therapy.* New York: Basic Books, 1967.

Hickok, J. E., & Komechak, M. G. Behavior modification in marital conflict: A case report. *Family Process,* 1974, *13,* 111–119.

Hirsch, S., & Leff, J. *Abnormalities in parents of schizophrenics.* Oxford: Oxford University Press, 1975.

Hoffman, L. W. Deviation—amplifying processes in natural groups. In J. Haley (Ed.), *Changing families: A family therapy reader.* New York: Grune & Stratton, 1971.

Hoffman, L. W. Changes in family roles, socialization, and sex differences. *American Psychologist,* 1977, *32,* 644–657.

Holt, M., & Greiner, D. Co-therapy in the treatment of families. In P. J. Guerin, Jr. (Ed.), *Family therapy: Theory and practice.* New York: Gardner Press, 1976.

Howells, J. G. *Principles of family psychiatry.* New York: Brunner/Mazel, 1975.

In her own words: An interview with Dr. Irene Goldenberg. *People,* April 3, 1978, pp. 56–58.

Jackson, D. D. *The etiology of schizophrenia.* New York: Basic Books, 1960.

Jackson, D. D. Family rules: Marital quid pro quo. *Archives of General Psychiatry,* 1965, *12,* 589–594. (a)

Jackson, D. D. The study of the family. *Family Process,* 1965, *4,* 1–20. (b)

Jackson, D. D. The myth of normality. *Medical Opinion and Review,* 1967, *3* (5), 28–33.

Kanner, L. Emotionally disturbed children: A historical review. *Child Development,* 1962, *33,* 97–102.

Kaplan, H. S. *The new sex therapy: Active treatment of sexual dysfunctions*. New York: Brunner/Mazel, 1974.

Kempler, W. Experiential psychotherapy with families. *Family Process*, 1968, 7, 88–99.

Kempler, W. *Principles of gestalt family therapy*. Oslo, Norway: Trykkeri, 1973. [Published in the United States in 1974 through The Kempler Institute, P. O. Box 1692, Costa Mesa, Calif. 92626.]

Laing, R. D. Mystification, confusion, and conflict. In I. Boszormenyi-Nagy and J. L. Framo (Eds.), *Intensive family therapy: Theoretical and practical aspects*. New York: Harper & Row, 1965.

Laing, R. D., & Esterson, A. *Sanity, madness and the family*. Middlesex, England: Penguin, 1970.

Langsley, D. G., & Kaplan, D. M. *The treatment of families in crisis*. New York: Grune & Stratton, 1968.

Langsley, D. G., Machotka, P., & Flomenhaft, K. Avoiding mental hospital admission: A follow-up study. *American Journal of Psychiatry*, 1971, 127, 1391–1394.

Langsley, D. G., Pittman, F. S., Machotka, P., & Flomenhaft, K. Family crisis therapy: Results and implications. *Family Process*, 1968, 7, 145–158.

Laqueur, H. P. Multiple family therapy: Questions and answers. In D. A. Bloch (Ed.), *Techniques of family psychotherapy: A primer*. New York: Grune & Stratton, 1973.

Laqueur, H. P. Multiple family therapy. In P. J. Guerin, Jr. (Ed.), *Family therapy: Theory and practice*. New York: Gardner Press, 1976.

LeBow, M. D. Behavior modification for the family. In G. D. Erickson & T. P. Hogan (Eds.), *Family therapy: An introduction to theory and technique*. Monterey, Calif.: Brooks/Cole, 1972.

Lewis, J. M., Beavers, W. R., Gossett, J. T., & Phillips, V. A. *No single thread: Psychological health in family systems*. New York: Brunner/Mazel, 1976.

Liberman, R. P. Behavioral approaches to family and couple therapy. *American Journal of Orthopsychiatry*, 1970, 40, 106–118.

Liberman, R. P. Behavioral methods in group and family therapy. *Seminars in Psychiatry*, 1972, 4 (2), 145–156.

Liberman, R. P., Levine, J., Wheeler, E., Sanders, N., & Wallace, C. J. Marital therapy in groups: A comparative evaluation of behavioral and interactional formats. *Acta Psychiatrica Scandinavica*, Supplement 266, 1976.

Liberman, R. P., Wheeler, E., & Sanders, N. Behavioral therapy for marital disharmony: An educational approach. *Journal of Marriage and Family Counseling*, 1976, 2, 383–395.

Liddle, H. A., & Halpin, R. J. Family therapy training and supervision: A comparative review. *Journal of Marriage and Family Counseling*, 1978, 4, 77–98.

Lidz, R., & Lidz, T. The family environment of schizophrenic patients. *American Journal of Psychiatry*, 1949, 106, 332–345.

Lidz, T., Fleck, S., & Cornelison, A. *Schizophrenia and the family*. New York: International Universities Press, 1965.

LoPiccolo, J., & LoPiccolo, L. (Eds.), *Handbook of sex therapy*. New York: Plenum, 1978.

Low, P., & Low, M. Treatment of married couples in a group run by a husband and wife. *International Journal of Group Psychotherapy*, 1975, 25, 54–66.

MacGregor, R. Multiple impact psychotherapy with families. In J. G. Howells (Ed.), *Theory and practice of family psychiatry*. New York: Brunner/Mazel, 1971.

MacGregor, R., Ritchie, A. N., Serrano, A. C., & Schuster, F. P. *Multiple impact therapy with families.* New York: McGraw-Hill, 1964.

Malcolm, J. A reporter at large: The one-way mirror. *New Yorker,* May 15, 1978, pp. 39–114.

Martin, P. A. *A marital therapy manual.* New York: Brunner/Mazel, 1976.

Masters, W. H., & Johnson, V. E. *Human sexual inadequacy.* Boston: Little, Brown, 1970.

McPherson, S. R., Brackelmanns, W. E., & Newman, L. E. Stages in the family therapy of adolescents. *Family Process,* 1974, *13,* 77–94.

Mendelsohn, M., & Ferber, A. A training program. In A. Ferber, M. Mendelsohn, & A. Napier (Eds.), *The book of family therapy.* New York: Science House, 1972.

Miller, J. G. The nature of living systems. *Behavioral Science,* 1971, *16,* 277–301.

Miller, J. G. *Living systems.* New York: McGraw-Hill, 1978.

Minuchin, S. *Families and family therapy.* Cambridge, Mass.: Harvard University Press, 1974. (a)

Minuchin, S. Structural family therapy. In S. Arieti & G. Caplan (Eds.), *American handbook of psychiatry II: Child and adolescent psychiatry* (2nd ed.). New York: Basic Books, 1974. (b)

Minuchin, S., Baker, L., Rosman, B. L., Liebman, R., Milman, L., & Todd, T. C. A conceptual model of psychosomatic illness in children. *Archives of General Psychiatry,* 1975, *32,* 1031–1038.

Minuchin, S., & Barcai, A. Therapeutically induced family crisis. In C. J. Sager & H. S. Kaplan (Eds.), *Progress in group and family therapy.* New York: Brunner/Mazel, 1972.

Minuchin, S., Montalvo, B., Guerney, B. G., Jr., Rosman, B. L., & Schumer, F. *Families of the slums: An exploration of their structure and treatment.* New York: Basic Books, 1967.

Minuchin, S., Rosman, B. L., & Baker, L. *Psychosomatic families: Anorexia nervosa in context.* Cambridge, Mass.: Harvard University Press, 1978.

Mishler, E. G., & Waxler, N. E. *Interactions in families: An experimental study of family processes and schizophrenia.* New York: Wiley, 1968.

Montalvo, B. Aspects of live supervision. *Family Process,* 1973, *12,* 343–359.

Moos, R. H. *Combined preliminary manual: Family, work and group environment scales.* Palo Alto, Calif.: Consulting Psychologists Press, 1974.

Mudd, E. H. Marriage counseling. In A. Ellis & A. Abarbanel (Eds.), *The encyclopedia of sexual behavior.* New York: Hawthorn, 1961.

Napier, A. Y., & Whitaker, C. A. A conversation about co-therapy. In A. Ferber, M. Mendelsohn, & A. Napier (Eds.), *The book of family therapy.* New York: Science House, 1972.

Napier, A. Y., & Whitaker, C. A. *The family crucible.* New York: Harper & Row, 1978.

Nass, G. D. *Marriage and the family.* Reading, Mass.: Addison-Wesley, 1978.

Papp, P. Family choreography. In P. J. Guerin, Jr. (Ed.), *Family therapy: Theory and practice.* New York: Gardner Press, 1976.

Papp, P. (Ed.), *Family therapy: Full length case studies.* New York: Gardner Press, 1977.

Patterson, G. R. *Families: Application of social learning to family life.* Champaign, Ill.: Research Press, 1971.

Patterson, G. R., McNeal, S., Hawkins, N., & Phelps, R. Reprogramming the social environment. *Journal of Child Psychology and Psychiatry,* 1967, *8,* 180–195.

Pittman, F. S., III. Managing acute psychiatric emergencies: Defining the family crisis. In D. A. Bloch (Ed.), *Techniques of family psychotherapy: A primer.* New York: Grune & Stratton, 1973.

Rapoport, R., & Rapoport, R. N. Work and family in contemporary society. *American Sociological Review,* 1965, *30,* 381–394.

Rapoport, R. N., & Rapoport, R. The dual-career family: A variant pattern and social change. *Human Relations,* 1969, *22,* 3–29.

Reevy, W. R. Educational and professional training of the marital counselor. In H. L. Silverman (Ed.), *Marital counseling: Psychology, ideology, science.* Springfield, Ill.: Charles C Thomas, 1967.

Reiss, D. The family and schizophrenia. *American Journal of Psychiatry,* 1976, *133,* 181–185.

Ritchie, A. Multiple impact therapy: An experiment. In J. Haley (Ed.), *Changing families: A family therapy reader.* New York: Grune & Stratton, 1971.

Ritterman, M. K. Paradigmatic classification of family therapy theories. *Family Process,* 1977, *16,* 29–48.

Robinson, L. R. Basic concepts in family therapy: A differential comparison with individual treatment. *American Journal of Psychiatry,* 1975, *132,* 1045–1054.

Rosenblatt, B. Historical perspective of treatment modes. In H. E. Rie (Ed.), *Perspectives in child psychopathology.* Chicago: Aldine-Atherton, 1971.

Rubenstein, D., & Weiner, O. R. Co-therapy teamwork relationships in family psychotherapy. In G. H. Zuk & I. Boszormenyi-Nagy (Eds.), *Family therapy and disturbed families.* Palo Alto, Calif.: Science & Behavior Books, 1967.

Rubenstein, E. Childhood mental disease in America: A review of the literature before 1900. *American Journal of Orthopsychiatry,* 1948, *18,* 314–321.

Sander, F. M., & Beels, C. C. A didactic course for family therapy trainees. *Family Process,* 1970, *9,* 411–423.

Satir, V. *Conjoint family therapy.* Palo Alto, Calif.: Science & Behavior Books, 1967.

Satir, V. *Peoplemaking.* Palo Alto, Calif.: Science and Behavior Books, 1972.

Satir, V., Stachowiak, J., & Taschman, H. A. *Helping families to change.* New York: Jason Aronson, 1975.

Saving the family. Newsweek, May 15, 1978, pp. 63–90.

Shapiro, R. J. Problems in teaching family therapy. *Professional Psychology,* 1975, *6,* 41–44.

Shapiro, R. L. The origin of adolescent disturbances in the family: Some considerations in theory and implications for therapy. In G. H. Zuk & I. Boszormenyi-Nagy (Eds.), *Family therapy and disturbed families.* Palo Alto, Calif.: Science & Behavior Books, 1967.

Shean, G. *Schizophrenia: An introduction to research and theory.* Cambridge, Mass.: Winthrop, 1978.

Silverman, H. L. Psychological implications of marital therapy. In H. L. Silverman (Ed.), *Marital therapy: Moral, sociological and psychological factors.* Springfield, Ill.: Charles C Thomas, 1972.

Simon, R. M. Sculpting the family. *Family Process,* 1972, *11,* 49–57.

Skolnick, A. S., & Skolnick, J. H. Introduction: Family in transition. In A. S. Skolnick & J. H. Skolnick (Eds.), *Family in transition: Rethinking marriage, sexuality, child rearing, and family organization* (2nd ed.). Boston: Little, Brown, 1977.

Skynner, A. C. R. *Systems of family and marital psychotherapy.* New York: Brunner/Mazel, 1976.

Slavson, S. R. *A textbook in analytic group psychotherapy.* New York: International Universities Press, 1964.

Sluzki, C. E., & Ransom, D. C. (Eds.). *Double bind: The foundation of the communicational approach to the family.* New York: Grune & Stratton, 1976.

Speck, R. V. Family therapy in the home. *Journal of Marriage and the Family,* 1964, *26,* 72–76.

Speck, R. V., & Attneave, C. L. *Family networks.* New York: Pantheon Books, 1973.

Speck, R. V., & Rueveni, U. Network therapy: A developing concept. *Family Process,* 1969, *8,* 182–191.

Spiegel, J. P. *Transactions: The interplay between individual, family and society.* New York: Science House, 1971.

Spiegel, J. P. The family: the channel of primary care. *Hospital and Community Psychiatry,* 1974, *25,* 785–788.

Stachowiak, J. Functional and dysfunctional families. In V. Satir, J. Stachowiak, & H. A. Taschman (Eds.), *Helping families to change.* New York: Jason Aronson, 1975.

Stier, S., & Goldenberg, I. Training issues in family therapy. *Journal of Marriage and Family Counseling,* 1975, *1,* 63–68.

Stierlin, H. *Separating parents and adolescents.* New York: Quadrangle, 1972.

Strelnick, A. H. Multiple family group therapy: A review of the literature. *Family Process,* 1977, *16,* 307–325.

Strupp, H. H. *Psychotherapy and the modification of abnormal behavior.* New York: McGraw-Hill, 1971.

Stuart, R. B. Operant-interpersonal treatment for marital discord. *Journal of Consulting and Clinical Psychology,* 1969, *33,* 675–682.

Stuart, R. B. Behavioral contracting within the families of delinquents. *Journal of Behavior Therapy and Experimental Psychiatry,* 1971, *2,* 1–11.

Stuart, R. B. An operant interpersonal program for couples. In D. H. L. Olson (Ed.), *Treating relationships.* Lake Mills, Iowa: Graphic, 1976.

Sundberg, N. D., Tyler, L. E., & Taplin, J. R. *Clinical psychology: Expanding horizons* (2nd ed.). Englewood Cliffs, N. J.: Prentice-Hall, 1973.

Towards a differentiation of self in one's family. In J. L. Framo (Ed.), *Family interaction: A dialogue between family researchers and family therapists.* New York: Springer, 1972.

Van Dusen, R. A., & Sheldon, E. B. The changing status of American women: A life cycle perspective. *American Psychologist,* 1976, *31,* 106–116.

Walrond-Skinner, S. *Family therapy: The treatment of natural systems.* London: Routledge & Kegan Paul, 1976.

Warkentin, J., & Whitaker, C. A. The secret agenda of the therapist doing couples therapy. In G. H. Zuk & I. Boszormenyi-Nagy (Eds.), *Family therapy and disturbed families.* Palo Alto, Calif.: Science & Behavior Books, 1967.

Watzlawick, P. A structured family interview. *Family Process,* 1966, *5,* 256–271.

Watzlawick, P., Beavin, J. H., & Jackson, D. D. *Pragmatics of human communication.* New York: Norton, 1967.

Watzlawick, P., & Weakland, J. H. (Eds.). *The interactional view: Studies at the Mental Research Institute, 1965–1974.* New York: Norton, 1977.

Watzlawick, P., Weakland, J. H., & Fisch, R. *Change: Principles of problem formation and problem resolution.* New York: Norton, 1974.

Waxler, N. The normality of deviance: An alternate explanation of schizophrenia in the family. *Schizophrenia Bulletin,* 1975, *14,* 38–47.

Weakland, J. H. Communication theory and clinical change. In P. J. Guerin, Jr. (Ed.), *Family therapy: Theory and practice.* New York: Gardner Press, 1976.

Weakland, J. H., Fisch, R., Watzlawick, P., & Bodin, A. M. Brief therapy: Focused problem resolution. *Family Process,* 1974, *13,* 141–167.

Weathers, L., & Liberman, R. P. The family contracting exercise. *Journal of Behavior Therapy and Experimental Psychiatry*, 1975, *6*, 208–214.

Wellisch, D. K., Vincent, J., & Ro-Trock, G. K. Family therapy versus individual therapy: A study of adolescents and their parents. In D. H. L. Olson (Ed.), *Treating relationships*. Lake Mills, Iowa: Graphic, 1976.

Wells, R. A. & Dezen, A. E. The results of family therapy revisited: The nonbehavorial methods. *Family Process*, 1978, *17*, 251–274.

Wells, R. A., Dilkes, T. C., & Trivelli, N. The results of family therapy: A critical review of the literature. *Family Process*, 1972, *11*, 189–207.

Whitaker, C. A. The growing edge in techniques of family therapy. In J. Haley & L. Hoffman (Eds.), *Techniques of family therapy*. New York: Basic Books, 1967.

Whitaker, C. A. Comment: Live supervision in psychotherapy. *Voices*, 1976, *12*, 24–25.

Who is the real family? *Ms. Magazine*, August 1978, pp. 43–48.

Woodward, C. A., Santa-Barbara, J., Levin, S., & Epstein, N. B. The role of goal attainment scaling in evaluating family therapy outcomes. *American Journal of Orthopsychiatry*, 1978, *48*, 464–476.

Wynne, L. C. Some indications and contraindications for exploratory family therapy. In I. Boszormenyi-Nagy & J. L. Framo (Eds.), *Intensive family therapy: Theoretical and practical aspects*. New York: Harper & Row, 1965.

Wynne, L. C. Methodologic and conceptual issues in the study of schizophrenics and their families. In D. Rosenthal & S. S. Kety (Eds.), *The transmission of schizophrenia*. New York: Pergamon Press, 1968.

Wynne, L. C. Some guidelines for exploratory conjoint family therapy. In J. Haley (Ed.), *Changing Families: A family therapy reader*. New York: Grune & Stratton, 1971.

Wynne, L. C., Ryckoff, I. M., Day, J., & Hirsch, S. I. Pseudomutuality in the family relationships of schizophrenics. *Psychiatry*, 1958, *21*, 205–220.

Wynne, L. C., & Singer, M. Thought disorder and family relations of schizophrenics, I and II. *Archives of General Psychiatry*, 1963, *9*, 191–206.

Zuk, G. H. Family therapy. *Archives of General Psychiatry*, 1967, *16*, 71–79.

Zuk, G. H. *Family therapy: A triadic-based approach*. New York: Human Sciences Press, 1971. (a)

Zuk, G. H. Family therapy. In J. Haley (Ed.), *Changing families: A family therapy reader*. New York: Grune & Stratton, 1971. (b)

Zuk, G. H. Family therapy: Clinical hodgepodge or clinical science? *Journal of Marriage and Family Counseling*. 1976, *2*, 299–303.

Zuk, G. H., & Rubinstein, D. A review of concepts in the study and treatment of families with schizophrenics. In I. Boszormenyi-Nagy & J. L. Framo (Eds.), *Intensive family therapy: Theoretical and practical aspects*. New York: Harper & Row, 1965.

NAME INDEX

Ackerman, N. W., 81, 102–104, 106, 108–109, 112, 117, 129, 138, 139, 141–142, 143, 150, 166–170, 195, 197, 198, 199, 234
Adler, A., 111
Alger, I., 105, 203–204, 212–213
Ard, B. N., Jr., 92
Ard, C. C., 92
Arnold, J. E., 129
Attneave, C. L., 105, 209–211, 246
Auerswald, E. H., 244–245

Back, K. W., 94–95
Baker, L., 3, 9, 17, 34, 37, 59, 62, 119, 121–122, 181, 209, 241–242
Bandler, R., 118, 172, 174–175
Barcai, A., 209
Bateson, G., 36, 52, 54, 86–87, 103, 106, 114, 175
Beavers, W. R., 39, 41–46, 84, 230
Beavin, J. H., 36, 57–58, 114
Beck, D. F., 51
Beels, C. C., 104, 117, 142, 167, 172, 228
Behrens, M. L., 139, 141, 143
Bell, J. E., 63, 103, 105, 108, 140, 153, 154, 163, 166, 194–198, 199, 200, 244, 245
Berger, M. M., 212, 229
Berkowitz, B. P., 127
Bertalanffy, L. von, 29, 82, 106, 112, 115
Bion, W. R., 94
Blechman, E. A., 185
Bloch, D. A., 33, 80, 84, 134, 136–139, 150
Bodin, A. M., 105, 228, 229
Bolman, W. M., 245
Boszormenyi-Nagy, I., 25–26, 90, 103, 105, 112, 237
Bowen, M., 3, 80, 85–86, 89–90, 96, 99–100, 103–104, 106, 108–112, 129, 150, 166, 170–172, 198, 199, 229, 234, 235, 244
Bowlby, J., 195
Brackelmanns, W. E., 50
Brody, E. M., 50

Cleghorn, J. M., 226–227
Cohen, M., 246
Cohen, R. E., 245

Constantine, L., 226, 228
Cooper, D., 150
Cooper, S., 93
Cornelison, A., 87–88
Cromwell, R. E., 92

D'Andrade, R. G., 21
Day, J., 69, 89
Dezen, A. E., 240–241, 243
Dilkes, T. C., 240
Dorlac, C., 209
Doyle, A. M., 209
Duhl, B. S., 214
Duhl, F. J., 214
Duvall, E. M., 14–15, 79

Epstein, N. B., 246
Erickson, G. D., 228
Erickson, M. H., 178
Esterson, A., 53

Feld, S., 91
Ferber, A., 104, 117, 142, 151, 167, 172, 224
Ferreira, A. J., 65, 68, 150
Fisch, R., 105, 115, 178, 233
Fisher, L., 147, 149
Fleck, S., 21–22, 54, 87–88
Flomenhaft, K., 105, 207, 240
Fogarty, T., 235
Foley, V. D., 84
Fournier, D. G., 92
Fox, R. E., 243
Framo, J. L., 90, 103, 105, 108, 113, 135, 150, 158–159, 163, 203–204, 230
Franklin, P., 153, 154
Freud, S., 4, 76, 80, 106, 111
Fromm-Reichmann, F., 85

Gazda, G. M., 94
Gladfelter, J., 233
Glick, I. D., 23, 65–67, 135, 144, 151, 232
Glick, P. C., 11–12
Goldenberg, H., 25, 93, 95–97, 101, 162, 202, 223, 245, 246
Goldenberg, I. T., 25, 202, 231, 246
Goldstein, M., 90

Gossett, J. T., 39, 41–42, 230
Graziano, A. M., 127
Greenberg, I. A., 94
Greiner, D., 238
Grinder, J., 118, 172, 174–175
Grotjahn, M., 102
Guerin, P. J., Jr., 96, 112, 228, 235
Guerney, B. G., Jr., 60–61, 101, 121, 241, 246
Guerney, L. F., 242, 246
Gurin, G., 91

Haley, J., 4, 8, 14, 17, 19, 52, 59, 86, 101–103, 105, 113, 115–117, 129, 140, 143, 151, 154–156, 158, 164, 166, 175–179, 183, 194, 198, 199, 224–225, 229, 231, 233, 236, 247
Halpin, R. J., 226, 233
Hawkins, N., 127
Healy, W., 93
Hickok, J. E., 127
Hirsch, S., 69, 87, 89
Hoffman, L. W., 21, 65, 102, 166, 175, 229
Hogan, T. P., 228
Holt, M., 238
Howells, J. G., 16, 19–20, 140–142

Jackson, D. D., 29–30, 33–34, 36, 52, 57–58, 86, 89, 96, 99–100, 102, 105, 108, 113–116, 126, 129, 175, 234
Johnson, V. E., 216–218
Jones, M. A., 51

Kanner, L., 93
Kantor, D., 214
Kaplan, D. M., 206
Kaplan, H. S., 217–218
Kempler, W., 140, 143, 153, 156–158, 164, 234
Kessler, D. R., 23, 65–67, 135, 144, 152, 232
Klein, M., 94
Komechak, M. G., 127

Laing, R. D., 52–53, 150
Langsley, D. G., 105, 206–207, 240
Laqueur, H. P., 105, 201–203
LeBow, M. D., 105, 123
Leff, J., 87
LePerriere, K., 33, 80, 84, 136–139, 150
Levin, S., 226–227, 246
Levine, A. G., 129
Levine, J., 188
Lewis, J. M., 39, 41–42, 230
Liberman, R. P., 123–124, 126, 129, 148–149, 150, 166, 187–190, 198, 199, 200, 203–204
Liddle, H. A., 226, 233
Lidz, R., 85

Lidz, T., 85–89, 100, 106, 108
Liebman, R., 122
LoPiccolo, J., 218
LoPiccolo, L., 218
Low, M., 204
Low, P., 204

MacGregor, R., 105, 204–205
Machotka, P., 105, 207, 240
Malcolm, J., 182, 232
Martin, P. A., 92, 136
Masters, W. H., 216–218
McNeal, S., 127
McPherson, S. R., 50
Mendelsohn, M., 224
Miller, J. G., 29, 35, 82, 84
Milman, L., 122
Minuchin, S., 3, 9, 17–19, 34, 37, 39, 59–62, 85, 101, 103–104, 106, 119–123, 129, 150, 166, 179–183, 197, 198, 199, 209, 229, 232, 241–242, 246
Mishler, E. G., 102
Montalvo, B., 60–61, 101, 121, 232
Moos, R. H., 145–148
Moreno, J., 94
Mudd, E. G., 91

Napier, A. Y., 28, 113, 116, 156, 236, 237
Nass, G. D., 11
Newman, L. E., 50

Olson, D. H. L., 92

Papp, P., 106, 166, 215, 229
Patterson, G. R., 127–129
Phelps, R., 127
Phillips, V. A., 39, 41–42, 230
Pittman, F. S., 105, 207, 240
Popenoe, P., 91
Preston, T. A., 231
Prosky, P., 153, 154

Ranson, D. C., 87
Ranz, J., 151
Rapoport, R., 19, 22
Rapoport, R. N., 19, 22
Reevey, W. R., 91
Reiss, D., 86
Ritchie, A. N., 105, 204
Ritterman, M. K., 119
Robinson, L. R., 134–135
Rodnick, E., 90
Rosenblatt, B., 93
Rosman, B. L., 3, 9, 17, 34, 37, 59–62, 101, 119, 121–122, 181, 209, 241–242
Ro-Trock, G. K., 240, 242, 246
Rubenstein, D., 93, 96, 235, 236
Rubenstein, E., 93
Rueveni, U., 210

Ryckoff, I. M., 69, 89

Sander, F. M., 228
Sanders, N., 188, 203–204
Santa-Barbara, J., 246
Satir, V., 9, 31–32, 102, 103, 104, 113, 115,
　117–118, 129, 150, 151, 154, 166, 172–
　175, 197, 198, 199, 234
Schumer, F., 60–61, 101, 121
Schuster, F. P., 105, 204
Serrano, A. C., 105, 204
Shapiro, R. J., 228
・Shapiro, R. L., 49
Shean, G., 87, 89
Sheldon, E. B., 22
Silverman, H. L., 92
Simon, R. M., 214
Singer, M., 89
Skolnick, A. S., 9, 11, 21
Skolnick, J. H., 9, 11, 21
Skynner, A. C. R., 224, 231
Slavson, S. R., 94–95
Sluzki, C. E., 87
Spark, G. M., 25–26, 112, 237
Speck, R. V., 105, 209–211, 246
Spiegel, J. P., 90, 134, 245
Stachowiak, J., 50, 117, 172
Stier, S., 231
Stierlin, H., 45
Strelnick, A. H., 202
Strupp, H. H., 239
Stuart, R. B., 126–127, 129, 166, 183–187,
　198, 199

Sundberg, N. D., 83

Taplin, J. R., 83
Taschman, H. A., 117, 172
Todd, T. C., 122
Trivelli, N., 240
Tyler, L. E., 83

Van Dusen, R. A., 22
Veroff, J., 91
Vincent, J., 240, 242, 246

Wallace, C. J., 188
Walrond-Skinner, S., 108
Warkentin, J., 150
Watzlawick, P., 36, 57–58, 105, 114–115,
　144, 178, 233
Waxler, N., 86, 102
Weakland, J., 52, 86, 105, 113–115, 175,
　178, 233
Weathers, L., 189
Weiner, O. R., 235, 236
Wellisch, D. K., 240, 242, 246
Wells, R. A., 240–241, 243
Wheeler, E., 188, 203–204
Whitaker, C. A., 28, 100, 102, 105, 113,
　116, 150, 156, 233, 234, 235–237, 247
Woodward, C. A., 246
Wynne, L. C., 69–71, 86, 89–90, 100, 103,
　105–106, 137–138, 150, 154

Zuk, G. H., 96, 101, 105, 135, 154, 166,
　191–194, 198, 199, 200

SUBJECT INDEX

Ackerman Institute for Family Therapy, 102, 234
Adolescents, 4, 13, 20, 23, 37, 39, 40, 49, 53, 135, 137, 138, 178, 180, 181, 182, 188–189, 204–206, 214, 242
Albert Einstein College of Medicine, 228
Alliance, *see* Coalitions
American Association of Marriage and Family Therapists, 91
American Group Psychotherapy Association, 95
American Institute of Family Relations, 91
American Orthopsychiatric Association, 90, 93
Anorexia nervosa, 62, 121–123, 181–182, 209
Antisocial personality, *see* Sociopath
Anxiety, 4, 14, 81, 110, 117, 134, 140, 144, 176, 217, 236
Asthma, 62, 122
Autonomy, 40, 42, 45, 62, 70

Behavior:
analysis, 123–124, 148, 226–227
theory, 123–129, 198, 199
therapy, 123, 176, 183–190, 199, 204, 216, 218
Biopsychosocial model, 112, 166–170
Blamer communication style, 117–118, 174
Blended family, 10, 11, 27, 244
Boston Family Institute, 214, 234
Boundaries, 37–38, 43, 44, 46, 47, 49, 59, 62, 71, 72, 82, 120, 121, 122, 129, 137, 149, 150
Brief therapy, 105, 114, 246

Cases:
biopsychosocial therapy, 167–168
complementary relationship, 58
conjoint family therapy, 173
dealing with the identified patient, 159
double-bind recipient, 86
experiential therapy, 156–157
family myths, 68
father/daughter alliance, 50
feedback loops, 36
hospitalized adolescent and family, 53–54

Cases *(continued)*
intergenerational conflict (teenage pregnancy), 136–137
mystification, 53
obese teenager, 160–162
post-suicide family, 23–25
problem-solving therapy, 155
relationship definition, 30
scapegoating, 63–65
schizophrenic adolescent, 5–6
school difficulty, 6–7
shaping a couple's behavior, 125–126
social isolates, 138–139
symmetrical relationship, 55–57
triadic-based family therapy, 193–194
working out transactional patterns, 18–19
Centrifugal style, 45–46, 47
Centripetal style, 45, 47
Child guidance, 76, 93–94, 106, 246
Closed system, 38. 43, 45, 47, 82, 205
Coalitions, 22, 23, 37, 40, 41, 42, 44, 45, 47, 49, 120, 134, 143, 149, 152, 177, 178, 192, 208, 216
Cohabitation, 10, 27
Common law family, 10
Commune family, 10, 27
Communication:
family, 40, 44, 47, 50–51, 60, 83, 85, 101, 103–104, 148–149, 150, 172
pathological, 44, 46, 48, 50–59, 71–72, 86, 89
theory, 113–119, 129, 176, 177, 198, 212
therapy, 172–179, 227
Complementarity of roles, 81, 144, 149, 199 (*see also* Roles)
Complementary relationships, 54, 58–59, 72, 116 (*see also* Communication, pathological)
Composite family, 10
Conductors, 104, 142, 167
Congruent communication style, 117–118, 174
Conjoint family therapy, 92, 154, 172–175
Conjoint sex therapy, 201, 216–219
Contingency contracting, 187–190, 200 (*see also* Contracts)
Contracts, 128, 151, 185

Cotherapy, 202, 212, 231, 235–238, 247
Crises, 13, 27, 48–50, 92, 105, 152, 181, 182, 196, 204, 206–209, 218, 246

Delinquency, 14, 60–61, 72, 76, 101–102, 206, 218
Dependency, 31, 88, 149, 166
Depression, 4, 14, 23, 26, 84, 139, 143, 176, 210
Developmental tasks, 16–20, 42, 48, 49
Diabetes, 62, 122
Diagnosis, 106, 139–150, 164, 169, 170, 218
Differentiation, 109–112, 149, 150, 171, 199, 235
Disengagement, 48, 59, 60–61, 71, 72, 101–102, 121
Divorce, 9, 10, 11, 75, 92, 115, 206, 244
    (*see also* Emotional divorce)
Double-bind concept, 52, 72, 86–87, 106, 114, 129, 143, 175, 178
Dyads, 22, 37
Dysfunctional:
    behavior, 4, 25, 37, 62, 72, 106, 133, 154, 177, 180
    families, 25, 27, 31, 41, 42–47, 48, 52, 69, 71, 84, 85, 129, 165, 174, 180, 202

no → Eastern Pennsylvania Psychiatric Institute, 190, 234
Ecological perspective, 244–245
Effectiveness studies, 182, 187, 207, 218, 239–243, 245–246, 247–248
Emotional divorce, 89, 100
Encounter groups, 95, 97, 231
Enmeshment, 23, 48, 59, 60–61, 62, 71, 72, 101–102, 121, 122, 150, 181, 182
Entropy, 43–44, 46, 82
Equifinality, 29
Experiential therapy, 156–157
Extended family, 10, 11

Family choreography, 105, 201, 214–216, 219
Family crisis therapy, 201, 206–209, 218
Family Environment Scale, 145–148
Family sculpture technique, 105, 201, 214–215, 219
Family therapy:
    historical roots, 75–106
    indications and contraindications, 135–139
    process, 133–164
    stages, 152–163
    values and goals, 150–152
wash DC   ✗ Family Therapy Institute, 176, 233
Feedback, 34–36, 47, 84, 85, 95, 115, 122, 204, 219, 247
Films, 228, 233–234, 247

Fusion, 109, 110, 149, 171, 199

General systems theory, 76, 82–85, 106, 115, 203, 212
Grandparents, 10, 19, 37, 38, 50, 120, 121, 177
Group for the Advancement of Psychiatry, 90, 103–104, 152
Group therapy, 76, 94–96, 97, 106, 202, 230, 233

Homeostasis, 29, 32–34, 69, 81, 84, 112, 115, 119, 122, 129, 134, 135, 165, 169, 172, 181, 182, 235

Identified patient, 9, 27, 65, 76, 84, 136, 137, 138, 143, 152, 158, 202, 203, 223
Identity formation, 1, 23, 46, 49, 70, 71, 90, 113
Interlocking pathology, 108, 129, 133, 150
Intrapsychic conflict, 4, 8, 14, 80, 81, 108, 112, 133, 176, 178
Irrelevant communication style, 117–118, 174

Jewish Board of Guardians, 94–95
Joint Commission on Mental Illness and Health, 91
Judge Baker Guidance Center, 93

Labeling, 25, 192, 223
Life cycle, 13–16, 27, 46, 48–50, 65
Live supervision, 231–233, 247
    (*see also* Supervision)
Living systems, 38, 82–83, 84

Marathon, 230–231, 247
Marital Pre-Counseling Inventory, 183, 187
"Marital quid pro quo," 115, 126, 186
Marital schism, 88, 106
Marital skew, 88, 106
Marital therapy; *see* Marriage counseling
Marriage counseling, 76, 90–92, 106, 111, 136, 183–187
Menninger Foundation, 89
✗Mental Research Institute, 86, 87, 114, *Palo Alto* 233, 234
Metacommunication, 114, 177, 178
Multigenerational transmission process, *see* Three-generation hypothesis
Multiple family therapy, 105, 201–204, 218
Multiple impact therapy, 105, 201, 204–206, 218
Multiple marital couple therapy, 203–204, 218
Mystification, 52–53, 72

Mythology, 40, 44, 46, 48, 65–71, 72, 150, 180

National Institute of Mental Health, 86, 89, 137
National Training Laboratory, 95, 97
Network therapy, 105, 201, 209–212, 219, 246
Neuroses, 43, 44, 45, 47, 107
Nuclear family, 9, 10, 15, 27

Open systems, 38, 43, 82, 84, 122, 205
Operant conditioning, 124, 126, 187
Operant-interpersonal therapy, 126, 183–187
Optimal family functioning, 38–42, 44, 47, 75, 230

Paradigm, 8, 17, 107
Paradoxical intervention, 177–178
Parentification, 25–26
Philadelphia Child Guidance Clinic, 103, 179, 232, 234
Placater communication style, 117–118, 174
Positive reinforcement, 124, 126–127, 129, 150, 183
Power, 31, 37, 40, 42, 44, 45, 46, 83, 113, 116, 118, 120, 129, 133, 147–149, 176, 177, 178, 191, 198
Pseudomutuality, 69–71, 72, 90, 106, 137, 150
Psychoanalysis, 4, 76–82, 85, 87, 106, 107, 108, 109, 112, 113, 129, 166, 170, 176, 190, 199
Psychodrama, 94, 231
Psychodynamics, 88, 107–113, 129, 142, 198
Psychopathology, *see* Dysfunctional, behavior
Psychosomatic, 62, 121–123, 139, 182

Reactors, 104
Reproductive Biology Research Foundation, 216
Retirement, 19, 20
Roles, 14, 17, 20–22, 25, 26, 27, 37, 38, 44, 46, 49, 63, 65, 83, 102, 112, 120, 134, 149, 163, 168, 185, 208
Rules, 29–32, 33, 44, 46, 47, 83, 113, 115, 134, 167, 195

Scapegoating, 26, 27, 37, 48, 63, 65, 71, 72, 84, 89, 138, 143, 149, 150, 167, 180, 192

Schizophrenia, 4, 14, 43, 44, 45, 46, 47, 52, 53, 69, 71, 72, 76, 85–90, 96, 100, 101, 102, 106, 111, 114, 138, 175, 192, 201, 206, 210, 235
Schizophrenogenic mother, 85
Sculpting, *see* Family sculpture technique
Serial family, 10
Sexual dysfunction, 4, 136, 137, 142, 166, 216–219
Shaping, 124–126, 129, 187, 190
Silence, 51, 192, 203
Single-parent households, 9, 10, 27, 244
Social learning model, 127–129
Social network intervention, *see* Network therapy
Sociopath, 45, 47
Structural:
    theory, 119–123, 129, 198
    therapy, 120, 121, 179–182
Subsystems, 28, 37–39, 47, 49, 59, 62, 72, 83, 120, 121, 122, 129, 163, 180, 203
Super-reasonable communication style, 117–118, 174
Supervision, 212, 224–225, 229, 231, 235, 236, 247
Symmetrical relationships, 54–58, 59, 72, 116 (*see also* Communication, pathological)
Symptoms, 4, 6, 9, 14, 62, 81, 84, 85, 103, 104, 117, 134, 140, 143, 152, 156, 162, 165, 176, 181, 210
Systems viewpoint, 3, 4, 9, 13, 28–38, 43, 47, 51, 54, 81, 105, 112, 119–120, 121, 134, 188, 223, 244 (*see also* General systems theory)

Tavistock Institute, 94, 95
Three-generation hypothesis, 89, 96–99, 111
Token economy programs, 127
Triadic-based family therapy, 190–194, 200
Triangles 19, 110–111, 170–172, 216

UCLA Neuropsychiatric Institute, 188, 231
Undifferentiated family ego mass, 109, 150, 170, 171, 235

Videotape, 40, 41, 105, 167, 201, 212–213, 219, 229–230, 233, 247

Wiltwyck School for Boys, 60, 121, 179